BEYOND NIHILISM

Ofelia Schutte

BEYOND NIHILISM

Nietzsche without Masks

THE UNIVERSITY OF CHICAGO PRESS
Chicago and London

OFELIA SCHUTTE is assistant professor of philosophy at
the University of Florida, Gainesville.

THE UNIVERSITY OF CHICAGO PRESS, CHICAGO 60637
THE UNIVERSITY OF CHICAGO PRESS, LTD., LONDON

© 1984 by The University of Chicago
All rights reserved. Published 1984
Printed in the United States of America

91 90 89 88 87 86 85 84   1 2 3 4 5

LIBRARY OF CONGRESS CATALOGING IN PUBLICATION DATA

Schutte, Ofelia.
  Beyond nihilism.

  Includes bibliography and index.
  1. Nietzsche, Friedrich Wilhelm, 1844–1900.   I. Title.
B3317.S47   1984   193   83-9240
ISBN 0-226-74140-0

For my mother, Ofelia, and my aunt, Arminda

Contents

Preface

This study represents an attempt to read Nietzsche without masks. In saying this, I am well aware of Nietzsche's love of masks. Here the masks I am calling into question are not so much Nietzsche's as our own. His work may be understood in spite of masks because his use of masks is generally explicit. Our masks, on the other hand, are less easy to detect. We do not hide behind a Zarathustra or a Dionysus, but sometimes we hide behind conceptual frameworks, abstractions. These are to us what Zarathustra was to Nietzsche. If the deception on Nietzsche's part is to speak through a unique figure situated six thousand feet beyond man and time, ours is to fail to speak sufficiently as individuals. We rely on systems of thought through which others can speak. Yet we value such systems. We value the type of communication they enable us to establish, the facilitation of dialogue and discussion, and the commonly accepted criteria to which we may appeal if disagreements arise among us. Nietzsche would say that as long as we are not free to transcend our conceptual systems we have not yet fully understood him. As for us, we want both our intellectual systems and Nietzsche. Is there any way of mediating these differences, so that we can obtain a philosophical understanding of him without at the same time losing the rich, engaging aspects of his thought?

In my interpretation of Nietzsche I have placed a fairly strong weight on the significance of his metaphors. In my view, the metaphor is not a mask concealing the real Nietzsche (if one may speak of such a character). On the contrary, the metaphor is one place where Nietzsche's views are most likely to be found. His metaphors need not lead any interpreter astray. They can easily be understood and valued precisely for what they are, namely, figures of speech. Nietzsche's metaphors are potential bearers of truth. While a poetic view of truth and philosophical truth are not always compatible, my task is to determine where Nietzsche succeeds in integrating poetry and philosophy. I am interested in the type of contribution Nietzsche can offer to a broad concept of philosophical inquiry.

In addition to weighing Nietzsche's poetry favorably, I have approached him philosophically through the mediation of the concept of the Dionysian. If Nietzsche's Dionysian perspective is understood, everything he writes can be seen as part of a clearly identifiable perspective on existence. Aspects of his thought which at first appear obscure begin to lose their enigmatic character. All those truths whose authority is sustained through mystery lose their importance, while some of his more simple and direct statements stand out as the more profound. In some ways the knowledge we gain is not flattering to Nietzsche. It especially shatters the imagery of elevation and heightened awareness in which Nietzsche very often clothes his views. Yet he challenged us to understand him as a spokesman for the pagan god Dionysus. He invited us to search for the thoughts behind his thoughts. My study is a response to this challenge.

The interpretation I have offered is sympathetic to Nietzsche's ontological views but critical of his moral and political theory. Because of this critical element it differs from those philosophical readings which offer a primarily favorable view of his thought. Nietzsche's unsystematic method and enigmatic teachings (the *Übermensch,* the will to power) are bound to generate controversy regarding how he ought to be read. The philosophical community (especially in phenomenology and analytic philosophy) has tended to view Nietzsche's work in a positive light. This happens because, as philosophers, we reconstruct Nietzsche's theories in terms of our traditions and interpretative frameworks. We choose from among his many statements what is most illuminating or sensible. Scholars influenced by Heidegger or Kaufmann tend to follow this approach. Moreover, as long as the Nietzsche scholar addresses such issues as Nietzsche's theory of time or of language, his work remains enlightening. It is when we get to questions of power and violence that serious problems arise.

Nietzsche has received negative criticism from thinkers (both conservative and leftist) interested in the philosophy or history of culture. From a conservative standpoint he is criticized for either directly or indirectly advocating an end to morality. In this vein Stern has called attention to Nietzsche's role in German culture as an ideologist of power and violence. Leftist critics (such as Lukács) charge that Nietzsche's defense of a high culture violates both the moral dignity and the political interests of the working class. To these concerns I have added the issue of Nietzsche's perspective on women, which is of special interest to many readers today. One of the main targets of those who criticize Nietzsche's views on morality and culture is his concept of justice (including social justice). He destroys the notion of justice based on respect for persons. This allows him to establish an authoritarian system of values which in turn defends the right of the strong to overpower the weak. When Nietzsche is read from the standpoint of the history of culture, he does not fare as well as when his work is studied in connection with specialized issues in epistemology, ontology, literary theory, or existential psychology.

My study of Nietzsche's metaphysics and morality shows that these cannot be separated (except arbitrarily) from his theory of culture. It is possible to portray his views on culture favorably if only one draws attention to the role he gives to the artist or the creator of values. On the other hand, systematic studies of Nietzsche make little note of his views on slavery. He endorsed slavery and exploitation as structures which could be used to further the self-enhancement of artists and geniuses. To many of us who appreciate Nietzsche's other insights on creativity and art, his statements on slavery are not appealing. Therefore, they tend not to be discussed. Reading Nietzsche without masks, I take it, means that as philosophers we have a responsibility not to cover up for him, especially when issues of justice and injustice are at stake. His positive contributions to knowledge should be distinguished from the justification of cruelty which he offers in the name of the superior culture and the superior man. Moreover, it is not enough to have some books eulogizing Nietzsche while other books portray him as a proponent of violence. We need an interpretation that can speak both to the positive and to the negative aspects of his thought.

Although I have refrained from looking the other way when Nietzsche defends cruelty, my main goal has been to trace the implications of the more creative and constructive aspects of Nietzsche's thought. Whenever possible I have read him as contributing to a standpoint beyond nihilism. Yet, as the study progresses, the contradictions between Nietzsche's intent to overcome nihilism and his exaltation of nihilism become more accentuated. The reason for this increasing tension is that we are following the actual implications of his views. The conclusions I have reached result directly from the hierarchy of values Nietzsche justified in his late works. The controversial nature of his statements is not something I have invented, but something he himself produced.

Finally, although I have taken seriously Nietzsche's high estimation of metaphorical discourse, I should also offer the reservation that metaphors alone cannot heal us. As long as nihilism is present in human life, the contribution of rational discourse to knowledge (including self-knowledge) cannot be discarded. In a nihilistic culture, even if reason appears in an alienated state, it represents a strength rather than a weakness. By advocating the primacy of the instincts and the unconscious powers of the mind, Nietzsche sought to heal the nihilism inherent in alienated thought. But the undermining of reason for a new kind of faith in life can also lead to self-destruction. In an alienated world, neither passion nor reason is the sole depository of value. If one wishes to stand beyond nihilism it is wiser to consider how best to conserve the strength of both of these powers than to view one human capacity as fundamentally weak and corrupt, the other as strong and dynamic.

As is appropriate, I would like to thank those to whom I am indebted. The University of Florida provided financial assistance through two grants from the Division of Sponsored Research and Humanities Research Council. I have benefited from many informal discussions with Lucie White, Michael Ryan, Gayatri Spivak, Thomas Auxter, and J. Jay Zeman at different stages of development of this work. I am indebted to Karsten Harries and George Schrader of Yale University, who introduced me to the interpretative and critical study of Nietzsche's thought. Papers on topics related to this work have been presented for discussion on many different occasions, including meetings of the North American Nietzsche Society, the Nietzsche Society, and the Boston University Institute for Philosophy and Religion. I thank all who have participated in those programs for their observations and critical remarks. My colleagues in philosophy at the University of Florida, some of whom have already been mentioned, have offered criticism of my work at several departmental colloquia. Several individuals have read an earlier draft of this work and have offered valuable comments. In particular, I thank Professors H. Stefan Schultz of the University of Chicago and Marx Wartofsky of Boston University for their very helpful advice. I am also grateful to Professor George Kimball Plochmann of Southern Illinois University for his advice and observations on the earlier draft.

The Bibliography contains most of the scholarly sources, critical editions, and translations of Nietzsche's work that I have found helpful. It was not possible in a study of this type to address in particular all of the works on Nietzsche that I have read with interest. I take this opportunity to acknowledge the work of Harold Alderman, whose view of masks and metaphor differs from my own, yet whose commitment to the textual interpretation of Nietzsche, as shown by his analysis of *Thus Spoke Zarathustra,* is one I share and value. I have had occasion at Yale and at Florida to benefit from informal presentations by Jacques Derrida on a variety of topics. With gratitude I cite the feminist movement, in particular the work of Simone de Beauvoir, for raising questions about women's existential and social identity that call for continued analysis today.

I am also grateful for permission to use parts of Chapter 7, on Nietzsche's politics, that originally appeared in the *Journal of the British Society for Phenomenology* 14, no. 2 (1983): 139–57.

Eric Kubli and Mariann Bienz generously hosted my first visit to the Upper Engadine region of Switzerland in August 1979. I offer them my most heartfelt thanks in view of their hospitality on that memorable occasion. In the same spirit, I thank the staff of the Nietzsche-Haus in Sils Maria for their hospitality and kind assistance. Finally, I thank my students, both graduate and undergraduate, for their contribution and interest in keeping alive the spirit and challenges of Nietzsche's philosophy.

Introduction

This study explores Nietzsche's view of a philosophical approach to existence in which philosophy would constitute an affirmation of the life process in its totality. An alliance between philosophy and nihilism is at work whenever philosophy accepts a theory of truth and value which is rooted in the Platonic need to separate a "real" world of truth from the temporal nature of existence. And yet it has been an indispensable element in the Western philosophical tradition to devalue life and its ontological analogue, temporality. Whether the philosopher is trying to arrive at a theory of truth or of the good, something other than life is taken as more real or worthy than life because life's "opposite" is thought to transcend change. The most sublime result of this type of thinking is the Platonic invention of a world of ideas or eternal essences whose power is incommensurable with that of temporal existents. But for those who are skeptical of such a world of ideas the same Platonic alienation from the value of temporal existents will result in a death-oriented approach to human activity. The more explicitly nihilistic attitude is encountered, for example, in Schopenhauer, who characterizes the essence of life as an alternation between pain and boredom.

This thread uniting Plato and Schopenhauer is only one of the many manifestations of nihilism in Western culture. In *Twilight of the Idols* Nietzsche noted that perhaps the philosopher has a special predisposition to consider existence worthless.[1] This serves to alert the reader to two broader and more significant issues. The first is whether the highest values of Western culture—among which philosophical activity is included—do not exhibit, either covertly or overtly, a resentment against life. If this is the case, a second issue arises: whether another philosophical outlook can be attained which will establish a new foundation for all values in a spirit of affinity with life. Nietzsche believed that the time had come for philosophers to take the leadership in reversing the

1

nihilistic attitude toward values pervading every dimension of human existence.

In *Thus Spoke Zarathustra* Nietzsche identified nihilism as an emptiness that devours increasing amounts of life and yet fails to be satisfied with living.[2] The nihilism that Nietzsche uncovered roughly one hundred years ago is still with us today, both in the form in which he observed it and in more intensified forms. The tendencies in Western culture toward self-destruction have accelerated since the middle and late nineteenth century. At present, the highest political authorities in the world have the power to destroy and exploit human life in unprecedented ways. Nonhuman life is generally destroyed with great thoughtlessness because the attention given to the continuity and interdependence of all life forms is only superficial. The earth is rapidly being depleted of its natural resources, but the development of weapons systems is assured. These specific phenomena do not constitute nihilism as Nietzsche saw it. However, structurally they fit the description of the results to be expected from a consciousness guided by hatred and resentment against life. The destruction of future life-forms through the excessive and careless appropriation of presently available resources is a manifestation of what Nietzsche identified as a resentment against time.[3] The wish to avoid responsibility for the future, like the desire to avoid taking responsibility for the past, is a sign to emptiness. The challenge to arrest the power of nihilism is still before us.

NIHILISM AND THE DEATH OF GOD

Manifestations—sometimes extreme—of nihilism are found in every aspect of human existence today, whether psychological, social, economic, or political. And yet, the term "nihilism" is usually thought to refer primarily to the consequences of the loss of belief in God or in an absolute system of values. The question is not raised as to why nihilism does not refer to the death of the earth and of the values associated with caring for the earth. The prevailing interpretation of nihilism should be seen as characteristic of a culture still controlled by nihilistic values. In such a culture, nihilism is interpreted as a crisis in values of the type where "nothing is true, everything is permitted." Under a reassessed or transvaluated perspective on values, however, one would see the same situation in the following terms: nothing that oppresses me and dominates me is true; everything that allows me to express the love of life is permitted.[4] In other words, what the established values view as chaos, the new principles hold to be vitality and freedom.

The person still influenced by nihilism associates it with the loss of belief in God. But Nietzsche asks: What is the origin of the belief in a Being with absolute power to punish one? The full investigation of this question will take us further than Nietzsche can lead us. In this study I will challenge the ideology of authoritarianism, which binds together the values of Western culture. In a patriarchal culture, one is so dominated by the fear of punishment that one fears it in one form or another even if one knows that the old God is dead. This phenomenon takes place because God's role in patriarchal culture has been that of Absolute Patriarch. The patriarchally dominated conscience continues to feel guilty of violating God's authority even after the death of God. Moreover, under a patriarchally dominated aesthetics, the death of God is still material for tragedy. One mourns the death of the patriarch in art as well as in one's conscience through guilt. Nietzsche himself was highly influenced by these values, although in his theory of values he struggles to disengage himself from them. And so in *The Gay Science* and *Thus Spoke Zarathustra* the death of God is portrayed by Nietzsche as both a tragic event and as a precondition for the possibility of gaiety.[5] Where Nietzsche views the death of God tragically he is still appealing to the nihilistic consciousness, although through tragedy he hopes to reverse the values of nihilism in favor of an affirmation of life. On the other hand, when he afirms gaiety and laughter, and when Zarathustra states that he would believe only in a god who could dance, Nietzsche adopts a new perspective on values whose foundation is a celebration of the earth, the body, and the human capacity for creative activity.

Although Nietzsche does not make this explicit, it should be emphasized that in a patriarchal society nihilism signifies the death of the patriarch and of his absolute authority to control life. If the patriarch is dead, it is asked, who will replace him? Following the patriarchal mode of reasoning, Freud thought that the patriarch's sons would replace him but that the sons would always feel guilty for having done so. Nietzsche, who denied the guilt, proposed that the authority to rule and the responsibility for governance should pass from the representatives of God (the priests) to the "higher men" of the patriarchal culture. But it will be easy to see that whenever Nietzsche followed the authoritarian mode of reasoning, both the resentment and nihilism that he sought to cure become reinstated in his own thoughts and teachings. It is helpful when combating nihilism to look at those areas in Nietzsche's theory of values where he succeeds in overcoming nihilism. However, it is also instructive to see why he is not always able to overcome nihilism. Although the major thrust of his work is life-affirming, Nietzsche's reliance upon the value of domination when it comes to settling issues of authority in morality and politics places him back within the compass of nihilism. I will specifically show that when the theme of domination is exclusively pursued in his work, Nietzsche's understanding of life turns out to be self-destructive.[6]

Fundamentally, however, Nietzsche had a liberating attitude toward what is generally thought to be the cause of nihilism, that is, the death of God or the loss of belief in absolute values. He did not believe that the death of God would precipitate a great nihilistic moment in human history as long as the real meaning of the "event" would be understood. What needs to be understood, in Nietzsche's view, is that with the death of God a great symbol of dualism and alienation from the earth has been vanquished. When many of the best human values are projected onto the essence of a divine and otherworldy being, a dualism is generated between what is divine and what is earthly. The death of God, then, signifies the end of one important manifestation of the dualism between the light and dark aspects of existence. If put in the right context—that is, if not replaced by some other form of dualism—it can be seen as a liberating experience since it establishes the possibility of human integration. Such is the message of Nietzsche's Zarathustra, who sought to guide the journey toward integration by offering to human beings the life-based symbol of the *Übermensch*.

THE POWER OF DUALISM

The influence of nihilism, however, is so powerful that in *On the Genealogy of Morals* Nietzsche observed that human beings would rather will nothingness than not will.[7] If all of the values in a culture are rooted in nihilism, this would mean that everyone would rather be a nihilist than refrain from living. Nihilism acquires its power indirectly through the indoctrination of the human conscience in the dualism between good and evil.[8] This indoctrination is then reinforced through the use of punishment. And yet Nietzsche thought that he could reverse the power of dualism through a reassessment of all values and their relationship to life. Looking at the unity of life, Nietzsche tried to point out that dualism implies the division and separation of life from itself (i.e., of some aspects of life from others). If the ideology of dualism overpowers an individual, he or she is endlessly trapped in cycles of self-hatred and self-division. This leads to the fragmentation of one's creative energy. An individual's creative life becomes more limited, if it is not completely impaired.

If Zarathustra is correct that the dualism of good and evil is the most powerful structure supporting the positing of what is valuable, is it still possible to break the power of this dualism? It is not enough to declare that an otherworldly God is dead, for other forms of dualism are ready to take the place of this belief. Nietzsche saw that to uproot the power of dualism one would have to eliminate the fear of punishment or, better yet, the ontological justification for punishment. One would also have to construct a whole new theoretical outlook on existence. This outlook would be such that the self would not see itself in opposition to the world, and the temporal life of human beings would not be considered in opposition to an eternal life where, as an added feature, one would experience either an eternal reward or punishment. Finally, one would also need to be sufficiently healthy—that is, psychologically ready—to accept the new interpretation of existence. Nietzsche took it on as his philosophical task to refine this new interpretation of existence as much as possible so that his victories over nihilism, whether great or small, could contribute to the release of the love of life in other human beings. The systematic project through which Nietzsche chose to develop his interpretation of life was called the "Transvaluation of All Values." An analysis of its major premises will convey what Nietzsche meant by the overcoming of nihilism.

THE PROJECT OF THE TRANSVALUATION OF ALL VALUES

In his autobiography, *Ecce Homo,* Nietzsche relates how in August 1881, while taking a walk in the woods, he had the most inspiring idea of his life.[9] This was the idea of the eternal recurrence of all things. One of the implications of this idea is that the life one lives will recur eternally without a single element subtracted from or added to the whole. Although if one accepts this belief as true, one is no longer free from the life one has lived, Nietzsche viewed the joyful acceptance of the belief as a sign that life had been fully affirmed and nihilism overcome. As time went on, Nietzsche became more and more interested in preparing humanity for the acceptance of the idea of the eternal recurrence. Eighteen months after the moment of inspiration, with the completion of Book I of *Thus Spoke Zarathustra,* Nietzsche felt that he had taken the first step in that direction.

Thus Spoke Zarathustra is Nietzsche's first attempt at a transvaluation of all values. Reversing the values of the ancient prophet Zoroaster, who had proclaimed the eternal opposition of good and evil, Nietzsche's Zarathustra comes down from the mountain to announce the death of God and the possibility of self-healing. In an unpublished note from 1884 Nietzsche observed that some of the results of the change of values would be the following: "No longer joy in certainty but in uncertainty; no longer 'cause and effect' but the continually creative; no longer will to preservation but to power; no longer the humble expression, 'everything is *merely* subjective,' but 'it is also *our* work—Let us be proud of it.' "[10] The purpose of the transvaluation of all values, then, is to destroy the need for a belief in a world of being in order to make possible the complete and joyful acceptance of existence as a process of becoming. This philosophical project was part of a long-standing effort on Nietzsche's part to relocate the origin of all values in "life" and to give this analysis of existence an exceptionally positive value. In fact, when Nietzsche stated in his first work, *The Birth of Tragedy,* that only as an aesthetic phenomenon could existence be eternally justified, he had already begun to consider the possibility of a life-based justification of values.[11] In the late works, Nietzsche considered extending the principle of creativity to all of existence—not simply to specified artistic energies. Alternatively, he also suggested that the issue of justifying existence—even through such a principle as the creativity of all life—is only meaningful to a nihilistic consciousness. Existence as such does not require justification, and to raise the question of justification already shows a negation of life.

Aside from Nietzsche's pursuit of the question of the origin of values and the "value" of values in his published works, it is known that he worked on a separate project in which he intended to lay down the principles of his theory of values systematically. The latter project—sometimes called "The Will to Power" and finally in 1888 entitled "The Transvaluation of All Values"—was never completed.[12] Nietzsche abandoned the project of "The Will to Power" because he could not reconcile the systematic goals of the investigation with what he deemed to be a more authentic and intuitive conception of existence. "I mistrust all systematizers and avoid them," he states in *Twilight of the Idols*. "The will to a system is a lack of integrity."[13]

After rejecting the project of "The Will to Power" Nietzsche decided to organize the "Transvaluation" project differently. According to his last plans, *The Antichrist* was to have been the first book of a four-part series under the general title of "The Transvaluation of All Values." *The Antichrist* would have been followed by separate critiques of metaphysics and morality and a final work on the eternal recurrence. But instead of proceeding to these works Nietzsche turned to the writing of *Ecce Homo* and then to his last work, *Nietzsche contra Wagner*.

The themes and arguments that Nietzsche hoped to develop in his unwritten critiques of metaphysics and morality do not remain a secret. They had already appeared in various—even if brief—forms in Nietzsche's published works, extending as far back as *The Birth of Tragedy*. It is interesting, however, to devote some critical attention to these themes not simply in the context of a critique of past values—as they are generally interpreted—but insofar as they express Nietzsche's vision for a life-affirming ground of a future metaphysics and morality. Since all of Nietzsche's work, both published and unpublished, from the period from 1883 to 1888 is especially relevant to his vision of overcoming and transcending nihilism, for the purposes of this study I have treated his concerns in his late works as aspects of a single purpose, namely, the laying down of foundations for a theory of value which would express the philosopher's joyful affirmation of life.

A Dionysian Reading of Nietzsche

Nietzsche's transvaluation of all values and his attempt to overcome nihilism may be read from many different perspectives. Since his affirmation of life is always associated with the figure of Dionysus, I have chosen to approach Nietzsche from a Dionysian perspective. My fundamental question has been: for what (Dionysian) reasons did Nietzsche criticize the tradition, and what alternatives did he propose in its place? This reading therefore differs from all those that study Nietzsche in terms other than the Dionysian.[14] Such studies are helpful but they sometimes fail to enter into dialogue with Nietzsche's Dionysian voice. My task, however, is to explore the labyrinth of Nietzsche's Dionysian conception of existence.

There are analogies between the myth of Dionysus and the type of reasoning Nietzsche employed to inquire about the origin of values. Dionysus is the twice-born god. His birth and death always imply a rebirth.[15] Similarly, Nietzsche's theory of values often calls for values to be twice-born (within a historical cycle). Dionysian tragedy appears first in the case of the Greeks and later in the case of Wagner. Philosophy, too, could be twice-born—first in the spirit of Heraclitus and then in that of Nietzsche-Dionysus. In these cases Nietzsche attributes to the transformed genre or activity an even greater power than to the original. The human species will be reborn as *Übermenschen* and, indeed, it is the *Übermensch* who has the greater power in comparison to man.

Let us characterize Nietzsche's Dionysian method as regressive-progressive.[16] Nietzsche first looks back to the origin of something. Then he looks forward into the future for the second coming of what was found valuable in the past.[17] He employs this method of reasoning repeatedly. However, since its principles are not laid out explicitly, his method is often misunderstood. Because we do not think in Dionysian terms, we are only able to see half of the picture. Usually our attention is focused on Nietzsche's relationship to the past. Yet in all of the statements where he reviews the significance of his work he conceives of his contributions as directed toward the future.

Nietzsche's method of reasoning has been called genealogical, in response to his use of this term in *On the Genealogy of Morals*.[18] Deleuze, in particular, describes Nietzsche's genealogical method as the tracing (or identification) of forces which count toward making something valuable. For example, Nietzsche characterized values as originating in strength or weakness, in vitality or decadence. In this type of analysis he claims to be tracing the origin of a value, but he is simultaneously establishing a new hierarchy of values. What he calls vitality becomes the highest-ranked new principle of values; what he calls decadence, the lowest. According to this method of appraisal, something evil, like cruelty, can lose its negative status immediately if Nietzsche is able to connect it to vitality. A virtue, such as prudence, could also lose its status if it is genealogically associated with decadence. Strictly speaking, this method of reasoning should not be called "genealogical," for this term generally implies a looking backward to an origin without at the same time instituting a complete shift in the worth of values. In Nietzsche, genealogy equals the transvaluation of values. To indicate the total (backward/forward) character of Nietzsche's manner of reasoning, the more appropriate name would be "Dionysian."

Nietzsche's Dionysian reasoning involves a movement backward in order to gain the vitality to move forward. If he criticizes past values, this is done so as to gather strength to create future values. For instance, Nietzsche was not interested in Greek culture for its own sake. His major study of Greek tragedy was balanced by an interest in Wagner's creative work. Nietzsche has been criticized for linking his study of the Greeks to Wagner's operatic work.[19] However, this criticism is unsound and reflects a lack of understanding of the Dionysian regressive-progressive method of reasoning. The regressive quality traces a value to its alleged origin; the progressive aspect shows the value's impetus toward reproducing itself in some future context. Just as the eulogy of Wagner is an integral part of *The Birth of Tragedy,* so is the transvaluation of all values (and its implications for the future) an essential statement of his philosophy.

A further clarification regarding Nietzsche's regressive-progressive method allows us to see that Dionysus symbolizes both a force (vitality, creativity, tragic insight) and a type (whatever belongs to the species of the twice-born). When Nietzsche reflects on questions of value, he speaks alternatively of forces and types. The worth of a value is most often attributed to a Dionysian force (e.g., vitality). However, Nietzsche also refers to a worthy type as the measure or standard of value (e.g., the Dionysian artist, the higher man). The Dionysian critique of values, therefore, tries to keep reordering past and present hierarchies of value so as to facilitate conditions for the successful appearance of either Dionysian forces or types. We are especially interested in Nietzsche's application of these insights to philosophy.

According to Nietzsche, the philosopher (or Socratic type) will become strong and ennobled only as part of a new and hybrid species, namely, the artist-philosopher. Nietzsche sought a blend of the artist's vitality and the philosopher's wisdom in a new breed of artist-philosophers, whom he named "philosophers of the future." To these new philosophers Nietzsche entrusted the task of sustaining a culture's vitality, strength, and affirmation of life. Genealogically, the values of these philosophers would be traceable to Dionysian artistic powers. Typologically, they themselves would be living exemplars of the Dionysian artist-philosopher. And then, ideologically, their teachings would have as their subject matter the celebration of a Dionysian conception of existence. Nietzsche thought of himself as the forerunner of this type and looked to the future for the emergence of companions. Despite his longing for unity with others, however, he remained fundamentally alone.

A moderately phrased statement in *The Birth of Tragedy* tells us that "Dionysus possesses the dual nature of a cruel, barbarized demon and a mild, gentle ruler."[20] As Nietzsche observes, Dionysus cannot experience oneness in his scattered and dismembered sate. Yet his promised rebirth symbolizes the possibility of a restored oneness and therefore of self-healing. A reading of Nietzsche's Dionysian conception of existence will allow us to see both aspects of Nietzsche-Dionysus. We begin with the promise of self-healing and Nietzsche's vision of the restored self. Since Nietzsche could not sustain the standpoint of redemption, we will also come to an encounter with the cruel, barbarized demon.

1

Truth and the Dionysian

Nietzsche does not have a systematic theory of truth; if he did, he would be violating some of his major insights on the subject. However, he continually raises the question of truth by noting that all truth claims are perspectival.[1] Obviously, the method or perspective chosen to determine what is true would then indicate what type of truth is most valued. This is to say that the question of truth cannot be settled apart from the question of values or resolved in isolation from lived experience. In Nietzsche's idea of truth we find a record of his lived experience. His thought may be characterized existentially as that of someone who struggled with various interpretations of truth, who sometimes despaired of ever reaching an adequate notion of truth, but who most often accepted a view of truth which he described as Dionysian.

In this chapter, I begin to examine Nietzsche's attempt to ground philosophy in a Dionysian conception of existence. The initial inquiry will take us back to the first book by Nietzsche, *The Birth of Tragedy* (1872). This is where he first announced the call for a reevaluation of a Socratic culture in terms of a Dionysian vision of reality. In this work, he uses three symbols from Greek culture to identify the different processes by which the Greeks gave meaning and value to existence. Dionysus, Apollo, and Socrates represent, respectively, the power of instinct and self-transcendence, the power of image and perfect individuation, and the power of logic and reasoning. My analysis of Nietzsche's work also begins with the symbol he considered most valuable (Dionysus) rather than with the one closest to the philosophical tradition (Socrates). The claims of Socrates will not be ignored but, in keeping with Nietzsche's priorities, I begin with Dionysus. The aim of this method is to study Nietzsche's work from inside out; that is, from what he took to be at the center of his experience (Dionysus) to his representation of it by way of image (Apollo) and argument (Socrates). Through this method I hope to understand, on Nietzsche's terms, what it would mean to root philosophy in a Dionysian conception of existence. If Nietzsche is right in arguing that Socratic reasoning has illegitimately disenfranchised the voice of Dionysus, we want to understand everything that philosophy has missed through its reliance upon Socratic assumptions and procedures. On the other hand, having given Dionysus an unprejudiced hearing, we will move on to interpret Nietzsche's Dionysian insights from the perspective of reason.

EXISTENCE AND TRUTH

Gaining access to Nietzsche's Dionysian philosophy is not easy. At the core of his view of existence one finds insights which defy explanation through logic. In some respects Nietzsche's position is comparable to that of Kierkegaard in the *Concluding Unscientific Postscript* (1846).[2] In a sharp critique of Hegel's dialectical logic, Kierkegaard protested that logic as such cannot capture the existential aspects of human life. Kierkegaard noted that while an atemporal logical system is indeed possible, an existential logic is impossible. The experience of temporality—an indispensable characteristic of human life—does not fit into the abstract structure of logical activity. An exclusively logical approach to truth, then, is found to be too distanced from the complexities of temporal existence to yield an adequate interpretation of reality.

The experiences of joy and suffering, the ambiguities to be found in language, the individual's sense of powerlessness before the passing of time, and the role of passion and instinct in the formation of values, on the other hand, provide the data needed by the existential thinker. Although philosophy would normally align itself with the method of logic and reasoning, given the nature of these existential themes the question arises as to whether they would not be better explored through a combination of methods rather than through the use of a single one, such as the rational argument. For example, the work of Kierkegaard and Nietzsche, and more recently that of Sartre, has shown that the process of existential thinking tends to combine the use of argument with a keen interest in human psychology and a preference for literary or aesthetic modes of representation. The multidimensionality of the process through which existential truth is represented speaks to the existential philosopher's need to transcend logical distinctions and boundaries when articulating the phenomena related to value formation in human existence. The strength of existential truth lies precisely in its insistence upon considering the importance of the totality of a person's being, including the role of the passions and the unconscious. Still, beyond this, the power of the existential perspective can be either sustained or weakened depending on the manner in which the interrelationship among the various components of human life is understood and depicted. Nietzsche's journey through the dimension of the Dionysian provides us with an interesting example.

DIONYSUS

In the second Preface to *The Birth of Tragedy,* or "Attempt at a Self-Criticism" (1886), Nietzsche remarks that his first book is significant because it raised a challenge to Socratic knowledge by looking at science from the perspective of the artist and at art from the perspective of life.[3] This statement solidifies Nietzsche's commitment to perspectivism as well as his existential view of truth. By placing the artist in a mediating category between science and life, Nietzsche implies that the artist is closer to life (and therefore to the truth of existence) than the Socratically inspired scientist or philosopher. The revelation of life's truths, Nietzsche further claims, is given through the experience of the Dionysian.

The principal Dionysian truth, insofar as it affects the individual, is the agony of individuation.[4] The myth of Dionysus's being torn to pieces by the Titans symbolizes the essential tragic insight that individuation is the cause of human suffering. Here the body of the god of life (Dionysus) represents the totality of existence, while the shattering of the totality into parts symbolizes the violent separation of the individual from the whole. Individuation separates one from the whole of life and, as it were, condemns one to death. However, just as the state of individuation is regarded as one of suffering, so its transcendence or end is experienced as a source of joy. According to Nietzsche, the Dionysian redemption promises "the shattering of the individual and his fusion with primal being."[5] The artistic mediation of this insight, he also argued, was found in early Greek tragedy. In Attic tragedy the mystery-teaching of Dionysus is expressed, both as abysmal truth and as joyous hope. Tragedy teaches that everything that exists is one and that individuation is the original source of evil. However, tragedy also heals the shattered individual, allowing the individual to transcend the spell of individuation in the aesthetic experience and thereby to experience joy. The pain of individuation is the obverse of the joy in self-transcendence.

It should be emphasized that the Dionysian state of consciousness is not a destructive or chaotic state, as its association with the notion of intoxication might suggest. One is intoxicated not with chaos but with life, with energy, even with gentility. Nietzsche relates that under the Dionysian influence the alienation of human beings from nature and from each other is completely overcome. There is joy in self-forgetfulness and joy in union with other human beings and with the earth. All oppressive relations between human beings are eradicated. The slave is now a free human being; all the "rigid, hostile barriers that necessity, caprice, or 'impudent convention' " have fixed between human beings are broken.[6] The Dionysian therefore symbolizes the end of the ego-consciousness with its discriminating and divisive judgments. In the union of human beings with each other through forms of communication like song and dance the power of individuation is broken and the natural affinities among people are affirmed.

THE INDIVIDUAL'S CONTINUITY
VERSUS DYNAMIC CONTINUITY

Through the perspective of the Dionysian Nietzsche stresses that our conception of individual existence represents a disruption of the fundamental continuity and harmony of the individual with nature. If individuation is assigned the character of discontinuity and the end of individuation is assigned continuity, what view of continuity does Nietzsche have in mind? Generally, we tend to think of continuity as a mark of individuated existence, not the converse. For example, there is the continuity of the individual or self in time. As a rule, when the ego-consciousness is lost or suspended, this phenomenon is not called "continuity" but "discontinuity." Nietzsche inverts the accepted paradigm. The reason for this is that he found in the principle of individuation a discontinuity from the dynamic continuity of life.

What the Dionysian state makes available is the return to the dynamic continuity of life. This possibility, in turn, transforms and transfigures human consciousness. Individuated existence is "cursed" because its psychological agent, the ego, disconnects

itself from the total flow of energy found in life. The ego super-
imposes its need for continuity and survival upon the unrehearsed
movement of the life process. The "waves" of dynamic energy
found in life are either subdued or ignored under the model of
continuity demanded by the ego for its survival. The power of
the Dionysian state breaks down the rigid barriers of convention
between individuals. In place of ego-security, which demands the
preservation of conventional barriers between people, the Dionysian experience offers the dynamic continuity of existence,
whose natural rhythms cannot be substituted for extrinsically determined norms. However, before the dynamic process can be
fully experienced or appreciated, one must give up the belief that
continuity can mean only the continuity of the ego and its survival.
Not only is this view of individuation something that will necessarily alienate individuals from each other and from nature, but
it is also false. The individual will perish in time. Continuity for
the individual is always threatened by death or destruction. For
the Dionysian-identified consciousness, on the other hand, life
and death are continuous and necessary aspects of each other.

The identification of the Dionysian state of awareness with dynamic continuity also helps to explain certain aspects of Nietzsche's view of the Dionysian which, on first consideration, do
not seem to blend in well with the harmony between individuals
and nature of which he speaks. This is the principle of destruction
that is associated with the power of the Dionysian. Speaking of
the Dionysian transformation that an "exhausted" culture may
undergo if it allows a Dionysian art-form like tragedy to develop
fully, Nietzsche writes: "A tempest seizes everything that has
outlived itself, everything that is decayed, broken, withered, and
whirling, shrouds it in a cloud of red dust to carry it into the air
like a vulture. Confused, our eyes look after what has disappeared; for what they see has been raised as from a depression
into golden light. . . ."[7] Here the motif of Dionysian destruction,
transfiguration, and creativity, so prevalent in Nietzsche's late
philosophy, appears under a medley of metaphors. The shepherd
in Zarathustra's vision becomes transfigured in biting off and spit-
ting out the head of the serpent, and here Nietzsche points to the
transfiguration through Dionysian tragedy of a "feeble" culture
that "hates true art" and fears destruction through its power.[8]
However, if the Dionysian principle is interpreted as a principle
of dynamic continuity, the transfiguration would not be surprising.

Despite the destruction of the individuated forms, there is continuity in life. What continues is the life energy and those aspects of the individual that are alive with that energy. What is phased out of existence is what is overpowered by a stronger force of its own kind. In Zarathustra's vision, the Dionysian-inspired shepherd bites into the serpent's head. Thus the individuated form of the serpent is destroyed because it is not powerful enough to resist the shepherd. In the same way, if Dionysian art were to "sweep up" all superficial forms of art in the culture, our eyes (here a symbol of that through which individuated forms are perceived) would be confused and look for the forms that disappeared. In contrast to individuated-oriented perception, the Dionysian state of awareness presents one with "golden light"— a metaphor for nonindividuated appearance. These metaphors show the transition from the individuation-oriented view of continuity to the dynamic Dionysian view.

The emerging Dionysian powers in human consciousness transform all decadent, fragmented life into a dynamic unity. When the transformative effects of the Dionysian are stressed, however, the emphasis is placed on how *different* the Dionysian state is to the withered state which preceded it. This makes it seem as if the dynamic unity of the Dionysian is something exceptional or remote, whereas in reality it is the very foundation of being. It is only remote to us when we alienate ourselves from its power. Because Nietzsche often wishes to show the dramatic contrast between the decadence caused by alienation and the radiant unity of life itself, an incipient dualism is introduced into his analysis of existence. But it is the alienation from the Dionysian continuity which causes the dualism rather than the nature of life itself through its so-called "weak" and "strong" forms.

It is interesting that the idea of regenerative transformation, first developed by Nietzsche in the form of a mandate for art to transform a decaying culture, should in his late works be extended to a criticism of all forms of decadence, including the psychological, physiological, and political. In its positive form, this idea of regeneration will underscore Nietzsche's teachings on the *Übermensch,* the eternal recurrence, and the will to power. As Dionysian symbols, these were expected to transform radically both the consciousness of human beings and the structure of Western culture. Nietzsche's idea of regenerative transformation, however, contains a pattern which will later develop into a major

portance to
tion that all
strong life.
rior person
es of those
idea of the
principle of
inciple. It is
an important
hasis on the
life as well
e Dionysian
manipulated
on) from the

on which re-
energies, he
ve with me in
f the Socratic
to your hand,
down, fawn-
s is promised
, however, is
are presented
ther powerful
cratic. Let us

nature have in
ure."[10] This is
forms of art,
and Dionysian
unconscious.
is is associated
ection with the
that these un-
an unmediated
ndent upon the
means through

which the individual b

more powerful energie

gies directly connecte

posed to the individuat

from the fundamental

mony. By being artistic

in the natural process

of the human unconsci

energies are able to bl

rection of their creativ

of the time. Even whe

degree in conflict. Evi

that the Apollonian en

the tragic spectator tha

god.

Apollo stands for the

fected beauty of the i

stands for illusion, as D

ollonian illusion is to po

This gives the individua

of appearances. But an

convince the individual

service of the Apolloni

Apollonian principle (m

principle (manifest in m

Nietzsche observes that

onysian universality and lo

distracting the self from

the immense power of its

and its arousal of symp

process *deludes* the indi

its standpoint—as if this

and other Dionysian sy

hancing the Apollonian i

What Nietzsche is des

tween the Apollonian an

exemplified in an aesthet

combined for the sake of

as the Apollonian illusion

Dionysian foundation. Ev

the Apollonian, indeed, is

weakness in his thought. The decision not to give importance to the individual as such will be combined with the notion that all decadent life needs to be destroyed to make room for strong life. This means that it almost becomes a duty of the superior person to either destroy or manipulate without limit the lives of those who are judged decadent or antilife. In this case the idea of the dynamic unity of life is lost, for this can only be a fit principle of activity as long as it does not become a despotic principle. It is important to emphasize that the continuity of life is an important element in the Dionysian world view. Too much emphasis on the notion of regeneration results in a condemnation of life as well as in its exaltation. This distorts the meaning of the Dionysian teaching and allows the Dionysian experience to be manipulated by the individual as an escape (or pseudoregeneration) from the divisions inherent in the alienated self.

THE APOLLONIAN INFLUENCE

As Nietzsche speaks of the Dionysian transformation which reunites consciousness with the ground of all natural energies, he enthusiastically concludes: "Yes, my friends, believe with me in Dionysian life and the rebirth of tragedy. The age of the Socratic man is over; put on wreaths of ivy, put the thyrsus into your hand, and do not be surprised when tigers and panthers lie down, fawning, at your feet."[9] The reconciliation of all opposites is promised to the Dionysian initiate. This ultimate redemption, however, is difficult to achieve, for the Dionysian energies of life are presented by Nietzsche as being in direct opposition to two other powerful tendencies of existence—the Apollonian and the Socratic. Let us look first at the Apollonian-Dionysian duality.

What the Apollonian and Dionysian energies of nature have in common is that they are both "art impulses of nature."[10] This is sufficient to allow them to blend at times in some forms of art, such as Attic tragedy. Furthermore, the Apollonian and Dionysian impulses are related by Nietzsche to forces of the unconscious. Apollo is linked to the dream image, while Dionysus is associated with states of intoxication. There is a further connection with the unconscious, however, in that Nietzsche claims that these unconscious states represent nature's art impulses in an unmediated manner.[11] The unconscious energies are not dependent upon the single unit or the individual, but rather are the means through which the individual blends in with the whole. They are also the more powerful energies the individual has. They are creative energies directly connected with the dynamic rhythms of life, as opposed to the individuated ego-consciousness which stands removed from the fundamental source of truth, creativity, power, and harmony. By being artistic impulses of nature and thus being grounded in the natural process of creativity, and by being twin expressions of the human unconscious powers, the Apollonian and Dionysian energies are able to blend together occasionally although the direction of their creative powers drives them to different ends most of the time. Even when they blend together, they are to some degree in conflict. Evidence of the conflict is shown by the fact that the Apollonian energies are always attempting to persuade the tragic spectator that Apollo, not Dionysus, is the superior god.

Apollo stands for the principle of individuation and the perfected beauty of the individual phenomenon. But Apollo also stands for illusion, as Dionysus stands for truth. Part of the Apollonian illusion is to portray the individual as eternally beautiful. This gives the individual a great feeling of security in the world of appearances. But another part of the Apollonian illusion is to convince the individual that the Dionysian exists only for the service of the Apollonian. This happens in tragic art when the Apollonian principle (manifest in the drama) uses the Dionysian principle (manifest in music) to enhance the dramatic effects. Nietzsche observes that the Apollonian "tears us out of the Dionysian universality and lets us find delight in individuals," thereby distracting the self from fulfillment in Dionysian oneness.[12] With the immense power of its image, its concept, its ethical teaching, and its arousal of sympathy for the individual, the Apollonian process *deludes* the individual into seeing the world solely from its standpoint—as if this were the only standpoint, as if music and other Dionysian symbols found their purpose only in enhancing the Apollonian image of being.

What Nietzsche is describing is the conflicting interaction between the Apollonian and Dionysian art impulses of nature as exemplified in an aesthetic work (like opera) where the two are combined for the sake of a single aesthetic effect. As powerful as the Apollonian illusion is, however, it cannot exist without a Dionysian foundation. Eventually the recognition must come that the Apollonian, indeed, is in service to the Dionysian and not the other way around. Nietzsche develops this insight by saying that all of the heroes of Attic tragedy (the individuated forms in which the audience takes delight) are really masks of the god Dionysus. It is really Dionysus who allows for the individual representations because the individuated characters (like Oedipus) are fundamentally representations of himself. The Apollonian principle ignores this debt to the Dionysian insofar as it can. Whether the Apollonian art impulse stands alone, as in the art of sculpture, or whether it merges with the Dionysian, as in classical tragedy and Wagnerian opera, its function is always to cover up the ground of truth—the Dionysian ''waves of the will''—with the beauty of individuated forms. This beauty is so attractive (for Nietzsche art was always a promise of happiness) that the audience or spectator is moved to blend with that beauty rather than with the dynamic and (to the individual) frightful ground of existence. Thus the Dionysian impulse toward blending and unity is put in the service of the Apollonian and diverted from its natural course in the unindividuated rhythms of life.

THE SOCRATIC DISRUPTION OF NATURE

Although the Apollonian energy has as its end the displacement of the Dionysian by delighting the individual with the beauty of forms and mere appearance, the Apollonian and the Dionysian are interdependent forces, ''interwoven artistic impulses,'' as Nietzsche remarks before he embarks on a discussion of the Socratic.[13] The duality between the Apollonian and the Dionysian is like that between the sexes (Nietzsche's comparison).[14] The Apollonian and Dionysian impulses complement each other in the creative process, whose greatest offspring is tragedy. Despite their opposition, Apollonian and Dionysian energies are of a similar kind. For Nietzsche they symbolize nature's process of creativity, which in human beings is directly manifested and expressed in the powers of the unconscious.

The appearance of the Socratic principle kills tragedy and, by implication, all artistic creativity, both from within and from without. Because it is a principle extrinsic to art (opposing thought to art) it overpowers art from without. And yet, as a formal principle, it succeeds the Apollonian impulse from within. The Socratic principle signifies the demand for the intelligibility of all things, including tragedy. According to Nietzsche, the Socratic is the new antagonist of the Dionysian and an alienated substitute for the Apollonian principle, which somehow disappears in the process. The form of beauty that Apollo used to provide now becomes the intelligible form demanded by Socrates. Nietzsche remarks: "Now we should be able to come closer to the character of *aesthetic Socratism,* whose supreme law reads roughly as follows, 'To be beautiful everything must be intelligible,' as the counterpart to the Socratic dictum, 'Knowledge is virtue'."[15] Euripides, who has internalized aesthetic Socratism as his inspirational voice, is depicted by Nietzsche as abandoning the dual Apollonian-Dionysian creative process and installing in its place a conveniently intelligible drama. Nietzsche goes on to say that Euripides' tactic of employing the gods to lend credibility to the truth of the Euripidean plot is a similar strategy to that followed by Descartes when the latter certifies that the empirical world exists because God is incapable of deception.[16] The artificial and fake god of intelligibility takes over Dionysus, the god of creative energy. The means used by the Socratic god of intelligibility to defeat the Apollonian-Dionysian alliance is the power to explain, control, and predict events in reality. Once the god's messenger who opens Euripides' plays is brought in to decipher and predict the outcome of all the events in the drama and the audience is satisfied to receive the meaning of life in an intelligible formula, the future power of science over human life and culture has been assured.

The Socratic disruption of the creative processes of nature is mediated by the need to control reality not as reality was known to the Dionysian initiate but as the reality of the world that appears before us—the world as object of knowledge. Reality is no longer the dynamic process out of which we spring (the Dionysian) or even the image contemplated in place of the ground of our existence (the Apollonian). Now reality is an object to be analyzed and manipulated. Now it must fit certain predetermined frames of thought rather than express, through art and the symbolic dream-process, truths that resist intelligible comprehension. These frames of thought are a version of the Apollonian principle of individuation in that, in spite of the universal claims given to knowledge, the knowledge of which Socrates speaks is one that facilitates the functioning and enhances the power of individual existents. Knowledge gives power to the individual, with the exception of knowledge as self-transcendence—a form of knowledge which Nietzsche indeed celebrates as a dimension of the Dionysian.[17]

But generally, what is known is either in the form of particulars or abstraction from particulars and, further, it is existentially made conformable to what can be known by individuals. The rules of logic deal only with discrete symbols and propositions. The Dionysian principle of dynamic continuity is violated to such an extent that Dionysus's only recourse is to revenge himself upon humanity by condemning it to perpetual fragmentation.

The creative balance of nature is such that one cannot disrupt the natural process without also provoking some type of reaction. The extreme case of the Socratic violation of nature's creative art impulses would, as a counterreaction, result in the dismemberment of the ego and, hence, in madness. Madness, then, is the perpetual Dionysian threat which a Socratic culture must experience. The most immediate form of threat, however, is fragmentation or dismemberment. The loss of the unified Dionysian ground of existence and the transfer of the center for synthesizing experiences to the thought process constitutes a violation of nature as well as a violation of all truly creative possibilities for human beings. Hence Nietzsche's later analysis of reason as a form of decadence. In *Twilight of the Idols* Nietzsche attributed the origin of the Socratic trust in reasoning to the disintegration of the instincts.[18] In light of what he says in *The Birth of Tragedy* this means that when the unconscious stops functioning in a creative manner, the intuitive sense of continuity is lost for human beings and the aesthetics of reason is put in its place.

THE AESTHETICS OF REASON

Still viewing science from the perspective of the artist, Nietzsche points to the beginning of Socratism—or the rise of the theoretical human being—as a phenomenon that both destroys tragedy and also, to some extent, creates a new art of its own. What theory does is to appropriate the creative energies of nature and apply them to a theoretical rather than artistic justification of existence. But since in Nietzsche's view any activity that attempts to give meaning to existence is fundamentally an aesthetic activity, reason itself is seen as performing an aesthetic function, giving meaning to the life of the individual by allowing the individual to have an intelligible understanding of life.[19]

In *The Birth of Tragedy* Nietzsche gives two views of what might be called an "aesthetics" of reason. Under the first aspect reason gives form and meaning to things but is fundamentally sterile because it functions in alienation from the dynamic richness of the artistic process. Here the aesthetics of reason has as its goal the purification of experience and the acquisition and accumulation of knowledge based on criteria of order and cleanliness. On the other hand, Nietzsche also claims that there is a fundamentally artistic activity in the theoretical process insofar as its aim is to give meaning to life. Where theory abstracts from life, Nietzsche calls it alienated. However, if theory springs out of a need to serve life, Nietzsche praises it as artistic in the fundamental (nonalienated) sense of the term.

Alienated reason's paradigm of aesthetic form is the logical method. The logical method thrives on clean proofs. It also keeps empirical knowledge in order by logical categories through which empirical data are classified and collected. The unconscious is rejected for its truth value, even if it is acknowledged as essential to the artistic process.[20] Theory equals form. The poet, whose creativity admittedly is linked to inspiration, is banned from Plato's republic. However, Nietzsche's main target is not Plato but Euripides. In his dramas Euripides allows the emotions some degree of expression, but Nietzsche observes that emotion is only accepted in its immediacy, that is, for its immediate effects. When the actor is nothing but the mouthpiece of the emotion he is evoking, this means that emotion is nothing but emotion, that it has no relation to the transcendent ground of truth. Thus Nietzsche notes that the Euripidean drama is at once cool and fiery—cool in its design and fiery in its effects. The coolness is a degenerate replacement for the Apollonian principle of contemplation, while the fieriness takes the place of authentic Dionysian ecstasies.[21] The same phenomenon, one might add, occurs in the fragmented artist that Euripides represents. The mind is cool, the passions fiery. The unconscious energies cannot make their way unhindered to conscious activity without being censored. The standard of mental cleanliness demands that all superfluous elements be kept strictly separate from thought. Alienated thought can only absorb what is decontaminated from the sensual elements of existence. Pleasure and pain are recognized as real, but their reality is in the realm of immediacy, where they are allowed to exist as long as they do so unproblematically. In no way can pleasure and pain signal to the metaphysical truths of existence, such as the pain of individuation or the pleasure of integration

with that which transcends the self. When such creative integration is lost, what is unintelligible to the alienated mind (e.g.,
passion, instinct, dream) is declared to lack ultimate significance.
The individual gives attention only to what is "real," namely,
what can be made subject to the individual's comprehension, what
is safe to experience.

But reason does not only expect that reality conform itself to
the standards of thought. It even seeks to *correct* existence. Compared to the formal beauty of thought, reality is a defect that
needs to be corrected. Nietzsche's critique of Socrates is intensified: "Wherever Socratism turns its searching eyes it sees lack
of insight and the power of illusion; and from this lack it infers
the essential perversity and reprehensibility of what exists. Basing
himself on this point, Socrates conceives it to be his duty to
correct existence. . . ."[22] An alienated type of aesthetic duty develops. Part of what it means to correct existence is to deny the
instincts their life-affirming power. Nietzsche believed that the
life-oriented nature of instinctual activity is manifested in the drive
toward self-transcendence. Again, this is a Dionysian teaching
which links self-transcendence to the end of individuation, and
therefore to the highest Dionysian good. But rational activity,
placed at the service of ego-sustenance and power, perceives the
instinctual drive toward self-transcendence as an anarchic threat
to its control.[23] This phenomenon is a symptom of the Dionysian
curse on the Socratic type. Whoever turns away from the life-
affirming, ego-transcending voice of the instincts is condemned
to a state of perpetual fragmentation, such that one is always on
the edge of being threatened with dismemberment unless one
keeps the life instincts under ever vigilant and tight controls. One
of the most effective instruments of control over authentic instinctual needs is the use of reason and morality. This is the
phenomenon that Nietzsche thought he observed in Socrates. The
instincts, symbolized by Socrates' daimon or voice, never urge
Socrates toward self-transcendence; on the contrary, they urge
him toward either self-containment or self-sufficiency. The instinctual imperative received by Socrates comes in the form of a
dissuasion, of a "no." Here lies the major difference between
Socrates and the Dionysian initiate who, on the other hand, is
ready to merge with the dynamic flow of life and even say "no"
to the needs of individuation if an important choice has to be
made regarding how one's energies are to be directed. But wher-

ever Socrates is the spectator and judge of existence, Dionysus must bow down to Socrates' control.

Socrates' ultimate power was to be able to accept his death without any apparent need of the Dionysian teachings.[24] In the Socratic type theory, rather than passion, is the one acceptable mode of self-transcendence. Socrates' triumph is that he made death intelligible to him and thus faced it calmly. He corrected the harshness of the natural phenomenon of death by giving it a theoretical analysis which satisfied his intellect and thus persuaded both himself and his companions that he possessed the meaning of existence. At this point, according to Nietzsche, Socratic theory, by justifying individual existence, turns its process into an Apollonian (illusion-oriented) venture. The very activity of making the life of an individual meaningful is an aesthetic process; even the abstract activities of logic and science, therefore, serve the aesthetic drive when they are used to give meaning to life. However, Nietzsche delimits the value of reason by suggesting that theory is valuable only insofar as the theoretician is an artist whose materials are logic and reason rather than song or dance.

Just as the occasional merging of the Apollonian-Dionysian opposites was found to take place in tragedy, so the even less likely blending of the Socratic and Dionysian impulses remains a possibility for Nietzsche. Toward the end of his extraordinary commentary on Socrates, Nietzsche raises the possibility that perhaps the opposition between Socrates and Dionysus is not necessarily trapped in a contradiction. Certainly there were many other aspects of Socrates' being that Nietzsche himself recognizes as having been left unexplored.[25] However, while there may be a blend between the Socratic and Apollonian principles insofar as scientific theory may replace traditional myth as the justification of the meaning of life, still it is difficult to imagine a merging of the Socratic and Dionysian *on Dionysian terms*. For this merging it would not be enough for the theoretician to "set some time aside" for the purpose of engaging in Dionysian activities, as Socrates did toward the end of his life when he decided to "practice music."[26] What is Dionysian cannot be compartmentalized or wrapped into such a tidy package. *For the proper blending of the Socratic and Dionysian the meaning of time itself would have to change.* The individual's relationship to time would have to be reconsidered from a standpoint in which the individual no longer wants to be in control of time. Eventually this transvaluation of the meaning of time will be addressed through the teaching of the eternal recurrence and Zarathustra's healing message against that which cripples the dynamic continuity of existence for the individual, namely, the alienated human being's resentment against the passing of time.[27]

Perhaps the only blending that is possible between the Socratic principle of intelligibility and the Dionysian idea of a world of endless flux and energy in which consciousness must ride the waves of unconscious creativity is to create a Dionysian philosophy which would give some degree of intelligibility to the basic Dionysian insight of the dynamic continuity of life. Indeed, this is the task to which Nietzsche applied himself in the period of the transvaluation of all values. The teachings of Zarathustra, the work on the will to power, and the critique of all previous values in religion, morality, and metaphysics represent Nietzsche's attempt to root philosophy in a Dionysian conception of existence. In this context the notion of philosophy itself must change, not with respect to the love of wisdom but with respect to the method philosophy has used to keep the love of wisdom tied only to some aspects of existence and not to the totality. Logic must still exist in the philosophy of the future, but it must not be given the exclusive voice as to how reality is to be interpreted. The notion of intelligibility must be made broader and must be given roots in the earth. In brief, a transvaluation of philosophy itself is demanded.

NIETZSCHE'S CRITIQUE OF LOGIC

The Dionysian transvaluation of all values requires the transvaluation of logic. From the standpoint of the Dionysian, Nietzsche views classical logic as a product of fragmentation, dismemberment. Furthermore, he views the process of abstraction from everyday reality as a process which, though it may aid the survival of individuals, still remains a fiction. What logic can piece together may be quite elegant, but Nietzsche believes that a fundamental distortion of reality has taken place.

His first objection against logic is that it has inverted the natural relationship of unconscious to conscious thought. Consciousness should be the overflow of the unconscious process or, at the least, conscious and unconscious should be interdynamic aspects of a wavelike rhythm, as in the rhythm of tides. Under such a model the conscious thoughts of human beings would be like a musical pattern of tones, playing tunes of high or low intensity in accordance with the overall rhythms of life. These figurative allusions appropriately convey Nietzsche's idea of the relationship of the individual to the totality of life. In his early work, following Schopenhauer, Nietzsche thought that the closest symbolic structure to the essence of life was music.[28] In his late writings, he refers to his state of mind prior to the writing of *Zarathustra* as the discovery of a new kind of music.[29] It is understandable that music, with its structure of theme and variation, its crescendoes and dissonances, should provide a model analogous to that of lived experience. Logic, on the other hand, gains its power from the exclusion of such life-rhythms, although its clear and precise method could also be characterized as its distinctive tune. However, it was not a tune that Nietzsche found very meaningful.

The second objection Nietzsche holds against classical logic has to do with the logical method itself, although the weaknesses he attributes to the method are related by him to the detached relationship between logic and life. Here all of the themes of the Dionysian interpretation of existence surface once more. In place of dynamic process, logic is interested in formal security and conventional boundaries. In place of dynamic unity, the logical method appears to assume a universe made up of discrete elements whose structures may be known or controlled through logical laws. In place of Dionysian universality and the end of individuation, there is the logical universal drawn in abstraction from flux. And finally, in place of expressive, poetic modes of communication, logic aims at straightforward, unambiguous discourse.

As an alternative to the logical method the Dionysian state of consciousness offers forms of communication such as song and dance. Nietzsche's Zarathustra teaches one not to believe in a god that does not dance.[30] The godliness of which Nietzsche speaks is that of the creative process of life, which is never self-contained. The rhythms and movement of song and dance, like those of life, elude classification. A refrain from the poetry of William Butler Yeats vividly captures the Dionysian vision:

> O chestnut-tree, great-rooted blossomer,
> Are you the leaf, the blossom or the bole?

O body swayed to music, O brightening glance,
How can we know the dancer from the dance?[31]

The subject-object distinction that rules discursive thought is suspended as the dynamic unity of life is perceived.

As we move away from aesthetic experience and back toward logical discourse, we may proceed to integrate either the Dionysian or the Apollonian perspectives with the Socratic, and thus actualize the aim to integrate reason and life. However, this type of integration may not always be attained. For example, in his late works Nietzsche charged that even the best-intended attempt toward integration may be thwarted. Even if the two potential antagonists, reason and life, were reconciled, integration could be hindered as a result of the conventional rules of grammar. His argument is interesting because it shows how a conventional practice may come to obstruct the resolution of the Dionysian-Socratic duality.

Nietzsche claims that the subject-object dualism which his Dionysian perspective seeks to eliminate may be potentially kept alive by the rules of language. Especially relevant is the case of those languages whose syntactical structure demands a strict separation between subject and object or subject and verb.[32] Nietzsche's point is that as long as one is psychologically dependent upon subject-verb and subject-object structures of grammar, one is implicitly allowing the splitting of subject and world to take place. If, in addition to this, one proceeds to a metaphysical reification of the grammatical elements that function as subject and predicate, the result is a picture of the universe where grammar, logic, and metaphysics reinforce their power by confirming each other's roles. Thus Nietzsche remarks that human beings will remain dependent on God as long as they have faith in grammar.[33] That is, whether God is conceived as noun (subject) or verb (process), or both, his existence reflects the ultimate reification of the subject-verb syntactical structure. Conversely, as long as human beings fail to raise critical questions regarding what truths, if any, may be inferred from grammar, they will continue to relate to grammar as if it were God.

Although the use of such arguments proves that Nietzsche was perfectly capable of using reason and logic to articulate his Dionysian vision of existence, he was reluctant to believe that these arguments as such were sufficiently powerful to reverse the effect of convention upon thought. In other words, even where logic could be used in defense of the Dionysian perspective, Nietzsche seems to have viewed logic more as an enemy than as a friend. For example, even though logic can help to clarify the illicit transfer of grammatical structures into metaphysical mystifications, Nietzsche depicts logic as an accomplice of grammar. In the same vein, he trusts only poetry and other artistic uses of language as options for counteracting the paralyzing effect of grammatical conventions. Even where logic serves the Dionysian good, poetry or tragedy alone bears the credit for doing so. This situation, one should add, does not follow from the use of the Dionysian perspective as such, but only from Nietzsche's reluctance to let go of a special faith in artistic genius.

Despite Nietzsche's generally insightful critique of logic, then, a few things need to be said in logic's defense. Without intending to repress or in fact repressing the importance of the Dionysian perspective, we can easily say that we are indebted to logic (and grammar) for providing certain structures of thought which guarantee the intelligibility of what is communicated verbally. The distinction between subject and object may not be conducive to expressing the nature of becoming, but as long as it is not thought of as an absolute or taken to refer to a fixed set of categories it is a useful and valid tool for making the world intelligible. Moreover, it cannot be expected that the relationship between self and world will always be one of mystic Dionysian oneness. There is a political and ethical issue at stake with respect to whether logic should be denied a voice in questions of truth. What can be expected is that the standpoint of logic and classical reasoning will not be considered absolute and that its limitations will be made explicit. However, if one goes on to suggest that these limitations disqualify logic from serving as a standard of knowledge, this is to move well beyond the original criticism. The criticism concerned itself with the abstract nature of logic and its severance from the unconscious processes of the organism. However, once these points are made (and they are made according to the fundamental rules of logical reasoning), one can still go on using logic. What one adds are some qualifications as to the extent of its validity.

Perspective and Politics

Now let us consider, hypothetically, the more extreme option of silencing logic. Could this tactic be justified, even in the name of Dionysian integration? Nietzsche has shown that the silencing of the unconscious in matters of truth constitutes a significant distortion of the nature of knowledge. We could argue that the silencing of logic would create a similar problem. However, it seems that in some cases the logical method has become so powerful as to completely silence the voice of the unconscious. For example, one could hold that unconscious desires can be appropriately expressed only in dreams and then add that dreams have no bearing on truth. This would be an extreme case of silencing the unconscious. What would happen if, as a countermeasure to this type of move on the part of the alienated reason, one were to propose exactly the opposite? What would happen if one were to attempt to silence logic, suggesting that its only allowable expression would be in grammar, but declared that grammar (like the dream) has absolutely no bearing on truth? It appears from Nietzsche's analysis of thought as fiction and from his statements on logic and grammar that he is sometimes led to consider this position.[34]

Supposing this were Nietzsche's position, why is it that it seems so outrageous to silence logic's relation to truth in comparison to silencing the dream's relation to truth? Why is it that the silencing of logic seems to be such a sacrifice of truth when silencing the dream might be an equal sacrifice? The power of logic lies in its ability to provide a certain stability and regularity through which experiences can be given a meaning and function within the compass of the logical world. This leads Nietzsche to hold that the contribution of classical logic to knowledge lies in its regulative function rather than in the specific nature of its rules. In other words, as long as a formal structure is given through which consciousness can understand experience, the determining elements of that form are relatively arbitrary with respect to knowledge. For example, the laws of the excluded middle and noncontradiction might be arbitrary for knowing the world, but what is not arbitrary is that there must be some formal structure or other. Let us say that instead of looking at reality through the category of individuation one simply erased that category—would the same idea of noncontradiction continue to hold? Or suppose that instead of viewing things as either static or in process one viewed them only as process. Would it not still be possible to know the world? These hypotheses are compatible with Nietzsche's theory of perspectivism: "In so far as the word 'knowledge' has any meaning, the world is knowable; but it is *interpretable* otherwise, it has no meaning behind it, but countless meanings."[35] What is to some degree incompatible with a broad thesis of pespectivism is the predetermined erasure of some perspectives so as to assure the acceptability of others. Although for experimental purposes the suspension of some categories of thought would be interesting, to attempt the erasure of specific categories would explicitly amount to censorship.

The idea that knowledge is dependent on form but that its formal principle is relatively arbitrary is interesting. It allows for some intriguing theoretical experiments, for example, what would the world be like if the notion of individuation were erased from consciousness? How would reality then appear to consciousness? One of Nietzsche's major insights is that reality could be described as will to power—and nothing besides.[36] Nietzsche's experimental perspectivism has great possibilities for thought. But it also presents important theoretical and practical problems. The main problem is that of erasure and censorship. This is not to say that the categories we use now are not erasing and censoring other ways of looking at experience, especially Dionysian ways. Still, to invert the process and replace some censoring agents with others is not a satisfactory solution. One merely keeps reproducing the disease instead of looking for and treating the cause. The roots of the problem of erasure and censorship lie in one's unacknowledged resentment against life itself. When Nietzsche tries to force the *inversion* of all previous values he resorts to a domination theory of existence, meaning, and value to justify his aggressive violence against unwanted values. By claiming that whatever perspectives turn out to be the most powerful will necessarily dictate the elimination of all rival perspectives,[37] he ignores his responsibility to protect the totality of life. The question always remains: Powerful for whom? Healthy for whom? Domination in itself is an empty concept (like the fictional metaphysical essence) if it is used simply to justify something that already is proven to exist or to have value. On the other hand, if domination is used to justify the value of intellectual forms of aggression against life, then one is back at the Socratic scheme of subjugating and correcting existence.

It was mentioned earlier that the authentic blending of the Socratic and Dionysian impulses could only take place on Dionysian terms. Given the Socratic repression of the Dionysian and the resultant Dionysian exclusion of the Socratic, is there any reconciliation possible between logic and the Dionysian perspective on truth? In the process of making the Dionysian perspective intelligible, Nietzsche appropriates from logic not the logical method itself but two broader notions: the idea of regularity and the idea that for the world to be intelligible there must be some formal structure to give it meaning. But at the same time he maintains his attack on logic in the specialized sense of the term. The blending of intelligibility and the life principle is given the appearance of taking place in life itself rather than through the mediation of reason. Nietzsche achieves this effect either by calling his formal principle a law of life or by using poetical figures of speech such as personification to give life a human voice and have it explain its meaning.[38] In his late works Nietzsche attempts to make the Dionysian flux intelligible through the idea, presented in *Zarathustra, Beyond Good and Evil,* the *Genealogy,* and *Ecce Homo,* that life is a process of self-overcoming (*Selbstüberwindung*). This perspective on existence, rhetorically called a "law," constitutes the logic of Nietzsche's Dionysian philosophy. The principle informs Nietzsche's interpretation of life and history and provides the fundamental formal structure for his arguments against traditional metaphysics and morality.

The fact that Nietzsche minimizes his debt to reason and logic and relies instead on rhetoric and metaphor to present his most important insights does not necessarily mean that logic and reason have no part in the development of truth or that his insights are invalid. He chose his method of presentation for a reason—to convey a sense of the immediacy of life and to give the sense that life already has a meaning and does not need theory to impose a superfluous and abstract meaning upon it. However, Nietzsche's tendency to erase the need for logic also points to certain weaknesses. His theory is open to the great Dionysian ecstasies but also to possible extreme erasures of the principle of individuation. These perspectival possibilities, as well as limitations, will have important consequences for his views on human nature and for his ethical and political theories.

THE LOGIC OF SELF-OVERCOMING

Nietzsche was still determined to challenge Socrates when he developed the Dionysian logic of self-overcoming. Socrates claims that he has received his wisdom on the mysteries of love from Diotima, but Nietzsche's Zarathustra receives the secret meaning of life from life itself: "And life itself confided this secret to me: 'Behold,' it said, 'I am that *which must always overcome itself*.'"[39] To the phenomenon of growth and decay, of change and recovery-reorganization, Nietzsche gave the name "self-overcoming." The idea of self-overcoming unifies all of the processes of life and at the same time provides a criterion for what is and is not life. The concept of self-overcoming is broad enough to encompass the process of change in all of its manifestations, including the periods of relative stability. On the other hand, it may be applied more specifically to what is active, rather than reactive, in life. That which is active is able to transcend itself and keep an open-ended future before it. What is reactive simply perishes without self-transcendence. "Self-overcoming" is a perspectival formula through which Nietzsche can describe the whole of life while at the same time judging the value of particular aspects of life. The reason Nietzsche's formula is so flexible as to apply to both the totality of life and its various aspects, in allegedly descriptive as well as prescriptive ways, is that "self-overcoming" is a metaphor whose meaning cannot be narrowed down to a literal or non-ambiguous reference.

The various levels of metaphorical discourse implicit in Nietzsche's understanding of life tend to make his use of the term "self-overcoming" somewhat misleading although not altogether inappropriate. The first step in interpretation requires the acknowledgment of how the metaphorical process affects the meaning of Nietzsche's words. Because, through personification, life is portrayed as a speaker in dialogue with Zarathustra, it seems to follow that self-overcoming is given its meaning in the context of a human activity. However, this impression is false. The moral sense of "self-overcoming" is not necessarily something Nietzsche wished to deny, but it belongs to the borderline areas of life's teaching, not to its core. What Nietzsche is addressing here is not some type of human activity but the living process in all of its determinations. The "I" that speaks for life's self does not refer exclusively to a human self. On the contrary, it expands the meaning of the self by referring to any aspect of nature or culture functioning as a principle of order and of relative stability in time. Though appearing now to be standing firm, such a structure of power will be overcome. Therefore the "I" that speaks for life is not intended to match the human individual. What is overcome may be an aspect of an organism, a set of beliefs, a process, a goal. The "I" refers to the dynamic process of life. The irony inherent in life's "secret" is that the speaker gives form and stability to a process (the process of change, flux) by claiming that the formal structure of the process is to destroy all of the forms that it creates. So the formula "self-overcoming" captures the Dionysian unity of creation-in-destruction and of destruction-in-creation. The self is that which creates and that which is destroyed. Indeed, it is that which destroys itself in order to create something beyond itself.

Nietzsche's principle of self-overcoming is in direct opposition to the principle of self-preservation and survival. However, if life is self-overcoming, does that mean that self-preservation is not life? The logic of self-overcoming would say that, strictly speaking, there is no such thing as self-preservation. First, there is no such thing as a definable self. Second, the organism does not stand unchanged at any moment. The cells in the organism are being created and destroyed continuously and the total identity that one calls "self" is also developing and changing, although perhaps less explicitly. Nietzsche does not give much value to the notion of self-preservation even in the sense of protecting one's life from destructive changes. "What does not destroy me makes me stronger," he states in *Twilight of the Idols*.[40] For Zarathustra the principle of self-preservation is a manifestation of the principle of entropy. Those human beings who care to preserve themselves regress into the "last" human beings.[41] On the other hand, those human beings who choose the path of self-overcoming provide the bridge to the *Übermensch*. Self-preservation tends to be viewed as a reactive part of life. Any authentic act of self-preservation that would qualify as active (e.g., the overcoming of destructive forces) would be more appropriately relabeled an act of self-transcendence. In the total context of the meaning of life, Nietzsche views the preservation of life simply as a partial and somewhat illusory aspect of the total process of life's self-overcoming.

The Dionysian interpretation of self-overcoming requires the suspension of the principle of individuation, even when one speaks of the self. From the Dionysian standpoint the self is always in process. It speaks for the dynamic unity of the body, not for something that controls the body or that lodges in a different sphere from the body and the earth.[42] But there is also an Apollonian interpretation of self-overcoming which allows a more individualized reading without necessarily negating the fundamental notion of process. According to the Apollonian reading, "self-overcoming" means the drive toward self-perfection. The interconnection between self-perfection and self-overcoming is also an essential part of Zarathustra's message to humanity.[43] It should be emphasized, however, that Nietzsche's idea of self-perfection is aesthetic rather than moral. It sees the drive for perfection as a drive toward integration and wholeness, not as a moralistic and judgmental effort to be perfect in order to accumulate rewards for oneself or to acquire power for oneself to control or punish others. It is also important to remember that the Dionysian totality is still the foundation for Nietzsche's vision of the relation of individual form to the total process of life. As soon as the individual form is given preference over the totality, the intent of Nietzsche's teachings is lost.

On the Way to Metaphor

When Nietzsche's major teachings, like those on the *Übermensch,* the will to power, and the eternal recurrence, are read in a purely discursive way, one is back to the alienated Socratic standpoint of trying to make the world intelligible exclusively through logic. Because these teachings are meant to go beyond logic and somehow express the dynamic unity of life and the richness of nature's artistic/creative process, it is a futile procedure to apply a method of interpretation which is incompatible with what the teachings are trying to express. Even Nietzsche himself, when he tries to give purely analytical interpretations of the eternal recurrence or the will to power, is well aware that this method is not compatible with the full sense of his teachings. Only a highly poetical exposition of the eternal recurrence and of the *Übermensch* remains available in his published work, while the intention to give a systematic presentation of the will to power ended in failure and frustration. From this it does not follow that

Nietzsche's teachings are meaningless but rather that to arrive at their meaning one must follow a different method of interpretation.

The method of interpretation best suited for Nietzsche's teachings is a combination of critical analysis with a metaphorical reading of his major thoughts. If we assume that the metaphorical process is an Apollonian process of representation, the combination of the critical-analytical and metaphorical approaches would yield a blending of the Socratic and Apollonian impulses in a manner not theoretically foreseen by Nietzsche but attained by him to a greater or lesser degree in practice whenever concept and metaphor are inherent in one of his philosophical teachings. In an early, unpublished essay Nietzsche argued that all concepts are like smooth coins whose original engraving has been worn down after centuries of use.[44] He notes that metaphor is the essence of conceptual thought, that every concept is a forgotten metaphor. Still, it is one thing to talk about the origin of concepts and their erasure of lived experience, and it is another to make sense of the relationship between the delimiting and clarifying function of conceptual thinking and the enigmatic and overflowing function of metaphorical intuiting-imagining-thinking. A more balanced way of conceiving the relationship between the Apollonian, Dionysian, and Socratic aspects of consciousness is needed.

The Dionysian philosophy offered by Nietzsche in his late work is, at its best, a blending of concept and metaphor in the form of such symbols as the *Übermensch*, the will to power, and the eternal recurrence. Such symbols are conceptual and anticonceptual at the same time. They are conceptual insofar as there is a meaning in them which may be explained conceptually. But they are anticonceptual insofar as their meaning is to cancel the boundaries of divided thinking typified by the dualism between body and mind, subject and object, time and eternity. At times Nietzsche is able to offer the liberation of logic through metaphor. The metaphor, that which carries us beyond ourselves, is the appropriate symbolic verbal structure for conveying the Dionysian understanding of reality. Conventional barriers and boundaries between objects break down, as Nietzsche expects of a Dionysian experience. The subject who interprets the metaphors becomes engaged in the process of creating the metaphorical meaning or meanings, so that the conventional barriers between knower and known, observer-observed also break down. Metaphor is creative engagement and transference beyond the literal world—beyond the everyday world of the divided consciousness, beyond the world of the single unit, of the individual. Whether engaged in the creation or interpretation of metaphorical discourse, the Dionysian philosopher is necessarily engaged in the creative-destructive process of life.

Still, the placing of *all* of one's hopes for truth in the metaphorical process of interpretation is too extreme a reaction against the dualism found in conventional thought. Imagination is a powerful integrative symbolic agent but there needs to be some continuity between the work of imagination and the realities of lived experience. This continuity is usually provided by life itself, as the Dionysian view suggests. If, as mentioned earlier, life censors itself either with regard to the intuitive-metaphorical process or with regard to the logical process, no continuity or integration can actually take place. Nietzsche's dramatic manner of representing the battle between life and logic has certain advantages but it also has the disadvantage of making logic into an adversary of life. In his late philosophy Nietzsche sometimes falls into a new type of dualism, the dualism of that which is "prolife" versus that which is "against life." This is a divisive rhetorical tactic which cleverly protects his own views—no matter what they are—from reasonable criticism, simply because he calls his critics enemies of life. The affirmation of the unconscious and of the metaphorical process loses its meaning, however, if it is simply to be used as a ploy in a new type of dualism where logic degenerates into a dysfunction while logic's opponent is given free rein.

In order to avoid some of the extremes into which Nietzsche's thought sometimes falls as a result of his critique of logical reasoning, I propose that we come to a more receptive rather than contentious attitude toward the meaning and role of the Dionysian side of life. The Apollonian process of metaphorical representation and the Socratic logical-dialectical process need to be mediated by a Dionysian acceptance of life. This would make the Dionysian not the antagonist of the Apollonian and the Socratic (as depicted in *The Birth of Tragedy*) but actually the mediating and common ground of communication between the two. A Socratic tendency toward the intelligibility of existence, if it is tuned to a Dionysian acceptance of life, will also readily accept the metaphorical contribution to making the meaning of life intelligible. Similarly, a poetical representation of reality, if it is to be accepted in the context of the totality of life, cannot separate itself or make itself immune from logical investigation and criticism. After all, if Nietzsche is correct that life is the ground of meaning, then it is only through the recognition and acceptance of the totality of our lives that we receive the power to make sense of reality through symbolic structures, both logical and metaphorical.

Although the point may seem obvious, it is important to look upon life as the ground of continuity for logical and metaphorical (as well as all other) activity. Unless this is done, one will lose the thread through which the best insights into Nietzsche's philosophy are to be gained. A Dionysian philosophy must be able to attain clarity about the meaning of a perspective that transcends the dualism of good and evil. Every reversion to pure Socratism—to the need to give meaning to life in such a way that the authority of reason is not threatened—increases one's dependence upon dualism. The Dionysian task, then, is to liberate philosophy from an exclusive dependence upon the authority of reason and to free the philosopher-artist from the power of all authoritarian and dualistic perspectives on life.

2

Nietzsche's Critique
of Metaphysics

According to Nietzsche, the reconstruction of philosophy must begin with a reassessment of the meaning of metaphysics. He viewed the metaphysical tradition and its doctrines as a major symbol of the fragmentation of the human spirit.[1] Concerned primarily with metaphysical Idealism and its psychological and moral implications, Nietzsche set out to review the process responsible for formulating distinctions between eternity and time, reason and nature, mind and body. He saw as inherent in this process a great turning away from life. In particular, he perceived the metaphysical task to be the denying of life (temporality, the human connection with the earth) and the rechanneling of life's creative energies toward satisfaction in a meaningless beyond. Perhaps metaphysics was especially offensive to Nietzsche because he, too, sought a beyond as a ground of values. But his ground of values differed significantly from that of the traditional metaphysician. The metaphysical beyond to which Nietzsche objected rested on dualism, whereas he claimed a reality beyond good and evil, that is, beyond the human being's alienation from the flow of life. Nietzsche depicted the new reality through various theories and images like the will to power, the eternal recurrence, the innocence of becoming, and the *Übermensch*. The fundamental message behind all of these ideas is the same—the overcoming of nihilism, decadence, resentment against life, psychological fragmentation. He thought that if only the individual would open himself or herself to the flow of life, there would be no more fragmentation and dualism. This would require an overturning of nihilism, specifically, the overturning of the individual's resentment against the passing of time.

Nietzsche's critique of metaphysics presupposes a new morality. The new morality would need to transcend dualism as well as eliminate the need for a metaphysical justification of guilt and punishment. Nietzsche's critique of metaphysics is therefore closely allied to a critique of dualistic moral values. He argues

38

that, at the metaphysical level, reality is nothing but a continuum of appearances. Therefore, strictly speaking, all alleged metaphysical boundaries between good and evil are projections of human insecurity or, at worst, nihilism and resentment. Morality, metaphysics, religion, and other systems of value are signs of processes which either affirm the healthy continuity of life or else rupture it. Where Nietzsche criticized the metaphysical systems of Plato, Kant, and Schopenhauer, he did so primarily insofar as these could be proven to exemplify such a rupture.

The rupture of existential continuity can be traced to a dualism upon which traditional metaphysics and morality are founded. In order to move beyond them, Nietzsche criticized the polarization of opposites from which metaphysics derives its sustenance. The reconstruction of metaphysics, then, begins with a critical appraisal of what is wrong with these polarities. In this chapter and the next I will proceed to reconstruct Nietzsche's views on the dualities being-becoming, self-world, will-cause, and eternity-time. His critique of metaphysics revolves around these four dualities, as well as the duality thing-in-itself/appearance, which is in the background of the other four. Nietzsche responds to the tradition with the theories of the will to power and the eternal recurrence. Ontologically, both of these theories state the same thesis, namely, that all of existence is interpretable as energy that is ever-flowing. Nietzsche's goal is to bridge the metaphysical dualism between being-becoming, eternity-time, and self-world.

In his critique of metaphysics Nietzsche follows a genealogical and perspectival method of inquiry. Rather than dwell at length on the analysis of specific theories, he moves fairly quickly to the issue of the origin of a theory. Nietzsche approaches metaphysical issues through genealogical and perspectival questions—"What is the origin of the concept of being?" "From where do we derive the notion of a cause?" The genealogical question is tied to a perspectival approach that is set on exposing all "life-denying" values for what they are, no matter how sacred or well established these may be within the culture. In this way Nietzsche hoped to free the interpretation of life from all forms of ascetic, dualistic, and alienated conceptions of existence. But to free the interpretation, one must free the interpreter. The aim is to free the self to affirm itself and love life. In the last drafts of Nietzsche's "Transvaluation of All Values" the critique of traditional metaphysics was to appear under such headings as "We Yes-Sayers" and "The Free Spirit." The images associated with the proposed book titles clearly convey the type of perspective Nietzsche would be following in his critique of the tradition.

As a result of Nietzsche's goal and method, his critique focuses much more on the psychological analysis of the preconditions of various metaphysical doctrines than on the doctrines themselves. Nietzsche moves quickly from theory to interpretation and then to the psychology of the interpreter. His own perspective as a critic-interpreter is grounded in the affirmation of life. The result is a critique of metaphysics which cannot be disengaged from a critique of religion and morality, on the one hand, and, on the other, from a positive hope in a new conception of the self's relation to life.

BEING AND BECOMING

The fundamental metaphysical duality fought by Nietzsche is that between being and becoming. Long before Nietzsche thought of the term "will to power" to designate the reality of all that is in flux, he had already argued in favor of Heraclitus's conception of existence.[2] For Nietzsche, as for Heraclitus, existence is a process that is always in flux. Nietzsche's denial of being is related by him to three basic theses: (1) there is no reality over and above the reality of the physical world; the appeal to a metaphysical reality over and above the reality of the physical world is a fiction; (2) specifically, it is a fiction to use the term "being" for a metaphysical reality that is superimposed upon time and becoming; (3) more generally, it is misleading to use nouns (in the sense of names) to refer to what is in flux; the stability of things is not to be implied from the formal structure of language.[3] In other words, the attack on metaphysics is really an attack on certain inferences derived from the use of language, as in the invention of a world of stability and relative security. This stabilizing fiction dims the reality of the only world there actually is, the world of life that is always coming into being and passing away.

Nietzsche used the perspectival method of criticism long before he thought of the term "perspectivism" to describe his epistemological stance, just as his ontological views antedated the use of the term "the will to power." In his critique of being, Nietzsche combines the genealogical and the perspectival methods of inquiry. The question "What is the origin of the notion of being?"

is used to uncover a flaw in the perspective that posits being. In a commentary on Heraclitus dating from 1873, Nietzsche accuses Heraclitus's opponents of "myopia," thereby implying that the metaphysician is looking at things too closely; the metaphysician's gaze does not transcend that which gives him or her comfort and security in the world of change and flux. For Nietzsche, on the contrary, "being" could signify the arrest of life instead of its continuity or presence. Life is one, continuous and flowing—there is no static river into which one can step even once. But the concept "river" makes it appear as if there were the same river every time the term "river" is used. One is led to understand the reality of the river as fixed by the concept rather than as determined by the tangible reality that is subject to change. Briefly, then, the idea of being may be said to represent, first, the arrest of reality and, second, the erasure of what-is in favor of what the metaphysician would like there to be.

The invention of being has consequences which cannot be separated from psychological, moral, and even religious categories of experience. Nietzsche's analysis quickly moves into the issues of guilt and responsibility. According to Nietzsche, those who posit the notion of being are responsible for dividing reality against itself. First, reality manifests itself as a oneness which is perceived intuitively. When the concept appears, however, reality is split into what can be posited conceptually and what is intuitively perceivable. The concept, with its capacity for prediction, its transcendence over temporal flux, and its tendency to correct existence, begins to make existence appear as a flaw for not living up to what the concept claims it to be. Conceptual thought prefers to deal with perfect entities and finds satisfaction in them. The concept may stand to be embarrassed by actual existents. A miscalculation may take place which was not anticipated by the conceptual controls. Rather than admit that the error has occurred because the concept has arrested or erased the movement of life, conceptual thought tends to attribute the error to the temporal, sensual, or idiosyncratic nature of existence. When this simple psychological situation is transformed into a metaphysical doctrine, the result is a devaluation of all temporal existents and the simultaneous elevation of reality to the plane of being, of plenitude, of perfection. The extreme form of this type of self-deception is the doctrine that what comes to be, grows, and perishes is burdened with metaphysical guilt whereas that which detaches itself from existence stands against it as a savior to redeem it. Life is thought to be meaningless due to its temporal nature. Ideas, on the other hand, are thought to be that which gives life meaning and value. As mentioned earlier, in *Twilight of the Idols* Nietzsche characterizes the traditional philosopher as a nihilist whose basic conviction is the fundamental worthlessness of existence.[4]

The idea that being implies presence while becoming or nonbeing implies either absence or alienation from presence is a direct consequence of the imposition of metaphysical guilt upon the process of becoming. When temporality is laden with guilt, the unity of existence (which consists of the process of dynamic continuity) is perceived as a dis-unity by the metaphysician who wants a whole containing no gaps, no opposition, no fresh growth, but merely undifferentiated presence. Where being is given the character of the "one" and the "plenum," becoming is seen as that which is multifarious and empty. Nietzsche indicates that this constitutes the reversal of the original situation in which the "one" is all-that-is, namely, becoming.[5] In contrast to the otherworldly metaphysician, Nietzsche sees the plenitude in the multiplicity of existents. The oneness and plenitude assigned to being are too costly. They are attained at the price of denying the unity and fullness of the world of multiplicity and change. Nietzsche is in favor of presence, but presence as related to becoming, which is the only type of existence whose reality he accepts.

Nietzsche develops the investigation of the origin of human beings' flight from the presence of temporal existents through a combination of psychological and metaphysical insights. He questions why the demand for presence should take the form of a withdrawal and flight from change, growth, and perishing. Nietzsche's Zarathustra traces the problem to a divison that incapacitates the self. The self is kept from developing according to its nature, which is to affirm the dynamic continuity of life. According to Zarathustra, the blocking of authentic self-development is caused by a resentment against the temporal nature of existence.[6] The need for presence in the form of being is rooted in the powerlessness of the human being to control temporal existence. For example, one feels powerless or impotent over what is past. It is the greatest agony of the self that it cannot "will backwards." As one tries to overcome one's powerlessness to reverse the past, the self turns into its own torturer and burdens itself with guilt. Since the past has escaped it, the only way to claim it back is through the weight that the loss of the past can place on the acceptance of the present. In other words, a past that is not accepted and released *as past* is a restless past which comes to haunt the present development of life in the form of guilt. It bears upon the present the resentment against the "it was." And as every present moment turns into another "it was," the blocked will that wants to call back the "it was" can only do so by making the next moment "feel" guilty for being-there. In this way the present moment, with its fresh presence, fresh energy, and latent possibilities for the continued development of life, is laden with burdens and accusations and told that it *lacks* being because it has come without bidding and will leave again without bidding. The nature of life does not suit the demands of the alienated self whose psychological structure is to resent its lack of control over life. The alienated person represents a form of life which, by hating or distrusting itself, blocks its natural development.

Nietzsche's counterteaching to the resentment against time is "the innocence of becoming."[7] This image reveals Nietzsche's attempt to liberate becoming from its bondage to being. Metaphysical guilt would be eliminated through the acknowledgment that there is to be no resentment against the perishing and coming to be of existents. But Nietzsche's idea of the innocence of becoming would be misunderstood if it were thought to be confined primarily to an acceptance of the perishability of all things. There is a more subtle and vicious kind of resentment against time than that which seeks its fulfillment in the otherworldly notion of being. Zarathustra reveals that the most crippling form of resentment is the resentment against what endures.[8] The person subject to this type of resentment accepts Nietzsche's first premise that everything is in flux. However, he or she then proceeds to draw the inference that, given this state of flux, whatever claims endurance through time *deserves* to perish. At times Zarathustra feels overpowered by this nihilistic doctrine, attributed to the soothsayer and also associated with the teachings of Schopenhauer. "Everything passes away; therefore everything deserves to pass away. And this too is justice, this law of time that it must devour its children."[9] But Zarathustra calls this teaching "madness." The "revenge against time" is the crippling psychological structure of the sadomasochistic will that stops willing because it cannot accept the dynamic continuity of life. Whoever is affected by the revenge against time does away with the innocence of becoming (which allows both for the passing away of things and for the continuity of life) and imposes a moral judgment against continuity by declaring that, since there is nothing lasting in life, then everything deserves to perish. Since nothing lasts, let us not allow ourselves joy in our own children, for they will perish too. This is the meaning of the nihilistic mandate to stop willing. This madness is an act of revenge against life on the part of the individual who resents his or her powerlessness to control the passing of life. Rather than allow itself to go on willing through its "children," the vengeful will turns against life and condemns its children never to be born. "All [life] is empty, all is the same, all has been!"[10] Nothing that endures is appreciated because the only aspect of it that is assimilated by the vengeful consciousness is the fatality of its eventual disintegration in time. The recognition of mortality locks the will into a self-destructive hatred of life. The child that is "devoured" through this revenge against life is not only one's offspring, whether literal or symbolic, but most important the child within oneself. This is the child who stands for the dynamic continuity of life, the innocence of becoming, and, as I will point out in Chapter 5, the *Übermensch*.

Through the idea of the dynamic continuity of life, also expressed in *Zarathustra* as the process of self-overcoming, Nietzsche gives a different interpretation of the meaning of coming-to-be and passing away. Zarathustra's view of self-overcoming transforms the nihilistic rejection of temporality into a hopeful statement on the potential for self-development in human life.

SELF AND WORLD

The world has been explained as the Heraclitean world of becoming. "Things" do not exist. Everything is in flux. One gives names to things, one equates them with each other or calls them "identical" to what they were in the past, but only because otherwise the survival mechanism would probably be impaired.[11] The next important rupture of existential continuity to which Nietzsche addresses himself is the rupture between self and world. Nietzsche calls into question the relationship between memory and forgetfulness. When I remember that this chair in front of me is the same chair that I saw yesterday, I have actually forgotten that there is no such thing as "same" and no such thing as "thing." These terms are convenient fictions for referring to entities whose identity or limits need to be grasped so that my everyday life will proceed unproblematically. The analytical process is relatively justified in that, while naming things and separating them from each other will constitute a rupture of existential continuity in terms of the dynamic unity of life, I, too, as an individuated existent need to ascertain my continuity in a world where some degree of stability is required for psychological functioning. However, my continuity, as evidenced by what I choose to remember, does not necessarily coincide with the existential continuity of my life as it is actually lived. Memory is actually a form of forgetfulness.[12] By remembering certain things out of my past, I will always erase many others that I decide not to remember. The role of the transvaluator of values is to question the politics and wisdom of what is remembered and what is forgotten, that is, what is put into the foreground and what is placed in the background. The transvaluator of values wants to exchange foreground and background. He or she wants to call attention to what has been forgotten so that one can put into perspective the significance of one's established identity.

The question of authenticity emerges here. One is faced with a decision as to how to understand the historical and constitutional determinants of one's self. Nietzsche is saying that what I identify as my self through the foreground use of memory may not be my authentic self at all. To allow myself access to *all* that makes up the self I must relax the function of memory and let myself be truly open to the world at the present moment, suspending the desire to grasp the flux of life either as it moves forward or backward. This will allow the self or ego (*Ich*), which is generally in control of my identity, to suspend its control and understand its foundations.[13]

Conceptual clarity is highly valuable, but, as Nietzsche points out in *Thus Spoke Zarathustra,* it is only one of the many dimensions of life's pulsating energy. If one is to reach a proper understanding of oneself, the ego must suspend or relax its status as director of the organism and allow the organism to speak to it of its reality. Nietzsche sometimes uses the metaphor of listening to refer to this process of enhanced self-awareness. When the ego, which generally controls the organism, is in command of self-awareness, it will posit its understanding of itself according to what best furthers its interests. Because it can justify its interests through an appeal to reason, it gains at least a formal advantage over the unconscious self. On the other hand, the authentic process of self-discovery is marked by the ability to listen to the many signs of harmony, contradiction, or disharmony. Even if these originate in unconscious processes, they are not to be regarded as insignificant. Again, to borrow an image from music, one might say that the self engaged in authentic understanding of itself needs to have a fine ear for the tunes that the body and the unconscious are playing in it and for it. Nietzsche emphasizes that, just as the ego is not a detached observer of life but is rooted in the instincts and passions, the listening self is not at all a detached observer of its experience. As one listens, one must also make appraisals and judgments as to what will be preserved or transformed for one's self-development and what will be discarded. "Always the self listens and seeks: it compares, overpowers, conquers, destroys."[14]

What is this self? The self is the process of life as it is manifested in one's body and total experience. The name Nietzsche gives to this process is "the will to power." The process may be described metaphorically as a listening, seeking, conquering, and destroying. Every change contains an implicit appraisal of values, a kind of creating and destroying. The transvaluation of the notion of the self leads Nietzsche to the analysis of both self and world as will to power. With this idea Nietzsche shows the truth or, more appropriately, the falsehood behind the ego's perception of itself as separate from the world. He argues that the continuity between self and world has been disrupted by the conventional, superficial, and divisive designations "self" and "world" as two ends of a polarity.

In contrast to the ego-world disjunction, Nietzsche wants to say that all of reality is a unity, although not a dull unity. As the animals tell Zarathustra: "To those who think as we do, all things themselves are dancing."[15] In place of this panorama of the dynamic unity of life, the alienated consciousness divides self from world, gives up its full participation in life, and chooses a detached perspective from which it pretends to judge life through the time-honored duality of subject and object. The subject, detaching itself from the world of experience as much as possible, observes the world and then proceeds to act upon it as if the world (or object) were a receptacle for its acts rather than what makes the subject's activity possible. The unified field of reality is split into two camps,

with one side claiming all the power of a "director" and proceeding without further ado to use the other as that which is to
be directed. Many metaphors of this metaphysical paradigm come
to mind as examples. For instance, the world may be conceived
as an orchestra playing under the direction of God. Or to bring
the model closer to a paradigm of human rather than divine power,
the controller-controlled duality may be represented as the case
of a motion picture in which the actors appearing on the screen
(the controlled world) are also the directors of the film and the
preliminary judges of its quality. The metaphysics of Kant's system closely approximates this paradigm. As thing-in-itself I am
detached from my appearance on the screen, although I control
its performance. As moral self I disengage myself as much as
possible from any pleasure I may derive either from viewing the
film or from my performance in it. My function is to remain
completely indifferent to the film except to correct (i.e., exercise
further control over) any noticeable deficiencies in my appearance.

Nietzsche's idea of the will to power was meant to undo and
reverse this alienated subject-object paradigm. Nietzsche asserts
the continuity of all experience—from directing to performing to
evaluating to enjoying to being resisted in all of these activities
by opposing and contradictory tendencies in reality. The will-to-
power idea breaks down the discontinuity between subject and
object by affirming that in the world of becoming there is no such
thing as a detached self. The self is rooted in a world which, like
the self, consists of a play of forces.[16] But the idea of reality as
will to power, in spite of the explanatory function Nietzsche sometimes gives to it, is primarily a metaphor designed to heal the
disruption by metaphysics of existential continuity and the unity
of life. To see why the will-to-power idea cannot be treated as a
scientific theory one must look at Nietzsche's critique of causality.
Nietzsche at times seems to substitute the idea of force as will
to power for the notion of causality.[17] However, this is not because
he wants to make of the will-to-power idea a causal theory of
explanation but rather because he denies the existence of the will
and of causality. This leaves him with one category of explanation,
and that is force. Because for Nietzsche there is no such thing as
a will in the literal sense, "the will to power" tends to be used
as a loose metaphor whose meaning shifts according to the context
in which it is employed.

WILL AND CAUSE

Nietzsche denies the existence of causes in the transcendent sense and objects to the manner in which the empirical distinction between cause and effect is formulated. He rejects the Kantian model of reality because of the dualities between the thing-in-itself and appearance, or between freedom and necessity. Nietzsche does acknowledge that the empirical use of causality is useful to human beings. With some degree of tolerance, he calls this type of causal explanation a "conventional fiction."[18] What he finds virtually intolerable, however, is the transcendent notion of causality. His critique of the notion of causality consists primarily in an attack upon the metaphysical concept of the free will. In addition to this, he denies the existence of God, especially the notion of God as first cause and judge of the universe. In this way he tries to eliminate the dependence of human beings upon a religious model that uses the transcendent notion of causality—for example, the belief in free will and in the creation of the world by God—as a means of manipulating and punishing individuals.

Nietzsche's critique of free will and of causality rests upon his disagreement with the general portrait of the world as thing-in-itself and appearance. His rejection of free will is an aspect of his rejection of the thing-in-itself, or more precisely, of the notion of the soul as some form of in-itself which dictates its commands to the body-as-appearance. Nietzsche's departure from this model of reality follows from his denial of any level of existence beyond what he calls "becoming." However, his rejection of the thing-in-itself is not analogous to his denial of the concept of being. There is a significant difference between Nietzsche's affirmation of becoming and his modified acceptance of the thesis that reality is nothing but appearance. Whereas in the case of the duality being/becoming Nietzsche blends the two notions by accepting a world of becoming upon which he bestows attributes of fullness and presence, in the case of the thing-in-itself and appearances he denies not only the distinction but each of the two categories as adequate representations of the world. Like being, the thing-in-itself is a fiction. Unlike becoming, however, the Kantian concept of the phenomenal world is also considered by Nietzsche to be a fictional construct. The realm of appearances in the Kantian sense is too scientifically oriented to suit him. He disagrees with Kant's optimism that the phenomenal world may be known through science. Nietzsche believes that scientific prediction has only a limited value as a perspective. Kant's realm of appearances is a realm subject to manipulation, a realm lacking imagination and spontaneity. Nietzsche therefore substitutes for appearances (*Erscheinungen*) the notion of appearance as illusion (*Schein*). To Nietzsche the world is indeed a world of appearance, but appearance in the sense of what shines, what displays itself, what manifests itself while lacking a steady ground, illusion. The world of appearances must be sufficient justification for itself, since there is no special substrate like the thing-in-itself underlying the manifestation to guarantee its reality.

Nietzsche further claims that whereas to the onlooker the world presents itself as *Schein,* if pressed to give a name from "inside," *Schein* would call itself "the will to power."[19] Nietzsche's idea of the will to power replaces the Kantian in-itself and Schopenhauer's notion of the will as in-itself, while his notion of *Schein* replaces the Kantian *Erscheinungen* and Schopenhauer's sphere of representation (*Vorstellung*).[20] The curious thing is that for Nietzsche both *Schein* and "the will to power" refer to the same phenomenon, the world of becoming. They are two different ways of referring to a reality that transcends logical comprehension. The following note, omitted from *The Will to Power* collection, gives a fairly precise account of Nietzsche's metaphysical model of reality.

Against the word *'appearances' [Erscheinungen]* N.B. *Appearance* [*Schein*], as I understand it, is the actual and only reality of things—it is that to which all existing predicates first of all belong and that which relatively speaking can be designated best by all predicates and so even by antithetical predicates. With this word, however, nothing is expressed other than the *inaccessibility* [of reality] to logical procedures and distinctions: thus 'appearance' in relation to 'logical truth'—which itself however is only possible in an imaginary world. I do not set appearance in opposition to reality, but on the contrary I take appearance as reality (which resists conversion into an imaginative 'World of Truth'). A definitive name for this reality would be 'the will to power,' that is to say [a name for reality] designated from inside and

not from its incomprehensible fluid protean
nature.[21]

In this unpublished note from 1885, Nietzsche states that when
reality is approached from "outside"—that is, through conceptual
thought and logical procedures—reality is perceived as an illusory
appearance. However, reality appears *as illusion* to a perspective
which is itself an illusion. What is real, then, is not the illusory
perspective but what resists being idealized. What is real resists
conceptualization and idealization into a "World of Truth." If
such a standpoint of "truth" were suspended, the reality could
be known for what it is, something inaccessible to logical procedures and distinctions, something that embraces all predicates,
even antithetical predicates. Here Nietzsche is reiterating the notion of the Dionysian and its opposition to the Socratic, only now
he is using metaphysical language instead of images of Greek
heroes and gods. The same point obtains. The same role that
Dionysus played relative to Socrates is given to the notion of the
will to power relative to logic and discursive thought. The will to
power is said to be the self-given designation for that which resists
being assimilated into discursive thought.

What is it that discursive thought violates when it tries to understand reality? For one thing, it attempts to make everything
equal. It glides over individual differences; it glides over conflict
and ambiguity; it is not sensitive enough to that which does not
fit into its logical frame. The feet of logic never touch the ground,
as it were, whereas Nietzsche would like to see the metaphysician
rooted in the earth. What does the earth know about quantification? The earth knows of fertility, nourishment, or undernourish-
ment. It may offer its gifts profusely or it may have little or nothing
to offer at other times. It does not quantify its fruit, nor does it
impose quotas. It does not make judgments as to success in meet-
ing quotas of productivity or lack thereof. The earth simply grows
its fruit and nourishes it. Discursive thought, on the other hand,
imposes patterns of quantification upon reality as well as dualistic
value judgments as to what is functional or dysfunctional, what
is good or evil. These observations, although not always made
explicit by Nietzsche, are presupposed in his critique of the metaphysics of the will and of causality. His critique of empirical
causality rests upon his preference for quality over quantity as a
criterion for measuring reality. His arguments against the tran-

scendent notion of causality—free will—are tied to a critique of the dualism between good and evil and the psychological thirst for punishment.

With respect to the empirical notion of causality, Nietzsche declared that there is no such thing as a cause. He argues that the attribution of causality to a thing or event is a psychological projection based on our own delusions about the nature of the self or of the will. Our feeling of will and our intention to perform an act have been mistaken for causes. "We have absolutely no experience of a cause; psychologically considered, we derive the entire concept from the subjective conviction that *we* are causes, namely that the arm moves.—*But that is an error.*"[22] I separate myself from the deed I perform. I manipulate, will or intend some "effect" to take place. Perhaps this gives me a feeling of psychological power but, according to Nietzsche, it says little or nothing about what is actually going on in the world. He suggests that what goes on would go on independently of my stating with respect to it, "I shall do this." In *Twilight of the Idols* he writes: "The 'inner world' is full of phantoms . . . the will is one of them. The will no longer moves anything, hence does not explain anything either—it merely accompanies events; it can also be absent."[23] Once our faith in the existence of the will disappears, the will no longer moves anything for us. Other phantoms of the inner world whose existence Nietzsche disclaims are motives and the ego. A motive is "a surface phenomenon of consciousness, something alongside the deed that is more likely to cover up the antecedents of the deeds than to represent them."[24] This seems to be true enough in cases of self-deception. Nietzsche argues that we may be living in a permanent state of self-deception with respect to our ego-determined understanding of the world.

Nietzsche attributes the empirical conception of causality to a mistaken association between events that we think we will and events that we see following each other with regularity. He also extends the critique of the empirical conception of causality to a psychological critique of the need for science. A slightly different psychological model is invoked here although the psychological method of argument is maintained. Nietzsche attacks not the truth or falsity of the scientific claims but the scientific need to quantify energy. "Science has emptied the concept causality of its content and retained it as a formula of an equation, in which is has become at bottom a matter of indifference on which side cause is placed and on which side effect. It is asserted that in two complex states (constellations of force) the quanta of force remain constant."[25] Nietzsche implies that the quantification of "constellations of force" violates the nature of the forces in question and that the reduction of living energy to a formula says little about the reality in question. His arguments need not be taken to mean that he thought nothing of science, but rather that the realities which were important to him could not be captured by science. I will come back to this point in Chapter 4, when I analyze the will-to-power theory in more detail.

In a separate argument against causality, Nietzsche points out that the regularity of a type of event does not imply its necessity. From the fact that I observe certain things happening with predictable regularity I cannot deduce that they are compelled to occur that way or that they will necessarily occur that way.[26] Nietzsche states that certain things are predictable because they are part of processes whose patterns form more or less regular cycles. But the notions of cause and effect carry the suggestion that the cause somehow is responsible for the effect or that the effect follows necessarily from the cause. Like Hume, Nietzsche found the notion of a necessary connection relating cause to effect to be a psychological projection conditioned by habit. But he went further than Hume to suggest that the reason regularity is interpreted as necessity is that human beings are very much afraid of the unknown. We are afraid not to be in control of things; perhaps we are afraid of the depths of our own nature. Therefore, when confronted with something new in our experience, the dread of the new makes us want to associate the new event with some past experience rather than attempt to understand the new event on its own terms. "Thus one searches not only for some kind of explanation to serve as a cause, but for a particularly selected and preferred kind of explanation . . . *the most habitual* explanations."[27] As a result, certain causes or explanatory reasons become accepted and others are either discarded or not even allowed to emerge. Fairly soon one has locked oneself into a narrow but safe framework of explanation. "One kind of positing causes predominates more and more, is concentrated into a system, and finally emerges as *dominant,* that is, as simply precluding other causes and explanations."[28] Nietzsche notes how the prevalence of this psychological phenomenon occurs in everyday life, for example, the banker thinks only of business, the Christian of sin, and so forth.

Here perhaps lies one of the origins of the psychological power of totalitarian ideologies. It is the fear of what is different, the insecurity of not being able to control that which threatens the stability of the habitual world, that keeps us locked into narrow patterns of expectations and therefore of explanations. Even science can turn into a narrow pattern of explanation (and a ruling ideology) if one considers how strong a need science fulfills in guaranteeing human control over natural events. Nietzsche's joyful wisdom or gay science, on the other hand, begins with the psychological premise that one will remain open to theoretical adventures, to different and multiple ways of interpreting reality. The richness of life cannot be exhausted by the mind. This is something that should make the lover of knowledge joyful rather than somber. It is Nietzsche's hope to be able to effect this reversal of attitudes through the transvaluation of values.

Nietzsche's ideas may be carried further, into a critique of patriarchal religion. Whereas Christian metaphysics, with its great fear of insecurity and adventure, has given us a universe subject to the rules of order of a Father-God, Nietzsche's metaphysics of the innocence of becoming represents a liberation from such rules and from the repression of life's spontaneity. Nietzsche is aware, to be sure, that his counterproposals to traditional religion and science are especially threatening to the ego. The innocence of becoming is meant to provide a metaphysical model not subject to the control of the ego. There shall be no cause-and-effect model such that the cause-effect relationship derives its pattern from the ego's alleged control over its activities. From the standpoint of the innocence of becoming the ego is just a dot in the wide panorama of existence. Existence is indifferent to the ego, whose only power is to turn everything it can find into an image of itself and therefore to explain the meaning of reality in terms of surrogates of itself, from God to atoms. Fortunately for existence, there is much in life that resists the ego's control; but unfortunately for life the ego has sufficient power so that whatever resists the ego is charged with and punished for conspiracy against the "truth." The ego rejects the innocence of becoming and in its place has recourse to a metaphysics that inflicts guilt and punishment upon anything that resists its power or points to its self-deceit.

Nietzsche calls the official doctrine of free will a "metaphysics of the hangman."[29] He links the free will theory to the Christian doctrines of original sin and eternal punishment in hell. He notes in particular that whenever the instinct to punish and judge is powerful, "responsibility" is defined in such a way as to enhance the power of the judging and punishing party. Under patriarchal religion, "free will" has been invented so that the priestly class can manipulate the people with threats of God's punishment.[30] "You are free" means "you are responsible to me," which in turn means "you are dependent upon me." Another possibility not mentioned by Nietzsche, but also fitting under his model, is the situation where freedom is presented by one party to another as an act of generosity or as a gift. In this case "you are free" also means "you are dependent upon me," namely, "you are dependent upon me for this gift." Just as I am being told I am free, I am manipulated to remain in a state of dependency toward such a party. Thus the appeal to freedom may in reality function as masked rhetoric for the enforcement of dependence.

Nietzsche emphasizes here that this analysis of freedom and responsibility is contingent upon there being a strong instinct to judge and punish on the part of those who define the notion of freedom. I cannot be considered free or responsible, however, under a system where I shall "hang" if I do not use my freedom "correctly," that is, exactly as the judge-hangman has stipulated its meaning for me. Here Nietzsche has uncovered a striking psychological phenomenon. Under the system of patriarchal religion and of authoritarian power structures, freedom simply means obedience and dependence. Although Nietzsche does not refer to the myth of original sin, an analysis of some basic elements of this myth would serve to corroborate his point. "Of all the fruits of the trees in the garden you may eat except of the fruit of this tree" actually means, "you are free to obey or disobey, but if you go against my command or stated wish, you will be severely punished." So the patriarchal Father-God expels his children from the garden unless their willing is *identical* to his, that is, unless they are mirrors of his presence. "Freedom" in this case means "follow my rules to the letter, otherwise you will be free to leave." But exile, of course, means death. "If you eat of this fruit, you shall die." Later, the doctrine is modified, and exile from the Father's will is interpreted to mean eternal punishment in hell. Here we see a system of interpretation where the free will seems to be a ruse for the justification of unfreedom and punishment. If the speaker had simply said, "Do as I will or else I will have you exiled, dead, or eternally in pain," the same results would obtain. They would have been obtained through the use of force and without any need for the notions of responsibility or freedom.

What is corrupting the notions of freedom and responsibility here is their use within a structure which thrives on a tyrannical use of power. The reason there is a verbal appeal to the notion of freedom instead of the physical abuse of force is that this type of structure makes use of moral approval as a tactic for behavioral control. When Adam and Eve are "good," that is, obedient, God bestows every favor in the world upon them and they live in Paradise. As soon as they are no longer obedient, a messenger is sent informing them of death, pain, and exile. In this myth there is clearly expressed the ultimate power of moral disapproval and the tying of behavioral control to a metaphysics of responsibility and freedom. As a punishment tactic the use of moral disapproval combines the authoritarian use of force with the dualism of good and evil. The moral dictator-judge stands on the side of the good, while anyone who differs from the stated moral position is considered "evil" and thereby deserving of punishment.

The dualism of good and evil disrupts a healthy metaphysics as much as it does a healthy morality. Nietzsche's psychological analysis of the origin of metaphysical doctrines shows that where the dualism between good and evil is not strong, neither is the desire to punish. Nietzsche also observes, however, that one does not have to be a firm believer in free will to be affected by dualism. He claims that whatever side one takes on the issue of free will—whether one argues for free will or determinism—as long as the instinct to punish is strong, not even a deterministic theory will liberate one from it. In this case, the "enemy" will merely shift to another plane, for example, society.

> Some will not give up their 'responsibility,' their belief in *themselves,* the personal right to *their* merits at any price. . . . Others, on the contrary, do not wish to be answerable for anything, or blamed for anything, and owing to an inward self-contempt, seek to *lay the blame for themselves somewhere else.* The latter, when they write books, are in the habit today of taking the side of

criminals; a sort of socialist pity is their most attractive disguise.[31]

Nietzsche's metaphysical idea of the innocence of becoming should
be distinguished from separate arguments used by him to justify
conflict and violence. The point he is addressing here is the issue
of self-deceit, and his point is valid. That is, I am engaging in
self-deception if I conceive myself either as completely free or as
completely unfree. In the first case, perhaps I am suffering from
vanity. In the latter case, I may well be suffering from self-con-
tempt and, wishing to excuse or liberate myself from something
inside of me that distresses me, I blame the existence of the
condition in me to a condition in society or to some other external
influence. If, in addition, my desire to punish someone or something is strong, I will tend to judge myself or others very severely,
depending upon whether I accept responsibility for the situation
or lay the blame for it somewhere else.

Nietzsche calls for a reconsideration of what it means for the
individual to be part of the totality of a situation. The individual
is not responsible for the totality; neither is the totality responsible
for the individual. These two positions (roughly the "free" and
"unfree" will) are psychologically interdependent. Each one is
an attempt to rid itself of the burden implied by the other. The
"free" will, burdened with excessive responsibilities and placed
in a state of dependency to a higher authority, may seek to escape
the guilt imposed on it by making others completely responsible
for its shortcomings. On the other hand, the lack of subjective
power implied in the theory of the "unfree" will is also burden-
some to human beings because it makes them appear as mere
objects determined by an environment. Neither position is healthy
or sane. If God is dead, the need to make oneself responsible for
ruling and judging the universe should fade. So should the fear
of being judged by a higher authority than oneself. These alienated
psychological habits, as well as the idea of God, were, according
to Nietzsche, only projections of the ego.[32] Still, it is easier to let
go of one's dependence on God than of one's dependence on the
ego. To understand how Nietzsche attempted to solve this problem metaphysically one must turn to the ideas of the eternal recurrence and the will to power.

3

Models of Existential Continuity

Nietzsche perceived that the existential continuity of life is ruptured by values inherent in the metaphysical tradition. The aim of his critique of metaphysics is to question, renounce, and reverse all manifestations of self-division originating in the alienated self's disjunction from the flow of life. His counterproposals to alienated conceptions of value and of human activity are contained in the teachings of the will to power, the eternal recurrence, and the *Übermensch*. In each of these interpretations of existence there is no strict line of demarcation drawn between self and world, subject and object, mind and body, individual and cosmos, reflection and action, time and eternity. In Chapter 5 the role of the *Übermensch* will be considered in conjunction with Nietzsche's idea of what it would mean to transcend traditional morality. Although the will to power and the eternal recurrence are not unconnected to Nietzsche's views on the transcendence of morality, he preferred to associate both of these ideas with the reversal of nihilistic metaphysical values. The first step in understanding the degree to which these ideas may inform a life-affirming metaphysics, therefore, requires that one consider broadly some of the more significant contributions of these two teachings to a nondualistic interpretation of existence.

THE WILL TO POWER

The most misunderstood of Nietzsche's ideas is, probably, the will to power. It is not a fully developed theory, although it bears the potential for providing a synthesis in Nietzsche's thought. As Nietzsche states, it is the one idea that can support all predicates, even antithetical predicates.[1] "*This world is the will to power—and nothing besides! And you yourselves are the will to power—and nothing besides!*"[2] Here is an idea that bridges the gap between self and world, between the various functions of the self and the various aspects of the world. Problems immediately arise as to how to make sense of this idea. Nietzsche's own attempt to provide a systematic exposition of the will to power was unsuccessful. I shall address myself here to the spirit rather than to the letter of Nietzsche's teaching. A more elaborate theoretical discussion of the will to power follows in Chapter 4. In the context of a discussion of Nietzsche's critique of metaphysics, however, the most important point that needs to be considered is how the idea of the will to power can be said to provide a line of continuity between metaphysics and psychology. In other words, if one is described as being nothing but the will to power and the world is described the same way, what does this say about the relationship between one's nature, the nature of the world, and the metaphysical "world of becoming" whose intimate name is "the will to power"?

From a metaphysical angle, the will to power was not the only name that Nietzsche gave to the Heraclitean world of flux. He also called it "the innocence of becoming," "my 'beyond good and evil'," and "the eternal recurrence of all things." Each one of these names is a metaphor for an aspect of existence that needs to be emphasized in light of the problems in the tradition that Nietzsche wants to see corrected or healed. The innocence of becoming counteracts the nihilistic tendency to see temporal existence as a sort of punishment. "Beyond good and evil" refers to the possibility of transcending the dualism implicit in the moral tradition. "The eternal recurrence" refers to the eternal presence of each moment in time. "The will to power" refers to all energy in its creative-destructive aspect. However, Nietzsche's exposition of the idea of the will to power lacks a framework through which the continuity of life can be explained in a way that goes beyond the two principal models of theoretical explanation offered by him. These two models are the recurrence of energy states and the domination of some energy states by others. The implications of Nietzsche's position need to be explained further.

One way of tracing the continuity of life is through the notion of recurrence—"as it has happened before, so it will happen again." This maxim is not taken in the sense of cause and effect (which Nietzsche denies) but in the context of a cycle or pattern where, once one of the elements in the pattern emerges, the rest of the elements are thought to follow for no other reason than that they are all parts of the same cycle. This view, writ large, will be found in the idea of the eternal recurrence. Once a certain configuration of energy-states obtains, then all of the consequences of that particular configuration are thought to follow in the same sequence without the addition or subtraction of any differing elements. Generally, the recurrence model of continuity is Nietzsche's primary model of explanation from a metaphysical standpoint.

Nietzsche's primary psychological model of explanation, on the other hand, is the domination theory of order and interaction. Another way of attempting to explain the continuity between various aspects of existence is to say that energy states are related to each other through a structure of domination. In this case, B follows A because B is dominated by A. Given Nietzsche's critique of causality, he should refrain from offering this type of interpretation. However, he remains inconsistent on this point. If he criticizes the model of causality, saying that the ego's command may accompany an act but does not cause it, he should at least question the commanding-obeying model of activity as a form of explanation for all energy states in reality. In one position taken by Nietzsche he reverses the controller-controlled paradigm and notes that it is the body that controls the ego rather than the other way around. He also suggests that the commanding party is a constellation of forces rather than a discrete entity or faculty. But he does not free himself from the model of continuity-through-domination except through the paradigm of continuity-through-recurrence. This is why his explanations seem to fall into one of two different types. Under the recurrence model, there is no sense of separation between cause and effect, no dualism, no ego, no will, and everything is in flux and flowing. Under the domination model, the fundamental structure is the dualism between the strong and the weak, the active and the reactive, and there is much rhetoric about dividing the strong from the weak through great acts of willing and commanding regardless of statements made elsewhere about the nonexistence of the will.

There is also the model of continuity found in the idea of the will to power as self-overcoming. Here Nietzsche tries to combine the recurrence and domination views of power. Given his philosophical critique of the self and the will, however, one has to take the domination component of this idea as unessential and superfluous to the fundamental meaning of self-overcoming. In fact, by turning the metaphor of self-overcoming into a law of life—and therefore introducing the element of domination into the idea— Nietzsche hurts the inspirational nature of his own teaching. In his political morality, where the paradigm of domination reaches its highest expression, the idea of self-overcoming is put in the service of an oppressive rather than a liberating view of life.[3]

There is yet another model of continuity that Nietzsche only rarely considers. This is the model of inner and outer balance. In this case B follows A because the organism seeks to maintain an inner balance as it undergoes growth, tension, or change. It is superfluous and misleading to superimpose upon every physio-logical and psychological process the charge that the process is following a structure of domination. If one applies the notion of domination to the structure of every single event or interaction in reality, it will no longer be relevant to isolate some structures as specific cases of domination, for every structure will be the same. Domination will be a given from which there is no escape for anyone. But just as cause and effect are said to be superfluous categories with respect to the description of a series of events, so are the notions "stronger" and "weaker." Because Nietzsche wanted to overcome a purely deterministic or mechanistic model of explanation, it makes sense that he would have turned to par-adigms other than determinism to explain change. However, it was also his intent to heal a highly fragmented and alienated culture. And yet, tracing one's continuity in time through the models of recurrence and/or domination does not guarantee that one will cease being a highly fragmented person. A third model is needed to lend perspective to the partial relevance of the other two. I suggest that the will-to-power idea may also be interpreted from the standpoint of inner balance.

The standpoint of inner balance grounds one's continuity in time and the continuity between the self and the world in a struc-ture different from either the recurrence or the domination views of order. Under each model of explanation, one's activities in life may be the same but self-understanding is different. Under the domination model, I may trace my continuity in time through a list of my projects and activities. Since I have control over my projects, the record of my continuity will show the record of my control over things. Patriarchal history is written from this stand-point of control and domination. The cumulative record of proj-ects—whether failures or successes—is said to constitute one's history. In contrast, under the recurrence model there is no em-phasis placed on either victory or defeat but merely on being part of a cycle. I ride with the cycle; I rise or fall with its waves. There is no goal unless it be the cycle or circle's own goal.[4] The projects over which I have conscious control do not necessarily claim my identity. They are epiphenomena resulting from states of energy which I identify as aspects of the cycle through which I must pass. Therefore my continuity is tied to the states of energy I experience rather than to the use to which I put these energy states. I experience myself as being carried along by existence or as being part of a process larger than myself, rather than as commanding existence to yield to me what I will.

The structure of inner balance begins with positing a sense of wholeness within one's self. This wholeness is attributable to the capacity of the organism to stabilize itself and create an inner balance within itself based on the energy it has available to itself at any particular stage of its life. Wholeness does not mean that one is a totality unto oneself. On the contrary, one is aware that the energy available to oneself is a result of the specific types of interaction one chooses to have with one's environment. But the interaction is not conducted as a way of losing oneself in something larger than oneself (the recurrence model) or as a way of exploiting the environment to enhance one's power over it (the domination model). The continuity between self and world is based on the need of each organism to seek its own balance in light of its constitutional needs and the possibilities available in its environment.

The will-to-power idea can convey this sense by reminding one that one is not made up of several compartments each of which has a separate function that needs to be tended to. There is no separation between mind and body or between freedom and necessity. One is a continuous whole, although perhaps one is not aware of the continuity. The last thing one learns to know adequately is the nature of one's own self. Nietzsche's idea of the self as the total organism rather than a specialized function of it (e.g., the ego) opens up the possibility of a new view of existence. It follows from Nietzsche's views that inner balance cannot be sought through the ego or through what it judges to be balance— a structure of domination within the body subject to its control. A transvaluation of the notion of balance is needed. One finds the new meaning of balance in the practice of eliciting a sense of wholeness within oneself without doing violence to any of one's centers of consciousness. Thus a practice of internal honesty and directness is called for instead of the average state of distraction and self-deceit. The ego, relaxing its control, assumes a relationship of gentle receptivity toward the total organism. With the ego-mechanism of censorship lifted, the organism may create its own balance if conditions of health are present.

As one discovers the continuity within oneself through the will-to-power metaphor, "You are the will to power and nothing besides," one cannot stop at the borders of one's skin. One allows the continuity of all reality to make itself felt in one's body and consciousness. "And the world, too, is the will to power and nothing besides." Through the will-to-power metaphor the dynamic continuity of existence is affirmed and, if conditions appropriate to health are present, a creative balance between the organism and the environment can be reached.

Once this creative balance is reached, the model of the will to power as domination will be seen to be just as significant a rupture of existential continuity as the dualities criticized by Nietzsche, those of being-becoming, cause-effect, time-eternity, good-evil. Dominator and dominated, master and slave, the heroic and the decadent—these dualities have no place in healthy systems, whether they are biological or social systems. Domination is a desperate attempt to enforce order where no order exists. The existence of systems of domination cannot be denied. But if one is interested in healing fragmentation and alienation, as Nietzsche claims to be, then it follows that one must discard the positive role that Nietzsche gives to domination and substitute for it the notion of order, synthesis, and continuity based on the inner balance of the healthy body and a reciprocal and symbiotic balance between organisms and the natural and social environments of which they are a part. This does not mean that conflict and opposition will cease to exist within an organism or between living organisms and their environment. What it means is that when conflicts arise they will not be interpreted or forced to a resolution through a structure of domination. A conflict need not mean that two entities are struggling to the death to dominate each other (patriarchal culture's paradigm of conflict) but that life is rich and varied. Richness and variety are being expressed and need to be dealt with. It is only the fear of the new, as Nietzsche has observed, that keeps us tied to narrow expectations and to the paradigm of domination as an explanation for everything that moves.

Nietzsche's dependence on the notion of domination was not absolute. If his critique of metaphysical and moral dualism is respected, the value that "commanding power" held for him can be seriously questioned. The strength of Nietzsche's idea is that it resists systematization.[5] By offering the widest possible name for reality through the metaphor of reality as will to power, Nietzsche leaves it open to others to interpret this metaphor in ways that fit their experience of life, just as he tried to explain its meaning in ways that fit his own experience and observations. In this way the philosopher is not locked into a single interpretation of reality but always welcomes new perspectives, challenges, and even contradictions.

Eternal Recurrence

Nietzsche did not intend the idea of the eternal recurrence to be part of his critique of traditional metaphysics. Clearly, the reason for this is that through this teaching Nietzsche meant to set down a new myth which would inspire and guide human beings. In the sketches for the "Transvaluation of All Values" the teaching of the recurrence usually heads the fourth and final book of the series while the critique of metaphysics forms a separate book. It is appropriate, however, to indicate how the recurrence would function as the culmination of Nietzsche's critique of metaphysics. It is also important to show how this teaching is seen by Nietzsche as the symbol of the transition from a life-negating to a life-affirming view of existence. The continuity between Nietzsche's critique of the tradition and the teaching of the recurrence is indisputable.

The eternal recurrence stands as the inspiration for the principle of dynamic continuity and the acceptance of all forms of life. Nietzsche's teaching, expressed primarily in *Zarathustra,* states that the life one lives, exactly as one has lived it, will return eternally.[6] It returns together with the entire world of energy to which it belongs. From the point of view of the individual, the effect of Nietzsche's teaching is to lead one to perceive one's life as being lived an infinite number of times in the same way as it has been lived and is being lived this time. "I come again . . . *not* to a new life or a better life or a similar life [ähnlichen Leben]: I come back eternally to this same, selfsame life [zu diesem gleichen und selbigen Leben], in what is greatest as in what is smallest. . . ."[7] From the metaphysical point of view, the theory posits the infinite recurrence of great cycles of energy throughout infinite time.

> There is a great year of becoming, a monster of a
> great year, which must, like an hourglass, turn
> over again and again so that it may run down and
> run out again; and all these years are alike in
> what is greatest as in what is smallest; and we
> ourselves are alike in every great year, in what is
> greatest as in what is smallest.[8]

Essentially, then, Nietzsche teaches that an individual's life and a great cycle of becoming have a similar structure. Everything that is, recurs; and nothing can be subtracted from or added to the whole.

The primary significance of Nietzsche's teaching lies in its potential for inspiring us to value the totality of our finite lives as well as the totality of the ontological universe to which we belong. The question posed by Nietzsche is the following. Suppose that everything that could ever exist could be seen as coming together and being contained in one moment of time—and this moment is that moment, and there is no way to avoid this question or this moment. If that were so, what attitude would one take toward one's life (as a whole, from birth to death)? Moreover, what attitude would one take toward the entire universe, where one's appearance is merely that of a "speck of dust"?[9] For Nietzsche, there is no better response to this situation than to affirm the moment, together with the totality, as recurring eternally. However, since Nietzsche's teaching represents not only a personal moral choice but also a pronouncement about the nature of reality, a word should be said regarding whether he expected his readers to accept this teaching on its inspirational merits or whether other factors, such as the support of scientifically relevant data, should ultimately determine its validity.

Because the teachings of Nietzsche's Zarathustra are presented from a metaphorical and inspirational standpoint, it seems to go against the very essence of Nietzsche's message to suggest that it be rethought scientifically. The issue of whether any evidence must be collected before a person accepts Nietzsche's teachings is not raised in his published writings. And yet we know from his unpublished work that Nietzsche did not rule out the possibility of a logical formulation of the idea of the eternal recurrence.[10] He expected this idea to transcend reason, not to conflict with reason. It was to be monumental, overwhelming, mysterious, and inspiring, but not absurd. For this reason we will consider briefly whether Nietzsche's Dionysian teachings bear a specific logical relationship to separate but parallel pronouncements by science on roughly the same topics.

Of special interest is the relationship between Nietzsche's two major ideas of poetic inspiration in *Thus Spoke Zarathustra*—the *Übermensch* and the eternal recurrence—and results of scientific research available to Nietzsche and his contemporaries. Here the basic conjecture is that Nietzsche's ideas may be seen as poetic alternatives to specific scientific theories which were popular in his day. We know that his ideas were meant to be alternatives to religion; what is less likely to be noted is that poetry may also serve the same role with respect to science. In particular, the *Übermensch* and the eternal recurrence can be taken as expressions of Nietzsche's attempt to offer his contemporaries a vision of phenomena more comprehensive than could be attained by the sciences. For example, in contrast to Darwin's theory of evolution based on natural selection, the struggle for survival, and adaptation to the environment, Nietzsche offered the idea of a constant process of self-overcoming and evolution toward the *Übermensch*.[11] Here the process of evolution is depicted as something spiritual. Its features are drawn not simply from a study of the past, however noteworthy that may be. They are also developed with an eye toward humanity's future.[12] Instead of adaptation to the environment, Nietzsche emphasizes the transforming of the environment. The quest is, above all, not for survival but for creativity.

Nietzsche's theory may or may not be judged acceptable as an alternative or supplement to Darwin's. Still, it should be clear that Nietzsche intended to convey poetically something that, strictly speaking, does not concern science because it falls outside of its range. Similarly, despite having presented the idea of the eternal recurrence in a mystical and poetical form, Nietzsche did not mean it to stand in an either/or relationship to the scientific developments of his age. The teaching is at least superficially compatible with versions of the principle of conservation of energy which enjoyed popularity in Nietzsche's time.[13] However, Nietzsche could not have reduced the meaning of his insights to a scientific theory because the latter did not provide him with a framework he could use to affirm his timebound existence. The aesthetic representation of the meaning of life is his way of reconciling himself with finitude. If we insist that Nietzsche leave poetry behind for the sake of science, we deprive him of his greatest asset in overcoming nihilism.

THE TEACHING'S INTENDED EFFECTS

Let us return now to our discussion of the role played by the eternal recurrence in Nietzsche's reconstruction of metaphysics. If his critique of speculative metaphysics is to be successful in uncovering the process that leads the individual to postulate a dualistic and alienating system of values, it should leave a place for an alternative understanding of eternity and time. Of all ruptures of existential continuity perhaps the most significant is the individual's relationship to the lost past and to death. The idea of the eternal recurrence, if properly understood, should contribute to the healing of this rupture. My aim here is to look at the role or function of this teaching precisely in its capacity to take the person who accepts it beyond nihilism. I argue that Nietzsche's teaching is in some senses quite vague and, therefore, that the response it may evoke in individuals is unpredictable. Although in some cases the teaching may indeed take us beyond nihilism, neither its logical formulation nor a person's acceptance of it as a moral maxim indicates that it is humanity's highest formula of affirmation, as Nietzsche himself believed.[14]

The positive function of Nietzsche's teaching is to unite the separate metaphysical worlds of time, eternity, self, and world into one great synthetic relationship. Just as the recurrence is the greatest approximation of becoming to being, so it is the greatest bridge between temporal and eternal life.[15] Every passing moment recurs. Everything returns as it passes away. If viewed constructively, this could help create a synthesis between time and eternity at the level of the individual's self-consciousness. However, the effects of the teaching are meant to be more far-reaching than that. Nietzsche also intended it to stand at the midpoint of history, redeeming all future history from the alienation of values it has suffered in the past. Again, this could be construed positively. We could say that our sense of temporality is alienated and we need a new theory to enhance or modify it. In this context, Nietzsche imagined the impact of his theory to be so great as to divide

history in half, as Christianity had so far been given the credit
for doing. He also apparently believed that Zarathustra's profound thought would persuade life-negating people to stop living.[16]
Although the idea would inspire the strong to build a greater
culture, it would also be a paralyzing, rather than inspiring, thought
to others. It could be used as a weapon to destroy the weak.
Because the effects of the idea range from self-integration to potential self-rejection and self-hatred, we cannot accept Nietzsche's characterization of it as the ultimate sign of life affirmation.[17]

For the moment, let us refrain from raising conjectures about
the potential historical effects of Nietzsche's teaching. Before any
historical effect can be ascribed to Nietzsche's idea, it must first
have its impact on individuals. For this reason, we need to investigate in some detail the process by which a person comes to
understand it, and then to accept it or reject it. My thesis is that
the acceptance of the teaching as such is no guarantee of life
affirmation (as Nietzsche believed), and therefore it is not to the
acceptance or rejection of its objective, logical, or scientific meaning that we must look if we are to see how this teaching can take
us beyond nihilism. On the other hand, it is both appropriate and
justifiable to consider whether the life-affirming qualities Nietzsche attributed to his teaching might not be a function of the
process by which one comes to think about it. We are reminded
here of Kierkegaard's claim that the process by which a person
makes an ethical commitment says more about the nature and
quality of the commitment than the actual objective content of
the person's choice.[18] In other words, Kierkegaard considers the
pagan who devoutly worships an idol to have a much more authentic God-relationship than the Christian who routinely attends
church. In the case of Nietzsche's idea of the eternal recurrence,
I suggest that the process by which one enters into a relationship
with this idea, rather than its actual acceptance or rejection, contains the most important data regarding both the liberating and
the paradoxical aspects of Nietzsche's thought.

SOME HYPOTHETICAL RESPONSES TO
NIETZSCHE'S TEACHING

Let us consider, then, at the level of the individual, the psychological effects of Nietzsche's idea. The idea of the recurrence is
intended to heal the disjunction between time and eternity and

especially the resentment against the past which divides the consciousness of the alienated person. If I think of myself as returning eternally, I may feel psychologically closer to the cycles of life and nature—to the phases of the moon, to the sun setting and rising, to the cycles of the seasons, to the waves of the sea, to the reproductive cycle. This is the spirit of the teaching as conveyed to Zarathustra by his symbolic animals, the eagle and the serpent.[19] And yet, although closeness to the earth may heal important aspects of my alienation from life, this is still not to say that the eternal recurrence is a true idea. On the other hand, by reflecting on this idea I could become more conscious of the processes which tie me to nature. Because it gives a positive value to these processes, it enables me to be more receptive and open to life.

In *The Gay Science* and *Zarathustra* Nietzsche presents the idea of the eternal recurrence as a test of the spirit's affinity with life. Those who cannot endure life and wish to escape it in any form whatsoever, he thinks, would be unable genuinely to accept the idea.[20] The key to the acceptance and love of life is, first, whether one is willing to accept all of one's past to the point of reliving it countless times; and, second, whether one is willing similarly to affirm the repetition of one's yet unknown future. First one must accept all of one's past as recurring eternally, along with everything the past contains. This will include not only joy but suffering, not only what is exciting but what is petty and tiresome, not only what was in our control but what came to us in spite of our will, not only success but failure. Even without also having to accept the future before us in a similar manner, this is already a difficult test to pass. And yet, as Zarathustra suggests, the acceptance of the idea of the recurrence shows that one is healed from the fundamental illness of alienated human existence, the revenge against time and the "it was."[21]

Could the idea of the recurrence, though, not be another form of revenge against time? Could it not show an inability to let go of life as one must let go when one is not divine or eternal? Unable to control the passing of time, the alienated person might say to the past, "Well then, I will teach you not to escape me—I will make you recur for me over and over again." Certainly this is a psychological possibility. Zarathustra possibly even thought of it.[22] And it certainly would make a difference whether one accepts the idea of the recurrence with the intention of never letting go of time or whether one affirms the passing of time, letting go of it and yet accepting one's place in it. In Nietzsche's favor it might be argued that the teaching of the recurrence has certain built-in characteristics that would tend to prevent someone from accepting it out of resentment.

The individual who wishes to recapture the past has less costly ways to do this than to affirm the recurrence. It is possible, for example, to keep the past alive through memory or through activities that link it to the present. In this case, we have some control over aspects of the past with which we wish to stay in touch, while the more painful aspects may be discarded or deemphasized. But if one accepts the idea of the recurrence, one is committed to holding that *everything* will come again and pass away exactly in the same sequence. It is not as if one could tape the best moments one has had and play back just that tape over and over again. According to the teaching of the recurrence, not only will everything come back but it will also flee again as soon as its time is up. So while it is possible to accept the recurrence in an unhealthy state of mind—that of wanting to grasp time and hold it under one's control—the idea of the recurrence does not lend itself very well to this type of grasping. Meditation on the idea will refer me to the truth that existence is temporal and *all* of it will pass away, including myself.

Still, an important qualification which Nietzsche did not raise needs to be mentioned. Zarathustra's teaching as such is not powerful enough to overcome the spirit of revenge against life. I emphasize this point because the teaching is described in *The Gay Science, Thus Spoke Zarathustra,* and *Ecce Homo* so as to lead one to think that this is the highest statement of life-affirmation that can be made; and if an individual accepts this teaching, he or she has passed the ultimate test against nihilism. However, it is possible, both logically and psychologically, to affirm the recurrence out of a sadomasochistic drive to torture others or oneself. If that possibility is left aside, it may be noted that a person who is affected by the spirit of revenge against the past would probably have no sympathy for Nietzsche's teaching. Here one notes the important connection between the innocence of becoming and the eternal recurrence. To accept one's past without resentment means that the tendency toward punitive moral judgments has been overcome. On the other hand, it does not follow, in spite of Nietzsche's statements in *The Gay Science,* that the person who replies to the thought of the recurrence, "Never have I heard anything so dreadful," is necessarily affected by a strong resentment against life. Nietzsche does not acknowledge the possibility of a person loving life to the fullest and yet rejecting the idea of the recurrence for reasons that may perhaps be valid in that person's life. One may reject the exact repetition of the great years of becoming not because one hates life but because one hates injustice or cruelty. This is not a question of denying the ontological innocence of becoming but of recognizing that human beings are not so much innocent as "becoming." If one is directly implicated in seriously injuring innocent persons it would seem a sign of one's love of life not to wish to repeat one's existence. Acceptance of Nietzsche's teaching is not in itself an infallible test of one's love of life or of one's deliverance from the nihilistic attraction to punishment.

These points refer us once more to the thesis that the existential significance of Nietzsche's teaching lies not so much with its acceptance as with the process by which one comes to terms with its message. Herein lies the importance of eliminating all traces of resentment if one is to affirm the idea of the recurrence. We gather from reading *Zarathustra* that if there has been resentment in one's past, that resentment cannot be eliminated. The past will recur eternally as it was lived. There is nothing now that can change one's lived experience. What can be changed is that attitude one takes in the present and the future. This means that affirming the past without resentment is a present endeavor. One lets go of the past one can no longer control. Yet one also takes responsibility for claiming that this life and no other has been one's life. I take responsibility for my own history and for *all* of the selves within me that make up my history. If one of my selves is still the resentful self (like Zarathustra's dwarf), I need to decide whether to continue nourishing that self in the future or whether to deal with its claims adequately until it loses its reason for being there. This brings us to the other side of the impact of the idea of the recurrence—its transformative effect for the future.

A psychological life-affirming test similar to the one we have noted with respect to the past also works with respect to the future. If I have already lived my life innumerable times and also will live it again many more times after this life, how does this affect my attitude toward the future? Does it mean that I am trapped within a cycle from which there is no possibility of exiting? Is this a constricting or a liberating thought? Upon first hearing of the idea, one may be led to view oneself as deprived of all future choice. But the deterministic element in the theory need not violate a person's sense of human choice or creativity unless one insists, for example, on holding on to the type of Kantian dualism between determinism and freedom which Nietzsche sought to oppose. It is true that, according to Nietzsche, a person living within a "great cycle" is indeed necessarily tied to the web of events which determines his or her life. But as Nietzsche also says, "I myself belong to the causes of the eternal recurrence."[23] For Nietzsche, freedom exists within destiny as the freedom to become who one is.

With respect to facing the future, as with coming to terms with the past, there are psychological existential possibilities that suggest the wrong motives for either accepting or rejecting Nietzsche's teaching. For example, there is the psychological possibility that one will accept the thought of the recurrence because it gives one a feeling of security about the future. Instead of wondering whether I shall try doing something new, I can reassure myself that whatever happens has already happened before. This will keep me locked in a feeling of safety. On the other hand, if I thrive on adventure, perhaps the flavor of the adventure will be lost when I picture myself having done it an infinite number of times. Here the soothsayer's cry "All is the same, all has been" might paralyze me. But neither of these psychological attitudes toward the future is healthy. Both are reactive. In the first case, I am reacting to the fear of the new. In the second case, I am reacting to the dread of boredom. To the healthy self, the new does not have to be feared and life is not a boring phenomenon. Using the idea of the recurrence as a means of counteracting either of these tendencies could be too costly. In both cases, one would be locked into a fatalism more costly than either the fear of what is new or the dread of the habitual.

Because the idea of the recurrence appears to justify an extreme form of fatalism, its acceptance is counterproductive unless the appropriate conditions are present. Nietzsche would not give much value to a person's consideration of his idea if the process that led one to his teaching were born out of weakness, cowardice, or a fatalistic indifference toward life. If his teaching is to be considered from a nonnihilistic standpoint, this must be done out of strength, that is, authentically. One must be able to trust oneself and one's existential situation in life to such an extent that if confronted, for example, with the choice of a situation that has the appearance of bringing back the past in its most dreaded form, one can say, "Yes, I will walk through this gate," although one fears and trembles to be trapped forever in the painful situation of the past. Psychologically, however, the transfigurative power of such a decision may change one's life. In this way and in this way only is it possible to overcome the fear of the past repeating itself in one's life.

In reality the only way to test such a situation is to overcome the dread of a present decision which, if taken affirmatively, would seem to lead one into a repetition of the most painful experience in one's past. If one does decide to walk through the gate marked "Recurrence," one will find that something curious has happened. Had I refused to walk through and told myself, "No, this is too much like the past, I had better go on with my 'safe' life and take my 'safe' self into its future," I would have stayed locked in my revenge against time and the fear of the "it was." I would have never been able to transcend my past because my main effort would have been to *avoid* repeating its pain. I would be forever dependent upon something from which I desperately wish to liberate myself. On the other hand, by walking through the gate whose sign reads "Recurrence: the future is the past returning," it turns out that I confront the past with the full power of consciousness and a life-affirming will; thereby I overcome both its negative influence on me and my fear of its repetition. Accepting life completely at such a juncture is actually the only way to break open the future I had envisaged but could not reach previously because I was too busy making sure I could separate myself from my past. Thus the eternal recurrence symbolizes the dynamic continuity of life through which my self-division and alienation may be perennially healed.

Nietzsche does not talk about accepting the recurrence in terms of accepting a present experience which appears identical to another painful experience in the past. But the example is useful in that it illustrates a psychological testing process wherein one must decide whether to accept life in spite of the fact that it appears to come to one in exactly the same painful pattern as experienced in the past. Actually, "same" is a metaphor when one applies it to two experiences within a single lifetime. No two experiences are the same, no matter how similar they might seem.[24] Had I truly been in touch with life I would have perceived the differences between my past and my present experience. But the alienated self does not want to see differences, is not sufficiently receptive to life to perceive them. "All is the same, all has been." It is this voice of resentment against life that needs to be dealt with wherever it dwells—whether in my fears, in my nightmares, in my philosophical ideas, or in my hopes. If the appropriate conditions develop, the alienated conscience will eventually learn from the healthy conscience that its model of life is no longer applicable. When it perceives that it can no longer command the self or win any significant victories over the process of healthy awareness, the alienated voice will gradually fade away. Where it can no longer divide, it will self-destruct.

The psychological effect of affirming the eternal recurrence of all things is one of accepting the past and hopefully enhancing the meaningfulness of one's life in the future. If the theory is correct, our lives will come back an infinite number of times. If it is not correct, it is still a valid psychological point both to accept and to release the past regardless of whether we live the same life again. If one believes that one will be living the same life many times over, one will probably try to act in such a way as to make of one's life something one can value eternally.

Nietzsche's teaching calls for each individual to search within himself or herself to determine the choices one would make in life were the idea of the recurrence to be true. It is possible that the kinds of choices one would make as a consequence of the idea of the recurrence would differ significantly from the choices one would make if one were to think—as one normally does—that one's life will not be replayed. From the standpoint of the passing of time, one might tend to want to use one's time without wasting a moment, knowing that time that is lost will never come back again. From the standpoint of the recurrence, on the other hand, one may find the standpoint of the eternal self and turn to the wisdom of that self. There would be no adversary relationship between time and eternity, as is normally the case.

I have mentioned Nietzsche's belief that the acceptance of the idea of the recurrence, in addition to transforming and healing the inner self, would change the course of history. He believed that the idea would have the same dynamic impact upon history as it had had upon his life. Out of this idea there had come Zarathustra and the concrete vision of a transvaluation of all values.

Despite his belief, though, the idea of the recurrence does not have the power of a myth that could move a historical age. It is a symbolic expression of life-affirmation, but it is not an exclusive formula of affirmation, and (in spite of Nietzsche's expectations) it lacks the power to destroy the antilife forces in culture. It shows one alternative to an alienated treatment of time and to the fragmentation of the self in time resulting from a divisive opposition between time and eternity. Individuals are given a chance to meditate upon and to choose an image of life and energy that goes against the mainstream of modern Western culture, where it appears that we treat ourselves as we treat time. As we quantify time, we quantify ourselves; as we manipulate time, we manipulate our activities in time; as we "save" time, we fail to give sufficiently of ourselves to the immediate situation. The conception of time (and therefore of ourselves) as recurring eternally is a counteridea to the prevailing conception of time in modern culture. If everyone were to accept Nietzsche's view of time and act consistently with this view, the ground of historical values would change, as Nietzsche predicted. The change, however, cannot be imposed from without—as in the form of a myth or a political ideology. It has to come from within and to flow as freely from people's selves as the great waves of becoming may be imagined to flow throughout infinite time and space.

CONCLUSION

As we have seen, Nietzsche's critique of the metaphysical tradition can be highly liberating. His arguments against the various aspects of metaphysical dualism serve the purpose of freeing the individual to reconceive the relationship between self and world. It is through his rethinking of the meaning of metaphysics that Nietzsche begins to explore the fundamental insights needed for an ontology of self-healing. Although one cannot claim that the critique of traditional metaphysics can induce a person to reassess his or her identity in the general manner that has been suggested here, Nietzsche's critique is sufficiently concrete to point to problematic cases of fragmentation and alienation resulting from a disruption of the dynamic continuity of life. The importance of healing one's fragmentation and self-division is the main life-affirming message imparted by Nietzsche's critique of metaphysics.

Without the recovery of the self it is impossible for a person to turn into a genuine free spirit and authentically to affirm life.

It is much harder to appraise the implications of Nietzsche's teaching of the eternal recurrence. In some respects the teaching is very specific, while at the same time its presentation in the form of a revelation makes it quite vague. As in the case of the will-to-power idea, Nietzsche did not attach to the idea of the recurrence a set of interpretative guidelines designed to preserve the life-affirming intent of the teaching. As a result, neither the mere celebration of the idea of the eternal recurrence as the highest possible statement of life-affirmation nor its acceptance as an ethical teaching can be taken as definitive and infallible signs that all significant traces of resentment against temporal life have been overcome. In the context of Nietzsche's life and philosophical development, the teaching can be seen as expressing his singular and outstanding love of life and destiny. But, ironically, from the standpoint of the possibilities Nietzsche opened up for his readers, the affirmation of life seems to be better served by his questioning of the tradition than by his asking us to adopt his most life-affirming thought as a new teaching on the meaning of existence. In this respect, our response to the most valuable insights to be gained from his work need not coincide exactly with his expectations.

The Will to Power as Metaphor

One of the most controversial aspects of Nietzsche's philosophy is the interpretation of the idea of the will to power. The will to power stands at the center of Nietzsche's mature work as the principle which not only explains the nature of reality and of all change but as that which *is* reality itself. In a note from June/July 1885, Nietzsche states: *"This world is the will to power—and nothing besides!"*[1] The same idea is suggested in *Thus Spoke Zarathustra* and *Beyond Good and Evil.*[2] And yet, what meaning can be given to this term, "the will to power"? What meaning or meanings did Nietzsche give to it? Has Nietzsche's idea been properly understood by interpreters of his work? Because there has been such an obvious variety in the range of interpretations given to this principle, both by Nietzsche and by his readers, the question arises as to whether there is a philosophical significance for the differing interpretations. With faith in the seriousness and coherence of Nietzsche's philosophical enterprise I will dismiss at the outset the charge that the variety of interpretations is attributable to some self-destructive desire on Nietzsche's part to dwell in irrationality and contradiction.

In this chapter I will discuss four different interpretations of Nietzsche's idea of the will to power, noting why each one of them captures an aspect of Nietzsche's theory. Each of these theories contains an element of truth concerning Nietzsche's statements on the will to power, yet not a single one of them in its stated form can be reconciled with the others. I point out that this apparent paradox can be resolved if one distinguishes between two uses of the will-to-power notion in Nietzsche. In one case, power is used in the sense of domination, whereas in the other it is used in the sense of recurring energy. Although for Nietzsche these two senses of power were not mutually exclusive, I argue that in terms of transcending nihilism the use of power as domination is entirely unacceptable. For this reason I will be critical of all attempts to ennoble the value of domination by means of the will-to-power theory—whether these attempts stem from Nietzsche himself or from interpreters who accept the pro-domination spirit of his theory. On the other hand, to be fair to Nietzsche, I also argue against interpretations which reduce the meaning of his will-to-power theory to nothing more than a jus-tification of violence, domination, and cruelty. The latter position is correct in understanding one aspect of Nietzsche's view but fails to acknowledge the brighter side of his view of power.

THE BACKGROUND OF THIS INTERPRETATION

Nietzsche's many notes regarding the will to power and the aban-donment in 1887 of an attempt to unify his work according to a systematic version of this principle show that, while he considered the idea to be fundamental, he resisted adopting a systematic model of explanation as constitutive of his theory.[3] The reason why Nietzsche resisted systematization is not that his thought is essentially discontinuous, as has been argued most recently by J. P. Stern.[4] Such an interpretation deemphasizes the philosoph-ical importance of Nietzsche's work, particularly his critique of Western metaphysics. On the other hand, attempts to reduce all of Nietzsche's observations regarding the will to power to a single philosophical idea, although serving to maintain his reputation as a philosopher, do not do justice to the wide variety of phenomena that Nietzsche meant to include under this principle. Therefore there is a need for a method of interpreting the will-to-power theory that allows for a plurality of interpretations and at the same time is able to give a unified and coherent account of the ontological, moral, and political significance of this pluralism. Such a method, I suggest, is one that takes the will to power as a *metaphor* concerning the nature of reality. This approach co-ordinates the theoretical meaning of the will to power with Nietz-sche's epistemology and ontology. For Nietzsche's critique of all absolutes and, in particular, of the Kantian "thing-in-itself" shows that he conceives of reality itself as a realm of appearances punc-tuated by relationships of semblance—and what is more appro-priate to such a conception of reality than to hold that the meaning of reality-as-appearance is most truly conveyed through meta-phors? Under Nietzsche's epistemological theory of perspectiv-ism, knowledge is freed from dependence on "facts"—and therefore from literal meaning—at the same time that it is freed from a strict dependence on logic. What better way is there of affirming Nietzsche's view of knowledge than for the philosopher to gather within a few suggestive metaphors such as the will to power and the *Übermensch,* insights about reality that no one literal interpretation could claim to exhaust? Under the perspective of the will to power as metaphor, all other interpretations of Nietzsche are not only better understood but often are liberated from their most salient restrictions. The idea of the will to power as metaphor therefore brings a new and important synthesis to our understanding of what Nietzsche meant by the will to power, while it develops concretely a very interesting application of Nietzsche's perspectival theory of truth.

The reading of the will to power as metaphor can help to explain both the significant contributions as well as the limitations of several major interpretations of Nietzsche's theory. I have chosen four such interpretations for the diversity of standpoints that they advocate and represent, as well as for the widespread influence they either have exerted or are likely to exert on Nietzsche scholarship both in this country and abroad. Stern's recent work, published in England, will be contrasted with Kaufmann's reading of the will to power, for it is primarily with Kaufmann's reading that Stern juxtaposes his interpretation.[5] Deleuze's interpretation in *Nietzsche et la philosophie,* a study which has influenced much of the recent French and Spanish criticism of Nietzsche, will be seen as disputing Heidegger's highly influential interpretation of Nietzsche's work.[6] Despite their differences, however, all of these interpretations have in common the fact that they do not explore the possible philosophical meaning of the will to power as metaphor. My alternative theory of the will to power will be offered in light of this other possible meaning. I will show that with the help of this alternative reading one can explain some of the contradictions which still beset the four interpretations chosen for discussion as well as simultaneously rescue Nietzsche from some of the contradictions unreflectively contained in his work. Ultimately it is my aim to use the interpretation of the will to power as metaphor as a critical tool against nihilism in Western culture. The alternative reading will disassociate Nietzsche's theory from the paradigm of the will to power as domination. The latter paradigm controls, either wholly or in part, the other four interpretations to be discussed.

CRITIQUE OF TRADITIONAL INTERPRETATIONS

In order to clarify the theoretical differences affecting the various interpretations of the will-to-power theory, it has been helpful at times to categorize the various interpretations of the will to power as psychological, metaphysical, scientific/cosmological, and so on, according to whether the interpretation of Nietzsche's theory professes to be a hypothesis about human behavior, the nature of being, or the interrelationship of forces in the universe.[7] The helpfulness of these categories in providing a more specific and comprehensible theory than that found at face value in Nietzsche's texts and notes must be acknowledged. However, certain important questions remain unanswered by this piecemeal categorical approach. For example, if the will to power is taken to mean a will to self-overcoming in the moral sense, as argued by Kaufmann, does this not evade the significance of Nietzsche's attack upon traditional morality? If, on the other hand, the will to power is taken to represent a destructive, irrational force, a crude or subtle principle of domination, as argued by Stern, does this not make Nietzsche's interpretation of human reality so narrow as to become intellectually unacceptable and ultimately insignificant except for its destructive potential? If the will to power is interpreted from a metaphysical point of view, as Heidegger proposed, does this not subvert Nietzsche's critique of metaphysics as well as ignore all of the references to the psychological applications of the will to power found in Nietzsche's work? Further, if an attempt is made to give a scientifically oriented explanation of the theory as Gilles Deleuze has done, does this not subvert Nietzsche's strong critique of science? It would seem that despite the contribution to our understanding of reality rendered by these interpretations of the will to power, the method of choosing one aspect of his philosophy to the exclusion of others as overwhelmingly paradigmatic of the will-to-power idea results in leaving out some equally or even more important arguments in Nietzsche's philosophical project. The fact that important aspects of Nietzsche's theory are excluded from these partial interpretations of the will to power suggests that one must look for a more comprehensive method of interpreting his theory.

In an attempt to preserve what is valuable in these different types of interpretation while at the same time trying to reach a more fundamental standpoint which can synthesize these insights in a spirit of affinity with Nietzsche's many-faceted texts, I shall raise a question which perhaps will take us closer to understanding this apparently elusive idea of the will to power. Although one of the primary aims of Nietzsche's idea of the will to power is to overcome the moral dualism between good and evil, to what extent is there an implicit or explicit moral dualism underlying the interpretations of Nietzsche? Finally, I will also question whether one of Nietzsche's versions of the will-to-power theory does not itself embody a dualistic approach to existence. The overcoming of dualism, as I see it, is more fundamental to the spirit of the will-to-power idea than the complete overturning of morality. Nietzsche's rhetoric of extremism and immoralism must be challenged. It seems more sensible to remain true to another Nietzschean point, namely, that the assumptions behind any theory are value-laden, and that of all values none are more powerful than our implicit or explicit moral assumptions. The critical task therefore is not to attempt to eliminate the moral assumptions governing the interpretations of the will-to-power theory, but to examine without pretense what kind of role morality plays in the interpretation and to determine whether such a role supports or distorts Nietzsche's critique of the moral tradition that exploits the dualism between good and evil.

A Moral Reading of the Will to Power

Walter Kaufmann's influential analysis of the will to power as a drive for self-perfection raises the question of what it means to give a moral interpretation of the will-to-power theory. Kaufmann's interpretation should be seen primarily as a moral rather than as a psychological interpretation, as it is sometimes described.[8] This moral reading is attained by emphasizing the correct and important link between the idea of the will to power and the notion of self-overcoming.[9] However, once this important connection is upheld, the Nietzschean meaning of self-overcoming is misinterpreted and obscured by the strong influence of the traditional moral categories informing Kaufmann's interpretation. Kaufmann interprets "self-overcoming" to mean the power of rational self-restraint against the presence of a strongly passionate natural disposition.[10] Will-to-power as self-overcoming is identified with the control of irrational impulses within oneself, a moral paradigm which is contrasted by Kaufmann with a crude and

insensitive reading of will-to-power as the domination and manipulation of any individual by any other individual. (It should be
noted here that while the latter theme cannot be identified as the
principal meaning of the will to power, neither can it be ignored.)[11]
The will to power is said to signify the triumph of the self over
its wayward inclinations. Kaufmann's interpretation places Nietzsche squarely in the tradition of mind/body dualism which Nietzsche meant to reject. While Kaufmann attempts to explain this
contradiction through a theory of sexual sublimation similar to
that of Freud, the strong presence of dualism in his interpretation
raises serious questions about the adequacy of reading Nietzsche
in this way.[12] It can be argued against Kaufmann that the teaching
of self-overcoming must be taken in the context of Nietzsche's
overturning of the traditional model of the self in *Thus Spoke
Zarathustra*.[13] Moreover, the critique of the self is not only present
in *Thus Spoke Zarathustra* but is supported by innumerable other
texts from Nietzsche's will-to-power period.[14] The will to power
as self-overcoming therefore requires a much more thorough ex-
plication than one restricted to the traditional moral sense. In
contrast to Kaufmann's approach we must ask, first, what the
will to power as self-overcoming means if Nietzsche's repeated
arguments denying the existence of the self are taken seriously.
Second, we must question both the heuristic and moral validity
of the paradigm case of self-overcoming given by Kaufmann—
that is, "self-overcoming" as the control of reason over the passions. This type of interpretation does not take the reader beyond
the alienated moral standpoint of the dualism between reason and
sensibility, duty and pleasure, which unfortunately characterizes
most of the philosophical tradition. Although Nietzsche may borrow terms or concepts from these categories and use them in the
course of his writings, it is our task to give a critical interpretation
of his writings according to where Nietzsche seeks to lead us
rather than according to the concepts that he has tried to overcome. Our task is to understand the conjunction between the
principle of the will to power and the transvaluation of *all* values,
as opposed to explicating the will to power in terms of all of the
categories, values, and definitions posited before Nietzsche's
transvaluation. To accomplish this, we must inquire vigorously
into Nietzsche's view of morality and of the self before fastening
any traditional meaning upon the metaphor of "self-overcoming."

The Will to Power as the Drive to Conquer

Stern takes issue with Kaufmann along traditional lines, so that their agreement on the importance of traditional morality is more significant than their disagreement as to how Nietzsche can be judged by these standards. Like Kaufmann, Stern does not inquire into Nietzsche's critique of the self. Neither does he inquire fully into Nietzsche's attempt to offer a perspective on existence "beyond good and evil" even though a major part of Stern's study is devoted to Nietzsche's work by that title. Stern's concerns in the interpretation of the will to power are remarkably close to Kaufmann's except that where Kaufmann sees Nietzsche as taking the side of rationality, Stern highlights the strong impact of irrationality in Nietzsche's "discontinuous" aphorisms. Stern uses the metaphor "the discontinuous and catastrophic will to power" to sum up his vision of Nietzsche's understanding of reality.[15] This is tied to the more serious charge that Nietzsche's thought lacks credibility due to its lack of substance and coherence.[16] Stern dismisses the substantive content of much of Nietzsche's philosophical critique of the tradition by a conjunction of several charges revolving around the theme that for Nietzsche the only truths that matter are those that are spontaneous and lack continuity. The theme of discontinuity leads Stern to discuss the discontinuity between Nietzsche's "moral" individual and the moral standards of society, thus building up the conclusion that the values of Nietzsche's "noble" individual are both empty and irrelevant and that Nietzsche's conception of the good is not only empty but antisocial and thereby immoral.

Stern's devaluation of Nietzsche's philosophical enterprise therefore culminates in the interpretation of the will to power as a narrow principle explaining only the moral emptiness of the drive for conquest and domination by a highly antisocial individual. Adolf Hitler is taken as the paradigm of what the will to power would mean to individual behavior, but the behavior of anyone who would set his or her "willfulness" against the "law" would probably serve to exemplify Stern's conception of the will to power in the psychological sense. Stern charges that the will to power is the epitome of selfishness rather than the moral act of self-overcoming suggested by Kaufmann. Whether the notion of will to power is subtle or crude, says Stern, it is always a justification of ruling and domination. "The purpose of all self-overcoming that is not decadent is the validation of command."[17] The command is not subject to morality, for in place of morality Nietzsche puts forward the standard of the "discontinuous and catastrophic" occurrences of life. Stern concludes that Nietzsche fails to go "beyond good and evil" in his interpretation of existence, for in giving this account of the nature of existence he has posited the violence of the will to power as the ultimate good.

While Kaufmann's analysis of the will to power ignores all self-overcoming that is not moral, Stern fails to include moral acts as part of the reality that is the will to power. Stern therefore considers the transvaluation of values simply as the reversal of decent moral values and socially sanctioned moral codes. The result, in his view, is the portrayal of an irrational and destructive universe in which the principle of violation becomes the good while the principles of love, generosity, or harmony take on the character of evil. Of this type of interpretation the most important thing to be said is that one indeed finds a great many passages in Nietzsche where cruelty and domination are seen in the essence of the will to power.[18] This shows the existence of an unresolved tension in Nietzsche's theory of values. To help resolve this tension one must question the grounds for Nietzsche's portrayal of the will to power as the will to dominate, wherever this characterization occurs. One interesting thing about Nietzsche is that he did not pause before social conventions and allow religious moralities or socially acceptable notions of the good to be exempt from criticism for acts of violation and domination perpetrated against "the innocence of becoming" and the "healthy body."[19] It is extremely important to give the proper attention to the theme of cruelty and domination in Nietzsche's work. Not only is there a misguided justification of cruelty in his work, but we also know that the historical misinterpretation of these ideas has been costly. The more important question to raise with respect to the will-to-power idea, though, is one suggested by Nietzsche's perspectivism: what can be said regarding the historical and ideological origin of the perspective that makes one interpret life in terms of aggressive destruction, including aggressive self-destruction? Surely, according to Nietzsche's theory of perspectivism, one is entitled to argue that it is due to certain limitations in our perspective that we are forced to draw a destructive interpretation of life. For the interpreter's ideas and the conditions for the possibility of an interpretation are interdependent.[20] If Nietzsche speaks of violence, let us consider the degree to which violence has been made acceptable in our culture before we charge him in particular with irrationality and irrelevance. To avoid the contradictions resulting from the problem of violence that appears in the will-to-power theory, I will question whether there is a necessary and inescapable relationship between the principle of the will to power and the principle of domination. Although Nietzsche endorses domination in many aspects of his theory, this is not directly attributable to the idea of the will to power as such but to one of the models of explanation used to interpret it.[21]

THE WILL TO POWER AS A METAPHYSICAL THEORY

Let us turn now from explicitly moral interpretations of Nietzsche's theory to Heidegger's reading of the will to power as the culmination of the Western tradition of metaphysics. It should be noted that Heidegger's interpretation is pervasively moral in tone despite Heidegger's alleged lack of concern for Nietzsche's moral theory and for ethics in general. Heidegger purifies Nietzsche's critical/genealogical method of inquiry by shifting the discussion of all issues to a highly abstract or metaphysical plane. Even where Nietzsche is most explicit about the connection of some types of knowing to survival, Heidegger strongly rejects Nietzsche's association of knowledge with biological needs.[22] More interesting than Heidegger's attempt to rescue Nietzsche from "biologism" is his interpretation of what makes Nietzsche an "immoralist." Heidegger redefines morality in terms of metaphysics. The attempt to undo the distinction between being and becoming—this, and only this, is the meaning of all of Nietzsche's immoralism.[23] Reading this conversely, one could say that the meaning of Heidegger's critical effort to restore the primacy of being against Nietzsche's theory of will to power as becoming represents the overturning of immoralism for morality. In Heidegger's recalling of being to human consciousness there is an underlying moral tone stronger than that of many explicitly moral theories.

The only way to escape the limitations of Heidegger's method is to drop the highly select and contrived categories through which he has given meaning to Nietzsche's notes on the will to power. On the ontological level this means that the will to power as becoming must not be given the negative value of an "eclipse" of being.[24] Nietzsche's theory of reality as flux, or becoming, is not a forgetting of being in the Heideggerian sense. On the contrary, it is a recalling of the human consciousness to its origins in temporality. In other words, ontologically, the differences between Nietzsche and Heidegger are not too striking, except that Nietzsche's primary category is becoming, while Heidegger's is being. On the epistemological level there are more serious differences. For Heidegger, the will to power as knowledge is the creation of order out of chaos.[25] A strong polarity is thus established between knowledge and chaos. This polarity, however, is more in keeping with the Western philosophical tradition than with Nietzsche's actual theory. Nietzsche had emphasized the continuity between knowledge and all other aspects of existence precisely in terms of the metaphor that everything is will to power and nothing besides. What is forgotten in Heidegger's analysis is that the will to power refers to all plays of force—to all constellations of force.[26] Schematizing forces are the will to power, but so is everything that defies schematization. The following statement, left out of *The Will to Power* collection and already referred to in Chapter 3, is worth bringing once more to our attention:

> *Appearance* [*Schein*], as I understand it, is the
> actual and only reality of things. . . . With this
> word, however, nothing is expressed other than
> the *inaccessibility* [of reality] to logical procedures
> and distinctions. . . . A definitive name for this
> reality would be "the will to power," that is to
> say [a name for the protean nature of reality] des-
> ignated from inside. . . .[27]

When Nietzsche says that the will to power is the name that becoming gives itself insofar as it can never be known through logical categories, he is pointing to a much more fundamental aspect of the will to power than the mastery of chaos by knowledge that philosophers find so comforting. This satisfaction of mastering "chaos" keeps us from asking the more fundamental question raised by Nietzsche's will-to-power theory: How can we cancel the division between subject and object, self and world, good and evil? By way of contrast, this type of dualism prevents us from reaching a proper understanding of the will-to-power theory. Nietzsche's theory attacks and negates the metaphysical and epistemological dualism so prominent in our civilization. When

Zarathustra tells the lovers of knowledge that out of their will to truth there speaks a will to power, the intention is to counsel the thinker to turn inward, avoid self-deceit, and attempt to understand the physiological and unconscious foundations of theoretical knowledge.[28]

SELF-OVERCOMING AS THE INTENSIFICATION OF LIFE

Although Heidegger's method of interpreting Nietzsche seems at times to instantiate the very type of metaphysical reification of judgments that Nietzsche sought to demystify, there are some exceptional insights which Heidegger contributes to the interpretation of Nietzsche's theory. Among these is the interpretation of self-overcoming as *Selbststeigerung,* an analysis that may be further developed through the closely related notion of the intensification of life.[29] The intensification of life need not be seen solely in art but should be extended as a philosophical perspective from which one could begin to understand all of reality. This is the perspective taken by Zarathustra, who interprets all of existence as a process of will to power as self-overcoming. Here it is crucial to notice that in the process of intensification of life the boundaries of the self are not only dissolved but lose their authoritative and controlling function over the organism. Self-overcoming, therefore, involves the overcoming of the self in a very different manner from that envisioned by Kaufmann. What is at stake is the overcoming of the schematizing self, the self which in terms of power defines itself in contrast to the body and the passions, and which in terms of knowledge defines itself as the measure of all things, including the maxim that guarantees the validity of this measure.

Nietzsche's thesis of the will to power as self-overcoming is at once an affirmation of life through the notion of its intensification and a critique of the metaphysical notion of the self. Self-overcoming means the intensification of life by which all divisive (even if conserving) boundaries on life are destroyed or transcended. Self-overcoming involves the overcoming of the Apollonian principle of individuation and drive to permanence in favor of the greater reality of the Dionysian flow of existence in which the boundaries between subject and object, time and eternity disappear. Language, caught in the metaphysics of the self, must also be exposed for the ideology it perpetuates through its metaphysics of subject/predicate and its reification of boundaries. The task for

the "artist's metaphysics" with which Nietzsche meant to sup-
plant the metaphysical tradition is the construction of a theory of
meaning in which language no longer takes on this alienating
function. The result of this elimination of boundaries, when seen
by some conservative interpreters of Nietzsche (such as Stern),
appears to be the advocacy of silence (instead of language) for
access to being or truth.[30] Nothing could be more inconsistent
with the intent of Nietzsche's major teachings. Nietzsche explicitly shows how silence in a theory of meaning and asceticism in
a theory of action represent the concrete culmination of nihilism,
the "illness" that human beings need to overcome.[31] As we overcome nihilism we look for a different theory of meaning. To do
this, Nietzsche—at times explicitly, at times implicitly—turned
to a theory of truth and existence that may be concisely described
as an appeal to truth as metaphor.

Still, the idea that Nietzsche's most comprehensive attempt at
an explanation of reality should hinge on the turn of a metaphor
might disturb those who prefer a more scientific account of reality.
Our socialization has made it more acceptable to hold that metaphysics ought to be replaced by science than to hold that metaphysical meaning should be redirected to an affirmation of life
through metaphors. Perhaps the two paths are not mutually exclusive. But in the interest of addressing how the will-to-power
theory would look to an interpreter who takes the scientific over
the metaphorical interpretation as primary, one may consider Deleuze's interpretation in *Nietzsche et la philosophie*.

THE WILL TO POWER AS THE GENERATING
PRINCIPLE OF FORCE

In contrast to Heidegger, Deleuze accepts the will-to-power theory as an affirmation of a metaphysics of becoming—not as a
threat to being. Deleuze relates Nietzsche's metaphysical preference to a scientific explanation of reality. Here the will to power
is related to the more primitive concept of force, just as Heidegger
had related it to the more primitive concept of being. Deleuze's
method is significant in that one of the important tasks of any
interpretation of the will-to-power theory is to explain the nature
of the pluralistic complex of forces that makes up reality. Deleuze
discards the judgment of those who claim that Nietzsche had only
a cursory interest in science pursuant to giving a scientific proof

of the idea of the eternal recurrence.³² He believes it is much more interesting to analyze what Nietzsche found objectionable in science and how he would have freed science from life-negating theories and methodology. In Deleuze's view, what separated Nietzsche from science was a way of thinking about reality. As he says, Nietzsche believed (whether justifiably or not) that science tended to equalize quantities and to study force from an exclusively reactive standpoint. Politically, Nietzsche also associated the scientific method with utilitarianism and egalitarianism. It is primarily for these reasons that Nietzsche criticized science. But still this is not to say that the will-to-power theory would be incompatible with science. Compatibility is possible if the concrete and differential elements in the play of forces are given scientific attention, as against an abstract and uniform conception of force. In this notion of an interplay of forces Deleuze finds the primary meaning of the idea of the will to power.

Deleuze removes the interpretation of the will-to-power theory from the specific arena of metaphysics and morality, just as he interprets the theory without any special allusion or attention to individuals, their psychological makeup, and their political arrangements and structures. Because Deleuze does not rely upon the mistaken category of the self he does not need to do an extensive analysis of self-overcoming but appears to take Nietzsche's analysis for granted. He works primarily with four basic categories—active and reactive force, and affirmative and nihilistic will to power.³³ The terms "active" and "reactive" are predicated exclusively of force, while the qualities of affirmative and nihilistic will to power relate the activity of force to every other aspect of reality, including human experience. The interplay of forces upon which Deleuze founds his interpretation is never treated in terms of such un-Nietzschean metaphysical categories as "thinghood," "self," or "individual."³⁴ Differentiation is explained in terms of the qualitative differences among forces. The qualitative element that both differentiates and generates forces is then said to be the will to power.

The virtues of Deleuze's interpretation are several. There is in his account the joy of allowing for a plurality of forces in the universe and an affirmation of every process of becoming-active within the whole of reality. The will to power is neither limited to nor centered upon the sphere of human behavior. The interplay of forces is a continuum of power relations throughout all of reality. When consciousness is no longer taken as something separate from the rest of life, there is for the first time a real chance that the previous or present tie of consciousness to nihilism will be exchanged for the liberating power of active, creative force. According to Deleuze, this liberation comes from opening up the prison of consciousness to the life-affirming forces of the unconscious. Deleuze's interpretation is so close in spirit to Nietzsche's writings that it is difficult to raise strong criticism against it. But it is still our task to place this theory as well as the other already mentioned within the compass of a more inclusive interpretation. Deleuze's main limitation is to insist that in Nietzsche's theory of the will to power there is a significant theoretical difference between the act of determining the meaning (*signification, sens*) of something and the act of determining the value (*valeur*) of something. Deleuze claims that to interpret is to determine the meaning of something according to the "force" that gives it a meaning, whereas to evaluate is to determine the value of something according to the "will to power" that affirms or denies its value.[35] This distinction, however, belongs to Deleuze rather than to Nietzsche, and it deflects from Nietzsche's effort to develop a theory of meaning in which all meaning is taken as a sign of value ("Man would rather will nothingness than not will").[36] The weight that Deleuze places on the distinction between meaning and value (interpretation and evaluation) raises the question of whether the purpose of this distinction is not found in the need to protect from criticism those analytical elements presented under the nonevaluative label.

Let us, then, look more closely at some of the attributes of active and reactive force which are said to be purely explicative. According to Deleuze, active force is that which synthesizes, affirms, posits its difference in a creative manner, whereas reactive force is that which separates and renders the active impotent.[37] But these descriptions are already value-laden, as the terms "active" and "reactive" suggest. It is also said that active force by its very nature dominates—it synthesizes and creates by dominating.[38] Here, Nietzsche's association of domination with creativity is sustained by Deleuze. As a result, Deleuze's analysis presents as definitive the interpretative assumption that creativity and activity depend upon domination. Moreover, although Deleuze's categories of active and reactive force are ostensibly free from morality, an explicit moral judgment is brought into the

explanation of change. For example, Deleuze states that "becoming-active is affirming and affirmative, while becoming-reactive is
negating and nihilistic."[39] In the final analysis, Deleuze connects
three activities or forces in such a way that the three always belong
together. These are domination, creative-affirmative activity, and
active force. Thus the scientific interest in investigating the nature
of active force turns into a justification of domination. Domination, in turn, is ennobled through its association with creative
activity and active force. This means that Deleuze's account genuinely reproduces but does not satisfactorily resolve the conflict
already found in Nietzsche's theory between the affirmative concept of a play of forces and the dualistic notion of a struggle for
power between the weak and the strong. Despite its attempt to
ground itself in science, the distinction between becoming-active
and becoming-reactive drawn by Deleuze remains conceptually
tied to the old notion of the struggle for power between the forces
of good and evil. We have yet to see in what sense this is a nihilistic
struggle. The structure of domination needs to be viewed critically
rather than affirmed as life-enhancing.

BEYOND THE RIDDLE OF DOMINATION

Although Nietzsche attempted to overcome the dualism between
good and evil by means of the will-to-power theory, the interpretations of the will to power that we have examined seem to maintain a moral dualism whether they intend to do so or not. The
solution to this riddle is not to get rid of morality in the belief
that morality is an oppressive force reflecting slave values (as
Nietzsche sometimes held), but to liberate morality from the model
of domination intrinsic to the master-slave dialectic. The breakthrough in the interpretation of the will-to-power theory is not
the cancellation of morality but the cancellation of domination
and of the alienating dualism that perpetuates the tension between
master and slave. Before we can reach this breakthrough we must
be willing to give up the model of knowledge informing or influencing our previous interpretations—knowledge as mastery of
reality. It is the model of mastery, assumed into a theory of what
counts as knowledge, that leads us astray. But to eradicate this
view of knowledge is difficult.

In all of the above interpretations of the will-to-power theory,
with the exception of Heidegger's remarks on will to power as

the intensification of life, the model of domination is used inextricably from the interpretation of the will to power. In other words, even when Nietzsche's theory is not interpreted as a theory of domination, the alternative interpretation follows an unacknowledged model of domination. Thus Kaufmann, who argues specifically against an interpretation of the will to power as domination, does not see that his own countertheory of self-control is an instance of domination—indeed, of the domination of the instincts by moral and rational controlling interests. Heidegger does not acknowledge that his discussion imposes the domination of being upon becoming, but considers only the violation done to the truth of being when other truths are given priority. Deleuze freely admits that active force rules over its environment by dominating reactive force and by taking its greatest satisfaction from this rule. Stern limits the will to power as domination to the realm of the irrational and appeals to a dualism of good over evil to show that there is a realm of benevolence and justice in human life that lies outside the drive to dominance. However, when Stern absolves traditional spirituality and the law from being instances of domination, he misses Nietzsche's incisive critique of these social and cultural structures.

The logical options regarding the inclusion or exclusion of the principle of domination in Nietzsche's theory of the will to power are the following. (1) One may identify the will to power with domination and give it a negative value, by virtue of one's moral opposition to domination. This is the tactic followed by Stern. (2) One may identify the will to power with domination but give it a positive value, either by devaluating the need for a moral interpretation or by giving "domination" positive characteristics such as the exclusion of impotence and resentment. This is the approach taken by Deleuze and at times by Nietzsche. (3) One may disengage the idea of the will to power from the principle of domination by refusing to deal explicitly with the topic as much as possible. This is the approach followed by Kaufmann and, to some extent, Heidegger. All of these approaches are unsatisfactory, for they all interpret the will to power in such a way that the interpretation excludes other important or essential aspects of Nietzsche's total theory. There is yet the option (4) to include in one's interpretation Nietzsche's account of the will to power as domination, yet to accept the account critically in light of other passages where the will to power is unrelated to domination or free from domination. This is the method I have followed in giving a critical reading of the will to power as metaphor. In following this option, it is my intention to acknowledge the phenomenon of domination but at the same time to free the interpretation of Nietzsche's works from its power. While there may be skeptics who will fail to be convinced of the interpretation that follows, I shall at least attempt to suggest how this method serves to unify the central themes in Nietzsche's philosophy.

In order to free the will-to-power theory from a model of domination one must first go back to Nietzsche's critique of metaphysics and, together with him, reject the traditional concept of the self as well as the metaphysics of language governing traditional theories of meaning.[40] This involves an important shift in which the significance of metaphysics is replaced by a series of metaphors. "Self," "will," "subject," "object," and so on are terms whose previous metaphysical reference must be canceled and exchanged for a philosophically critical metaphorical reference. Zarathustra's cry "God is dead—the *Übermensch* shall live!" can be translated into the proposition "Metaphysical truth is dead—from now on metaphorical truth shall live." God as absolute and thing-in-itself had been a metaphysical truth, while the *Übermensch,* Zarathustra's principal teaching about humanity, is a metaphorical truth about the possibility of human fulfillment. The *Übermensch* is a metaphor for what it would mean to be a human being who is no longer fragmented by the forces of dualism and the condition of alienation from the earth.

That the will to power is a metaphor about reality is so obvious a conclusion to be derived from Nietzsche's writings that its truth has slipped by unnoticed. To say that the world is "the will to power and nothing besides" is not to say that, literally speaking, nothing exists except the will to power (however that may be explained). Rather, a metaphorical interpretation of this statement suggests two main points. First, since metaphors contain an implied likeness, what Nietzsche means is that the world is like "the will to power," and nothing excludes this likeness. Second, since metaphors bear the possibility of multiple interpretations, taking the will to power as a metaphor means that one must keep oneself open to the possibility of multiple interpretations of this image. While it is part of this theory to say that the will to power may bear many different interpretations, my aim is to look for the best interpretation we can offer. According to Nietzsche, good interpretations are those which arise without resentment against time, affirm life, enhance life, avoid self-deceit and the deceit of others, and are sufficiently comprehensive to give meaning to other interpretations.[41] A good interpretation of life must also exclude a justification of domination. Let us test whether it is possible to combine Nietzsche's perspective and mine.

A good place to begin is with the analysis of what the will-to-power metaphor is intended to express and achieve. Having analyzed what the metaphor is meant to achieve, I shall go on to examine the more precise meaning that is conveyed by its terms, in particular, the meaning of "will."

THE AIM OF THE WILL-TO-POWER METAPHOR

The immediate aim of the will-to-power metaphor is the cancellation of boundaries between self and world: "This world is the will to power—and nothing besides. And you yourselves are also this will to power—and nothing besides." In this cancellation the will to power idea becomes that link or implied likeness which, once posited, transforms the connection between self and world from a condition of alienation and self-deceit to a condition of integration and truthfulness. There is, however, more than one way in which this cancellation may be understood. Although Nietzsche does not seem to be aware of this, it is possible for the will-to-power idea to provide the link between self and world (or subject and object, or human beings and nature) in a way that does not lead to integration or truthfulness. This happens when the significance of the metaphorical elements in the will-to-power idea are forgotten. Paradoxically, it is when the metaphorical elements are remembered and joined to a philosophical self-criticism of the will-to-power idea that the full truth of this idea emerges. It will be helpful to show how such a critical interpretation of the metaphor may be contrasted with a naive reading. But first an overview of the general aim of the metaphor should be presented.

The will-to-power theory is an attempt to unify the nature of all human reality (from subconscious drives to the highest manifestations of culture) under one principle, the will to power. Just as important, it is also an attempt to unify and correlate the whole of human reality, understood as will to power, with the whole of reality outside of human nature. The result is the view that whatever is, is will to power. The unification of reality, or the self-overcoming of an alienated conception of humanity (humanity alienated from the rest of the universe), may be established in one of two ways for Nietzsche. One may either attribute to the rest of reality features comparable to those of human nature, or one may demythologize the "special" importance of human nature in the larger context of reality. In the first case there is a tendency to personify natural forces, while in the second case there is a tendency to depersonalize human activity and understand it on the basis of energy and force. It is a peculiar characteristic of Nietzsche's theory that both a reduction of human activity to natural forces and an elevation of natural forces to human activity appear to take place at once. This effect is achieved through Nietzsche's combination of a poetical use of language with a philosophical self-criticism of the fictions projected by his philosophical poetry.

DIFFICULTIES IN INTERPRETING NIETZSCHE'S METAPHOR

Now let us consider the simple or philosophically naive route to Nietzsche's use of the will-to-power metaphor. Let us suppose that the will exists and is something personal—that a will is always the will of a self or of a subject of consciousness. This view is commonly taken for granted in ordinary language although in his philosophical analyses Nietzsche opposed it vehemently.[42] Nietzsche used the common assumption to his advantage in collapsing the distinction between human beings and nature. Still, all arguments employing the assumption that the will exists rest on an illusion. It is not surprising that interpretations of the will to power making use of this illusion should eventually lead to contradictions. Two possible types of misunderstanding that are likely to arise will be mentioned briefly.

If the will is thought to be a definitive expression of personality or subjectivity, and if all reality is held to be will to power, the will-to-power theory would seem to be saying that all movement in reality is like the human (personal) act of willing. What could this mean? One possibility is to suggest that Nietzsche makes use of this analogy to explain all movement as determined by an *internal* center of power. For example, nature is said to move "from inside" just as it is felt that we do when we do something.[43] A variant of this type of interpretation is followed by Danto.[44]

This line of interpretation is correct insofar as Nietzsche proposed an alternative to both the theological and mechanistic explanations of change, using the will-to-power theory to rule out the external intervention of God as creator and "first mover" of the world as well as all other theories that separate and externalize cause from effect. But here one must be careful to note, as Danto has done insofar as his method allows, that Nietzsche proposed the alternative notion of all activity as a *process* where everything is so interrelated that it is an illusion to separate "cause" from effect, "thing" from process, "fact" from interpretation. This is why the notion of the will itself is an illusion and why it is both incorrect and misleading to say, without qualification, that behind every perceptible discrete event in the world there is a correspondingly discrete force or will to power. But beyond this, it is important to question what kind of theory of value, if any, is attached to this view of power.

A second type of misunderstanding resulting from the unreflective use of the will-to-power metaphor and the uncritical use of "will" within that metaphor may be observed when the comparison between human beings and nature is stated not in terms of force or power but in terms of consciousness and freedom. In this case, to say of all phenomena that they are "will to power and nothing besides" suggests, through the mediation of the traditional notion of "will," that all phenomena approximate certain activities of consciousness and freedom. Nietzsche himself is fond of using this approach, especially in poetic contexts where non-human elements in nature are personified and given a human voice. Much of *Zarathustra* is a case in point. At first glance this approach may appear to be a generous humanization of nature since, through the figure of personification, nature is given access to a "will" and to the process of deliberation, thus participating in activities that have been regarded as either exclusively or primarily human. But, in fact, there is much more to the metaphor than this, for the metaphor also suggests the converse. The use of metaphor for Nietzsche is always bipolar. Since the status of both terms is that of appearance (rather than one term resting on something more metaphysically substantial than the other), relationships of likeness among appearances are always correlative. In the case of the will-to-power metaphor this means that not only is nature like us but that we are like nature. But what does it mean to say that we are like nature? Does this analogy force us to give up morality?

The rhetorical (still unreflective) effect of the personified use of the will to power is the elevation of natural forces to a type of consciousness like ours. As a result, all the less rational aspects of human beings (for example, procreation, aggression, violence) are elevated to the status of "will," of consciousness. Given this elevation, what used to be considered less than human aspects of human beings are now considered on the same level as rationality and morality (each drive or instinct within us is a will to power). In fact, through the will-to-power personification of nature, natural forces may even acquire priority over the value of human purposiveness from which they take their name of "will." In the *Genealogy of Morals*, for example, Nietzsche argues that just as in animal life the strong predators must overcome their prey and fully enjoy their spoils, so must the strong and noble among human beings derive satisfaction from overtaking the weaker.[45] In the end, the glorification of the untamed will becomes an implicit assumption in an argument of much larger scope wherein irrationality and violence, especially if uncorrupted by a so-called decadent reason, are celebrated both in the natural world and that of human relations. What starts out as a personification (and thereby humanization) of extrahuman forces tends to turn around and effect a dehumanization of human beings or, at the very least, a devaluation of rationality. Nietzsche's elevation of nature through attributes such as nobility and strength should therefore be read quite critically.

In subsequent chapters we will have the opportunity to see in more detail how Nietzsche's erasure of the distinction between human and natural forces may further the dehumanized notion of humanity. But even though we note the danger in Nietzsche's view, we also observe that other, less guarded, interpretations of Nietzsche's theory can be offered. For example, a justifiable line of argument is to maintain that, if Nietzsche sought an overcoming of humanity, his goal was not to dehumanize humanity but to lift human beings from the illness or incapacitating character of nihilism.[46] It cannot be denied that there is some truth to this view. The problem in Nietzsche, as I see it, is that he does not always sustain this perspective. Therefore, to keep us from being swept away by an idealistic interpretation of Nietzsche, we must emphasize that Nietzsche's affirmation of life and nature cannot be viewed uncritically. Affirmation of life, in the full sense of the term, is only attained when there is a state of integration and creative balance between human consciousness and life. For this to be achieved there must be freedom from a nihilistic consciousness, as exemplified in the overcoming of otherworldly values. But there must also be freedom from a view of life that dwells on irrationality and violence or that legitimizes these as natural goods. Indeed, Nietzsche criticized human nature for the resentment bred within its consciousness and argued that human beings cannot be healed from alienation and nihilism unless they accept their finite place in nature with the full affirmation of life implicit in his teaching of *amor fati*. What this argument requires for its completion, in spite of what Nietzsche may sometimes say to the contrary, is the stipulation that nihilism is not overcome unless human beings overcome the need for domination in their relations with each other, with their own bodies, with nature, and with the universe. To heal the resentment that drives human beings to a condition of alienation it is not enough to cancel the boundaries between mind and body, self and world, or good and evil, although if the boundaries rest on relations of dominance, their cancellation is in itself a good start. What is also necessary and ultimately indispensable, is to cancel the ideology of conquest that is responsible for having alienated and continuing to alienate human beings from nature, from each other, from temporal existence— in short, from the meaning of the earth.

The reason why nihilism cannot be overcome unless the principle of domination is eradicated from our culture can be clearly seen by highlighting the many contradictions into which Nietzsche's theory relapses when it attempts the defeat of nihilism in a prodomination way.[47] For example, he is forced to say that by becoming more evil people will become more noble; that by endorsing violence and exploitation with a good conscience they will become more just; that by becoming subhuman they will become superhuman. He is forced to say that both extremes must be intensified at once, otherwise human beings are bound to mediocrity.[48] These riddles are paradoxes of domination and have no place in a theory of the will to power that retains consciousness of its metaphorical level and does not descend to the uncritical identification of the will to power with the will to conquer either others or ourselves, either chaos or decadence. The ideology of conquest is already a paradigmatic sign of moral decadence. Decadence itself interprets the will to power as a will to rule.

The precise derivation of Nietzsche's justification of violence from certain premises of the will-to-power theory cannot be dismissed as an aberration in his theory. Unless one disassociates the term "will to power" from its narrow meaning of will to domination or conquest, one will be misled into thinking that the essence of all that lives is the will to conquer. But if we remind ourselves of the genealogy of the will-to-power metaphor, we will see that we are dealing with a figure of speech the philosophical meaning of which is far from obvious. The simultaneous elevation of nature and submergence of consciousness into its·dark roots is a poetic device meant to break open the barriers and boundaries in human consciousness that have separated human beings from nature and from their bodies, thus cutting off from humanity both the love of the earth and the instinctual source of human creativity. If the will-to-power metaphor is forgotten and the phrase is understood literally, the transfigurative effect of the will-to-power emblem will be erased from consciousness.

A CRITICAL READING OF THE METAPHOR

Let us now take a different route to the metaphor that all is will to power and nothing besides. Considering that Nietzsche denied the existence of the will and of the separate existence of the subject of willing, let us start out, alternatively, with a philosophically critical interpretation of the will to power. Assuming that there is no subject and there is no will, one needs to explain the psychological phenomenon of the feeling that at least in some instances there seems to be something that can be appropriately described as the will to power. What is at stake in this case? As already shown with respect to his critique of causality, Nietzsche claims that in the specific case of the term "will" what is at issue is the (mistaken) feeling that one is willing something.[49] He considers this feeling to be something epiphenomenal. There is always a complexity of phenomena involved in a "doing," but there is neither an existentially separate "doer" nor a "deed." The doer and the deed are abstractions from life, as is the faculty of willing. So we are a play of forces in tune with or in struggle with other combinations of forces. Nietzsche claims that the will, in the psychological sense, is a metaphor for the exertion of force—or, more precisely, a metaphor for the feeling on the part of an individual that he or she is commanding something. However, a critical investigation of what takes place in willing reveals that the exertion of force involved in willing-as-commanding is not an event in itself but part of a "sea of forces" whose movement has been essentially characterized as self-transcendence or self-overcoming. For Nietzsche the positive sense of the illusion of willing-as-commanding is the sense of thriving that one experiences as one centers all of one's attention and energy upon the creation of something. This activity is ethically significant because it marks the transitional context between the exertion of power (as perceived momentarily by the individual) and the *overflowing* of this power into the continuing and long-term process of a life of creativity for the individual. In other words, the ethical significance of the will-to-power metaphor (when the metaphor is interpreted in the psychological sense) is the opening up of the individual to a more creative relationship with his or her environment. Besides freeing the psychological interpretation of the will to power from the charge of egocentrism, this model of interpretation also allows the critic to distinguish between a noncoercive model of creativity and a domination-oriented conception of psychological power.

The major difference between this interpretation of the will-to-power metaphor and the one discussed previously is that here the philosopher is critically aware that the use of the term "will" has no literal significance. The will serves to designate the idealized process of self-transcendence through which the inexhaustible re-creation of life is eternally renewed. When the term "the will to power" is used to explain the nature of the world of becoming (the nature of all movement and change), what is being attempted is what Nietzsche calls "an inside view of reality," namely, a view of reality that escapes the conceptual tendency on our part to freeze the process of life into fixed entities and to measure movement in terms of net losses and gains. "The will to power" is used for its connotation of the exertion and flow of power, not for its connotation of acts done by a personality with the aim of acquisition or expansion. There is something highly poetical in calling reality "the will to power," but in this nothing whatsoever is implied about the value of acquiring power or the existence of a will. To use Nietzsche's images: the world of the will to power is "without goal" and "without will" "unless a ring feels good will toward itself," "unless the joy of the circle is itself a goal.''[50] What has been at stake for Nietzsche is the attempt to give a life-affirming description of the world of becoming or flux.

METAPHORS AND TRUTH

When the will to power is liberated from the traditional notion of the will and self-overcoming is liberated from the traditional notion of the self, one is able to give an entirely different reading of Nietzsche's theory of the will to power. The correctness of this reading depends upon the close interrelationship between critical philosophy and metaphorical meaning. Metaphors alone cannot provide the understanding of reality that Nietzsche wants to give us, as can be seen by the confusion that takes place when his metaphors are read uncritically. But neither can philosophy alone provide for a Nietzschean understanding of existence. This raises the question of the importance that Nietzsche placed on the relationship of metaphor to truth.

From the time of *The Birth of Tragedy,* the analysis of the meaning of metaphors is essential to Nietzsche's theory of meaning and critique of established truths.[51] From the writings of the period of the transvaluation of all values (1883–88), one may deduce that metaphors represent the most truthful form of knowing because as relations of likeness between various forms of appearances they are perfectly in harmony with the ontological understanding of reality as a world of appearances and change. Metaphors express the truth of appearances as metaphysics had expressed the truth of the thing-in-itself which is no longer credible to us. Through metaphor various aspects of reality, previously thought of as separate, are given a new sense both of unity and multiplicity. A metaphor will reveal the unity of two aspects of reality once considered different. But at the same time it does not make this new metaphorical semblance so binding as to reify it into a fixed and permanent thing. Metaphorical relationships are pluralistic and open-ended. Any aspect of reality may be metaphorically related to an innumerable variety of other aspects and each metaphorical relation may be interpreted in multifaceted ways. These relations show the rich variety of perspectives through which reality may be interpreted by human beings who have shed the need for a Controller of Interpretations (God, Facts, Ego, System, Method). Nietzsche believed that when the metaphorical meaning of things and relations is forgotten and varieties of literal interpretations take over our understanding of things, we lose ground with the truth of existence as well as with the happiness that existence can give to human beings.[52] For all of these reasons it makes sense to say that in terms of Nietzsche's ontology and critical epistemology, the only philosophically coherent interpretation of the idea of the will to power is a metaphorical interpretation—that is, an interpretation which combines Nietzsche's critique of logic with his Dionysian affirmation of truth, life, and art.

NIETZSCHE'S DISTANCING FROM THE WILL-TO-POWER METAPHOR

While a combined metaphorical and critical interpretation of the will to power is most consistent with Nietzsche's ontology and with his conception of truth, one finds that Nietzsche himself often departs from this interpretation. Given his denial of causal explanation, Nietzsche needed another principle of explanation for the happening of events. The responsibilty for providing an alternative explanatory account of reality fell upon the theory of the will to power. A note from 1885 referring to Nietzsche's projected work, *The Will to Power,* explains the meaning of "will to power" as follows: "Under the not undangerous title 'The Will to Power' a new philosophy—or, stated more clearly—the attempt at a new exposition of all that happens shall herewith have its say."[53] In the space of just one sentence "the will to power" already means a variety of things: the title of a book, the main thesis of a new philosophy, the attempt to make that thesis good, the introduction of a new principle of causal explanation, and, most elusive of all, the meaning of the nature of reality ("all that happens"). However, when a metaphor like "the world is the will to power" is made to serve an explanatory function, the free-ranging use of its symbolism will be impaired. If, in addition, the explanatory use of "the will to power" assumes the existence of the will—which is denied in Nietzsche's critique of metaphysics—the result will be a theory of explanation that is, at best, a fiction. At worst, it is a theory beset by conceptual muddles.

It was mentioned in Chapter 3 that Nietzsche tended toward either a recurrence or a domination model of explanation and that he used the idea of the will to power in the context of both of these explanatory models. When the idea of the will to power is used in the context of a recurrence model of explanation, the ontological presuppositions of Nietzsche's thought are preserved without disruption. This means that the consistency of his ontological outlook is maintained. Under the recurrence model, "the will to power" does not refer to a literal *will* to *power* because the standpoint of recurrence has already discarded the relevance of an atomistic view of things. In this context Nietzsche observes that the will to power does not refer to a will or goal, that the process is its own goal.[54] When the idea of the will to power is used in the context of a domination theory of explanation, however, the ontological presuppositions of Nietzsche's thought are both suspended and disrupted. All change is interpreted as a struggle. Moments of peace are but intervals allowing the will to gather sufficient strength for new wars. Struggle, competition, and resistance are then called "the will to power." It should be emphasized, however, that the will-to-power metaphor does not force such an interpretation upon existence. Rather, the view of life as domination prevents the possibility of one's interpreting the metaphor in any other way. Under the domination model of explanation all existence is viewed as a struggle for competition and power and all change is thought to be reducible to the drive of each unit of life to manipulate and conquer others. Once one is locked into this explanatory model it is virtually impossible to transcend it because one has lost the sense of the flow of life. Instead of perceiving the richness and continuity of life, he perceives only the struggle of opposites. Because every experience is perceived as a possible defeat or victory, one's energy and attention are distracted from the full reality of events. The capacity to learn about existence through a receptive attitude toward life is thereby obstructed.

One cannot deny that there are conditions of domination in human reality. There is oppression, there is slavery, there is competition for power and privilege, and so forth. Some individuals dominate others, while others allow themselves to be dominated or are forced to submit to a power beyond their control. Nietzsche is especially astute when he observes the many manifestations of these phenomena. But should one make an ontological model of this condition and project these conflicts unto the structure of the entire universe? Would it not be better to suggest that where domination occurs new conflicts are brought into existence which would otherwise have no reason for being? Is not domination a nihilistic attempt to rewrite history and to deny the reality of what is? If the notion of order were reevaluated, one would notice that the world does not need to be ordered through domination for stability to be maintained. In fact, where order is maintained through domination and exploitation, the stability of life tends to be severely impaired. For example, the selected exploitation of natural resources has been shown to lead to severe cases of disbalance in the ecosystem.

When Nietzsche uses the paradigm of domination as a natural or an ontological category, his perspective needs to be questioned. The "commanding-obeying" notion of reality is not a given, although it is an important facet of social reality. Human knowledge can help to lend perspective to the uses and abuses of the concepts of mastery, domination, and command. For this to happen, knowledge must itself be free from being defined in terms of a structure of domination. Knowledge must be freed from having to fit the pattern of mastery over the unknown or over chaos (control and/ or exploitation of the "other") as is demanded by a domination theory of power. The analysis of knowledge as the assimilation of chaos (which Heidegger attributes to Nietzsche) reminds one of the terrifying myth of Saturn devouring his children. One need not accept the charge that Nietzsche's theory of knowledge conforms to this paradigm. A Nietzschean interpretation would show precisely the opposite. Knowledge is childbirth and self-overcoming; it is the result of the closeness between ourselves and the world. In knowledge the closeness and continuity between ourselves and the world can be experienced critically, imaginatively, and creatively. One sees this life-affirming view of knowledge, for example, in Zarathustra's dialogues with life, just as it is more analytically manifested in Nietzsche's critique of logic. A rejection of the model of knowledge as mastery of reality is essential to the liberation of Nietzsche's will-to-power theory from a fixation upon willing as commanding.

Another area which needs to be critically reevaluated with respect to the application of Nietzsche's the will-to-power theory is the area of individual psychology and social relations. Unfortunately, in these respects Nietzsche adheres quite firmly to a domination-based explanation of human behavior, especially in the context of social interaction. The moments when he departs from this view may be regarded as exceptional. Still, the fact that such exceptional moments are there shows that it is possible to develop a liberating moral theory out of Nietzsche's ontological framework for the transvaluation of all values. The fact that he himself did not carry this project through to a successful conclusion indicates that in the areas of morality, social relations, and politics Nietzsche could not concretely imagine a universe where the continuity and flow of life would be a part of one's daily social experience. Given such views about social life, it is understandable that Nietzsche should have chosen the path of solitude.

In conclusion, I reiterate that although the will-to-power metaphor is capable of sustaining many different interpretations, the most consistent philosophical reading of the metaphor is that which preserves Nietzsche's intention to heal the alienation of self from world. The intention in portraying the world and the self as will to power—and nothing besides—was to enlarge the horizons of one's experience and to allow the tides of becoming to reinvigorate the self with life's flowing energy. Nietzsche's teachings of the will to power, the *Übermensch,* and the eternal recurrence are directed toward this vision of life and human experience. Where dualism breaks this vision apart—whether the dualism is found in Nietzsche himself or in the interpretations of his writings—one is no longer dealing with what Nietzsche sought to heal in Western culture but with states of consciousness which are still in need of healing.

5

Beyond Good and Evil

When reconstructing the premises of Nietzsche's moral theory, it has been the habit of some of the more influential Nietzsche scholars in the United States to say that Nietzsche's method is that of a genealogist of morals and that his message amounts to a critique of "slave" values. Nietzsche's message has been interpreted primarily from a liberal point of view as an argument for the abolition of slave morality. This means that Nietzsche is viewed as a thinker who celebrated the freedom of individuals to be creators of values and to refrain from following the behavior patterns of the majority, or "herd." Second, it means that the principle of authenticity—"Become the person you are"—is taken as the highest maxim of Nietzsche's moral theory.[1] Although this interpretation of Nietzsche's work covers some of the most important themes in his critique of traditional morality, it also leaves much unexplored. Several other aspects of Nietzsche's statements in separate aphorisms and works, both published and unpublished, must be pieced together before a more complete picture of his intent can be presented.

The next three chapters of this study are my attempt to evaluate the ideas and values Nietzsche proposed to replace the life-negating moral values associated with Christian morality, Kantian morality, and utilitarianism. Because Nietzsche's attack on these ideas is fairly well known, the discussion will not dwell on his criticisms of the tradition.[2] What Nietzsche sought to create beyond the tradition will be addressed in three stages. In this chapter the meaning of the "beyond good and evil" that is to follow traditional morality will be considered. In Chapter 6, the implications of the transfer of moral authority from God to individuals will be analyzed. In Chapter 7, Nietzsche's ideas about the political use of moral authority will be explained and evaluated. My aim in these three chapters is to investigate the meaning and implications of Nietzsche's singular attempt to give direction to the future of humanity from an extramoral perspective.

NIETZSCHE'S "IMMORALISM"

Nietzsche describes himself as an immoralist, but is one obliged to take his rhetoric seriously?[3] Walter Kaufmann, who has given one of the most influential readings of Nietzsche's philosophy, has argued to the contrary. Kaufmann sees Nietzsche's critique of morality as a morally respectable critique of slave values. In addition, he restricts the meaning of "slave values" to a "state of being" of the moral agent. It follows from Kaufmann's interpretation that as long as one believes in anything, including Christian dogma, out of a feeling of strength, one need not consider oneself a believer in slave values. In Kaufmann's view, Nietzsche's critique of morality is compatible with a belief in Christianity. "The difference between Nietzsche's ethics and what he himself took to be Christian ethics is not ultimately reducible to different forms of behavior or divergent tables of virtues. . . . The basic distinction here is that between two states of being: the 'overfullness of life' and the 'impoverishment of life,' power and impotence."[4] This approach ignores all the instances where Nietzsche criticizes the "decadence" of Christian morality in order to defend an immoralist use of power.[5] Kaufmann assumes that Nietzsche opposed slave morality because slave values are not sufficiently moral. He is responsible for the wide adoption of this influential but inaccurate view of Nietzsche's theory.

Unlike Kaufmann, Arthur Danto emphasizes Nietzsche's attack on Christian values. But Danto goes on to add that Nietzsche can be considered an "immoralist" only in the "specific sense of opposing Christian morality."[6] Danto gives a politically liberal interpretation of Nietzsche's defense of aristocratic values. He argues that Nietzsche's analysis of the "herd" is outdated and that "masters are simply distinguished individuals of whatever sort who impose values on the world."[7] Danto views Nietzsche's references to a natural aristocracy as an oversight as well as a violation of Nietzsche's "perspectivistic message." However, while Nietzsche's reference to natural kinds (as Danto puts it) may be a violation of the spirit of Nietzsche's perspectivism, it is not a concrete violation of its logic. Nietzsche was well aware that he was giving an interpretation of existence, not a report on objective facts. Where Danto gives the most misleading portrait of Nietzsche's theory, though, is where he dismisses Nietzsche's defense of the aristocracy as a meaningless error which in no way

affects the substance of his moral theory. On the contrary, I will
show in Chapters 6 and 7 that Nietzsche's idea of the "order of
rank" (*Rangordnung*) is not only one of the central doctrines of
the transvaluation of all values but the structural paradigm supporting Nietzsche's immoralist perspective on values.

Because Nietzsche's critique of traditional morality is highly
complex, it requires very careful reading and interpretation. The
reason that the critique has not been understood well so far is
that the emphasis has been placed on what Nietzsche attacked
rather than on what he proposed as the goal of the transvaluation.
Too much emphasis has been placed on how he addressed the
past and too little emphasis on how he envisioned the future. In
reading Nietzsche's works I have tried to keep in mind that he
called himself an "immoralist" for more than purely rhetorical
reasons. To come to a full understanding of Nietzsche's immoralist perspective, it is necessary to see that his genealogical approach (the search for the "origin" of values) is only part and
not the whole of either his philosophical method or the intent of
his philosophical teaching. As a transvaluator of values, Nietzsche kept a constant eye on the present and the future, not merely
on the past. He was as interested in effecting specific social and
political changes by means of his theory of values as he was intent
upon investigating the psychological origins of values. He believed that the surpassing of morality and the beginning of his
"philosophy of the future" would go hand in hand. While *Beyond
Good and Evil* was subtitled "Prelude to a Philosophy of the
Future," from the information in the Colli-Montinari edition of
his notes we now know that it might have been subtitled "Attempt
at an Overcoming of Morality."[8] It is important, then, to determine
what sorts of changes Nietzsche intended to promote by means
of this effort.

Through the doctrine of the overcoming of morality Nietzsche
intended to achieve two principal goals. First, he aimed at the
eradication of dualism in Western metaphysics and morality. Second, he aimed at a reversal of values such that what was considered "evil" under the previous system of values would be
considered a source of strength under the future system. Given
these purposes, the question arises as to whether these two goals
might not be contradictory. The analysis to be given shows that
they are indeed contradictory, in that the second goal (the reversal

of slave values) simply turns the dualism of the tradition on its head.

Did Nietzsche know that in his attack upon traditional morality he was pursuing two different goals or that these two goals might be opposed? There seems to be no realization on his part that what he defined in the *Genealogy* as the opposition between "good and bad" (master and slave) was just as dualistic as the target of his attacks, the Christian's fixation on the opposition between good and evil. However, there is an indication in *Ecce Homo* that he was much happier with his work in *Thus Spoke Zarathustra* than with his work in *Beyond Good and Evil*.[9] In *Zarathustra* he had primarily concentrated on fighting dualism, whereas in *Beyond Good and Evil* he had concentrated on reestablishing a system of values based on the distinction between noble and base. However, since Nietzsche did not view the distinction between noble and base as dualistic or nihilistic, he was unable to see that he himself was responsible for reinstating the dualism which in a separate context he sought to overcome.

What, then, is the meaning of Nietzsche's immoralism? Here it is important to clarify what is immoralist in Nietzsche's perspective and what is not. Although both the eradication of previous values and the reversal of such values may be described as immoralist endeavors, in each case the charge against Nietzsche contains different presuppositions. In the first case, Nietzsche negates the moralistic position which relies upon the dualism of good and evil to warrant all its value judgments. The person who transcends this dualism is only an immoralist in the eyes of one who is still trapped in the dualistic moral perspective. In the second case, Nietzsche continues to be a dualist but reverses the value of his opponents' ideals. Nietzsche points to the struggle between masters and slaves for the appropriation of all values in Western culture. The position attacked by Nietzsche is that of the "moralist," namely, the slave or democrat who claims that all persons have moral dignity regardless of sex, class, or race. Nietzsche here defends the immoralist master or aristocrat who denies the slave's values. I maintain that when Nietzsche sides with the master and asserts that there is no such thing as human dignity, it is appropriate to identify him as an immoralist, that is, as someone who opposes the notion that all human beings have both a moral identity and moral rights which cannot be ignored at will. When he argues against the inhumanity of moral author-

itarianism and against dualism, though, there is no reason to call
him an immoralist, as the moral fanatic might be tempted to do.

THE THEMATIC DEVELOPMENT OF NIETZSCHE'S IMMORALISM

In 1885–86 Nietzsche decided to unify the meaning of all his works
through the theme of the overcoming of morality (*die Überwindung der Moral*). The aesthetic view of reality given in *The Birth
of Tragedy* was reassessed in terms of its contribution to an an-
timoral and anti-Christian doctrine of values. In the 1886 preface
to *The Birth of Tragedy* Nietzsche wrote: "It was *against* morality
that my instinct turned with this questionable book, long ago; it
was an instinct that aligned itself with life and that discovered for
itself a fundamentally opposite doctrine and valuation of life—
purely artistic and *anti-Christian*."[10] Nietzsche looked upon his
work in *The Dawn, The Gay Science*, and *Zarathustra* as proph-
esying the destruction of morality. In one of his unpublished notes
he summarized the theme of these works as follows:

> *The Dawn.* Morality as a sum of prejudices.
> *The Gay Science.* Scorn for European moralism.
> Z[*arathustra*]. View of an overcoming of morality.
> How might a human being who lived beyond mo-
> rality need to be constituted?[11]

While there were anticipations of the idea of the overcoming
of morality as far back as *The Birth of Tragedy* and in the two
works preceding *Zarathustra*, Nietzsche identified the turning
point of this idea with the emergence of the "Zarathustra type."
He applied the epithet "the annihilator of morality" (*der Ver-
nichter der Moral*) to Zarathustra.[12] Five years later he reiterated
the point in *Ecce Homo:* "The word 'overman' . . . —a word that
in the mouth of a Zarathustra, the *annihilator* of morality, becomes a very pensive word—has been understood almost every-
where with the utmost innocence in the sense of those very values
whose opposite Zarathustra was meant to represent."[13] Nietzsche's demand that he be read less innocently is still applicable
today.

If Nietzsche has been and continues to be misunderstood, this
is not entirely the fault of his readers. Nietzsche himself is responsible for some of the misunderstandings that have emerged

from his works. He repeatedly called himself both an heir to morality and an immoralist. Thus he invites controversy regarding his works, but also misunderstanding. The tension between his "moral" and "immoral" identities can be explained by examining two distinct conceptions he held regarding the overcoming of morality: the self-overcoming of morality and the overcoming of morality by the higher man. (Nietzsche usually referred to the latter idea simply as the overcoming of morality.) It is important for the reader to follow Nietzsche's separate use of these two ideas, especially because Nietzsche does not distinguish clearly between them. He fuses them together or presents them as complementary. One passage where he explicitly states their interrelationship appears in *Beyond Good and Evil:*

> But today . . . we immoralists have the suspicion that the decisive value of an action lies precisely in what is *unintentional* in it. . . . The overcoming of morality, in a certain sense the self-overcoming of morality—let this be the name for that long secret work which has been saved up for the finest and most honest, also the most malicious, consciences of today.[14]

Here the overcoming of morality is presented as the more encompassing of the two theses. This is not surprising, since in *Beyond Good and Evil* Nietzsche had abandoned the primacy of the notion of self-overcoming developed in the early parts of *Zarathustra*. Nietzsche's main interest in *Beyond Good and Evil* was to develop the foundation for a theory of values based on the idea of an order of domination and rank in nature and culture. Whereas in *Zarathustra* the symbols associated with the self-overcoming of morality had been the *Übermensch* and the eternal recurrence, in *Beyond Good and Evil* these important symbols are dropped. The notion of self-overcoming is used only in support of a hierarchical model of life where the sacrifice of the "lower" forms is demanded for the sake of the "higher" forms. The thesis of the overcoming of morality by the higher man is introduced to justify the social and political rise to power of these so-called "higher" men.

I will now turn to the thesis of the self-overcoming of morality (the less controversial of the two theses) and briefly examine its development in Nietzsche's middle and late works. A discussion of the overcoming of morality by the higher man and its political implications follows in Chapters 6 and 7.

THE SELF-OVERCOMING OF MORALITY

The self-overcoming of morality is an offspring of the self-criticism of morality prominent in Nietzsche's earlier writings, especially *The Dawn*. What starts out as a self-criticism eventually results in the self-destruction (*Selbstvernichtung*) or self-overcoming (*Selbstüberwindung*) of morality. However, what is destroyed is thought to be what is superficial, hypocritical, or inauthentic in morality. The lies within morality are supposedly crushed in favor of truth. Since morality's authority is supposed to have rested on a lie (the existence of God or of a moral world-order), the destruction of morality is actually a creative effort to arrive at a more honest foundation for values. But past dependence on an absolute or independent ground of moral values is still strong and the critique of morality appears to bring the collapse of a great order and a condition of chaos. Zarathustra, however, emphasizes that the chaos is pregnant with promise: "One must still have chaos in oneself to give birth to a dancing star."[15] While the self-destruction of morality (that is, the self-destruction of the self-assured moral consciousness) represents a destructive moment in the history of humanity, Nietzsche believed that this event would turn out to be highly affirmative of life.

The themes of self-destruction, affirmation, chaos, rebirth, and liberation from an alienating order characterize the thesis as Dionysian. Paradoxically, however, the idea of the self-overcoming of morality may also have a special appeal for a Christian audience. This is because the idea is presented from the point of view of *morality itself*. Morality's mandate of honesty undermines its own foundations. Nietzsche's presentation of the self-overcoming of morality often has a moralistic tone, one that would appeal to Christians. He uses a special type of moral rhetoric: "Morality itself, in the form of honesty, compels us to deny morality."[16] Nietzsche knew that persons espousing traditional moral principles could at least feel partly at home in this perspective, and he made rhetorical use of these moral overtones to gain a sympathetic hearing from traditionally schooled readers. In the 1886 preface to *The Dawn* Nietzsche stated that the final morality for conscientious human beings is the refusal to believe in something untrustworthy, whether that something is called God, virtue, truth, justice, or love of neighbor.[17]

Nietzsche's rhetorical eloquence also has an adverse consequence. He leaves unclear precisely what aspects of morality shall be destroyed and on what grounds. The moral appeal to the authority of conscience—like Luther's resistance against the Roman Catholic church—does not necessarily shake the foundations of morality. It merely transfers the authority of moral judgments to a different ground. As I will show, one needs to supplement Nietzsche's idealistic rhetoric by other considerations. Why is it impossible for a person to continue to believe in virtue? If belief in virtue or love of neighbor is no longer acceptable, is there any specific alternative to be put in their place, and why? These are the types of questions I shall be raising in my analysis of Nietzsche's overcoming of traditional morality. I am interested in the arguments he gave against morality but also in the procedure he used to set up new or alternative values.

Nietzsche had a double intent in disputing the authority of the moral world-order. He objected both to the ideology of this order and to the process by which the ideology is formed. For example, he objected to the ideology implicit in the belief in the Christian God. This means he was opposed to the notions of sinfulness, the need for redemption by Christ, the possibility of eternal punishment, and so forth. In addition, he objected to the process whereby this ideology gains acceptance in human consciousness. As hypothetical explanations for the alienation of consciousness Nietzsche offered the theories of the dread of becoming and the resentment against time. When considering the process of ideological formation, he emphasized the role played by unconscious processes and drives.[18] This method is comparable to certain materialist theories of ideological formation insofar as those theories attribute the origin of an idea (or its wide acceptance in a given epoch) to economic conditions, class structure, and the like. In Nietzsche's case, however, psychology carries a greater weight in explaining the origin of values. He sought a qualitative explanation of the origin of values. This accounts for his interest in ascertaining the quality of a person's character before attributing any validity to his or her judgments. According to his theory, nihilistic life would produce alienated and unauthoritative judgments, while self-affirming life would produce life-enhancing and authoritative judgments. Ideally, then, if a person were fully in-

tegrated with his or her life-affirming instincts, out of this integration there would emerge an authentic basis for morality.

Nietzsche's application of the genealogical method to psychology can be either critical or dogmatic. This method is a function of a broader regressive-progressive method which, as I stated
in the Introduction, links the investigation of the origin of values
to the creation of a future set of values or a future type. If Nietzsche's attitude toward the future value is dogmatic, so will be the
genealogical investigation that corresponds to its establishment.
As we have seen, every look Nietzsche takes toward the past or
the origin of a value is also part of a creative effort to institute
other (different) values for the future. The method he uses is
interesting but in itself cannot guarantee perfect results. Through
a self-critical use of the method one may indeed discover that one
suffers from a resentment against the passing of time. One could
detect that resentment leads one to adopt certain values that would
not have been adopted otherwise. These discoveries might lead
to a critical reevaluation of one's values. On the other hand, the
method could be used dogmatically. In this case one would not
ask oneself whether, in the absence of resentment, the same judgment concerning a value would be reached. Or one might ask
oneself such questions but act in self-deceit and, as a result, reach
the wrong answer. The noncritical approach to genealogy confines
the question of value to a mere either/or. Either the process leading to a value, or the value itself, fits a certain expectation or it
does not. Either it is "prolife" or "antilife." If it is prolife, it is
completely justified; if not, it is discredited. The criteria defining
the meaning of value are taken for granted and regarded as settled.
Whoever questions them is thought to be antilife.

We have seen that Nietzsche used the genealogical method
critically; he also used it dogmatically. For example, his opposition to democratic movements was so strong that he proceeded
to call "nihilistic," values such as compassion for the oppressed
and the equality of rights for all human beings. Predictably, he
proceeded to call "life-enhancing" the opposite values—hardness
against oneself and others, the use of power to dominate and
enslave the weak, and so on. Finally, he condemned anyone who
opposed his specific values as someone who was nihilistic or
decadent and therefore unworthy of having an authoritative moral
voice. The ideals of self-integration and life-affirmation are turned
into justifications of authoritarianism and extremism.

The model of self-integration as a foundation for moral judgments is valuable. Yet, before so much power is given to the ideal
of a life-affirming, integrated self, one needs to keep very clear
about the model of health one is following. Some—although by
no means all—of the specific things Nietzsche called healthy were
actually decadent and corrupt. It is therefore important not to be
swept away by Nietzsche's rhetoric and to inquire persistently
into the role he assigns to truth, once morality's authority is
undermined. Before one concedes whether Nietzsche is truly
speaking against deceptions inherent in the old moralities or
whether he is leading his audience to new deceptions (having
undermined their trust in the old moralities) one must follow
Nietzsche's ideas on the overcoming of morality very carefully,
especially the relationship between the overcoming of morality
and the future role of truth.

THE UNDERMINING OF MORALITY BY THE WILL TO TRUTH

In its positive form, Nietzsche's argument for the self-overcoming
of morality rests on two premises: the thesis that all great things
are engaged in a process of self-transcendence and the thesis that,
as the meaning of morality and truth develop historically, the
absolute foundation of morality is destined to be undermined.[19]
Although the argument for the self-overcoming of morality is fundamentally simple, difficulties stem from Nietzsche's use of different variations of the major argument. He led up to it in various
ways—psychologically, politically, metaphysically. He also used
different terms to refer to the process of self-overcoming—*Selbstüberwindung, Selbstaufhebung, Selbstvernichtung.*[20] This left him
free at times to emphasize the self-cancellation or self-destruction
of morality, while at other times he considered a less destructive
idea, such as the self-surpassing or self-transcendence of morality.
In any case, Nietzsche's central argument is that the development
of the moral conscience is bound to reach the point where honesty
orders that the belief in an independent foundation for morality
be abandoned. In other words, Nietzsche held that research into
the origin of morality destroys the credibility of an appeal to
morality as an independent or absolute foundation of values. Morality can no longer command absolutely, because one discovers
that there are no purely moral commands as such. Moral judg-

ments do not have an independent origin apart from the rest of one's physiological and psychological makeup, or apart from the political arrangement of society.[21] From this Nietzsche concluded that the power morality holds over a person's life needs to be analyzed from an extramoral perspective.

In *Beyond Good and Evil* Nietzsche argues that moral judgments are to be analyzed psychologically, just as a person's fears, ideals, dreams, and neuroses are to be understood through psychological investigation. Psychology is hailed as the principal scientific discipline of the future: "Psychology shall be recognized again as the queen of the sciences, for whose service and preparation the other sciences exist. Psychology is now again the path to the fundamental problems."[22] According to Nietzsche, by applying a psychological method to the question "How did morality arise?" the philosopher uncovers a conception of human nature much more realistic and profound than the accepted Christian interpretation.

Nietzsche did not give a single all-encompassing answer to the question of how morality arose. Still all of his answers have in common the use of the psychological method of explanation. In *Beyond Good and Evil* he suggested that herd morality arose out of fear, and in *On the Genealogy of Morals* he argued that the first morality of all, master morality, simply arose in self-affirmation.[23] By self-affirmation Nietzsche meant the habit on the part of the most powerful people in a society to consider their own choices noble in contradistinction to the general behavior of the less powerful. In addition to this predominantly political interpretation, Nietzsche considered an aesthetically oriented interpretation of the origin of morality. This interpretation considers moral activity as a manifestation of an Apollonian will to appearance. Morality is said to have originated in an effort toward beautification.[24] It was the determination on the part of human beings to appear less crude, more humane, more noble than they actually were. In other words, morality arose from the instinct to "cover up," from the desire to deceive oneself and others. Paradoxically, because of the strong desire to *appear* noble, morality gave legitimacy to an instinct which opposed the will to appearance—namely the will to truth. Although morality overpowered the extramoral drive for truth and made it fit under its rules, after many centuries the will to truth would have as its destiny the destruction of morality itself. Thus the Apollonian will to appearance is still considered by Nietzsche to be a powerful but not altogether overwhelming antagonist of the Dionysian nature of life. Nietzsche placed himself at the momentous turn in human history when the foundations of morality would collapse. He maintained that his philosophy of the will to power represented the "coming to self-consciousness" of the will to truth: "in us the will to truth becomes conscious of itself as a *problem.* . . . As the will to truth thus gains self-consciousness . . . morality will gradually perish."[25] It is more appropriate to say, however, that what perishes is morality's claim that the moral good is something uncontaminated by evil. What the will to truth shows is that the dualism between good and evil in unfounded. All values—no matter how sacred—originate in the mixture between the drive for survival and the drive for self-transcendence which are constitutive of human life.

The self-overcoming of morality, then, means the overcoming of deceptiveness regarding the origin and authority of traditional morality. Although traditional morality tends to be dethroned, it should be possible for morality to continue to operate in the service of life. But Nietzsche does not develop this point and instead emphasizes morality's perishing. Of special importance to Nietzsche, however, is the fate of the will to truth once it separates itself from traditional morality. In keeping with the principles of the transvaluation of all values, the will to truth does not lose value because it shares a common origin in life with the will to deceptiveness. The will to truth, on the contrary, is made stronger by this knowledge, steps down from its false sublimity and turns its activities to the service of life. Specifically, its task is to place human beings on a par with natural life and to strike down the vanity that makes them think they originate in something higher than nature.[26] It should be noted that Nietzsche's references to the will to truth, the will to appearance, the will to knowledge, and so forth, are an attempt to demythologize the abstract character of truth and knowledge. This rhetoric does not mean that Nietzsche believes in the existence of any such wills or in the will itself. The references indicate the complex of forces which manifest themselves in human life and which, in their specific forms, express the human process of self-transcendence.

Zarathustra's preaching to human beings initiates the return of the will to truth to the sense of the earth. In *The Gay Science* Nietzsche presents Zarathustra's attempt to overcome the old dualism between good and evil as a new tragedy of the human spirit.[27] The beginning of this tragedy is not unrelated to the destruction of the moral point of view which had protected human beings' metaphysical security by appeals to the fatherhood of God or humanity's redemption from death. It should be noted, however, that liberation from a patriarchal God and from a falsely sublime view of one's value should not be regarded as a tragedy but as a celebration of joyful wisdom.[28] What is tragic (under a transvaluated system of values) is not one's return to the earth but one's persistent and often sublime efforts to disassociate oneself from one's origins in nature. The resentment against the earth has created a dualism in the human spirit which has led the spirit to practice cruelty against the body because the body reminds one of the earth. The care for the body and the earth—that is, the absence of all exploitation against the body and the earth— is a prerequisite for the successful overturning of dualism. Nietzsche's "beyond good and evil," therefore, cannot be reached as long as the exploitation against life is condoned. But as the teacher of the *Übermensch* and the will-to-power ideas, Nietzsche's Zarathustra moves significantly closer to the affirmation of the earth than had the religious and moral tradition ruling Western culture. In this sense Nietzsche's need to move beyond the nihilistic and dualistic values of the culture had to be expressed as a movement beyond the human condition itself. The transcendence of good and evil is therefore promised through the symbolism of the *Übermensch* in *Thus Spoke Zarathustra*.

THE ÜBERMENSCH

It was mentioned that with respect to Zarathustra Nietzsche wrote: "View of an overcoming of morality." This statement is significant, for Nietzsche held more than one view as to what it might mean to overcome morality. The view depicted in *Zarathustra* is his most radical as well as most promising answer to the overcoming of dualism. The very first words that Zarathustra speaks to the people relate to the transcending of humanity in the *Übermensch*. "I teach you the overman. Man is something that shall be overcome. What have you done to overcome him?"[29] Since human beings measure themselves by the standards of morality, the overcoming of morality requires the overcoming of one's present understanding of the self. The important connection in *Thus*

Spoke Zarathustra is between the overcoming of morality and the overcoming of what it means to be human today. Self-overcoming is important in that it represents an exemplary way to achieve this goal.

The overcoming of morality (and of the human condition) symbolizes the end of the dualism between body and spirit that has fragmented the lives of human beings. Zarathustra referred to even the best human beings as a mixture of plant and ghost.[30] As Zarathustra implies, mind-body dualism has weakened both the body and the spirit through the power of a life-denying ideology. Dualism has characterized the philosophical tradition as well as all of Christian teaching. The overcoming of mind-body dualism is seen by Nietzsche as inducing a great overflow of creative power in human life. Creative power is life-affirming, in contrast to the life-denying cult of good versus evil in which the value of temporal life, the body, the passions, and the instincts is depreciated.

In place of the dualism between body and spirit Nietzsche teaches that all life is a process of self-overcoming or will to power. The best expression of what this teaching means in relationship to the self-overcoming of morality is found in Zarathustra's first speech on the three metamorphoses of the human spirit. Here Zarathustra describes how the human spirit, through self-overcoming, passes from an ascetic stage to the denial of all alienating values and finally to the overflowing affirmation of life. The symbols Nietzsche uses for each of these states are camel, lion, and child. "What is difficult? asks the spirit that would bear much, and kneels down like a camel wanting to be well loaded."[31] The burdened camel speeds into the desert and in its loneliness turns into a lion, whose task is to create for itself the freedom from all alienating values. The greatest enemy of the spirit-turned-lion, however, is the "Thou shalt." The overturning of morality— the overturning of the "Thou shalt"—is dramatic and abysmal.

> Who is the great dragon whom the spirit will no longer call lord and god? "Thou shalt" is the name of the great dragon. . . .
> Values, thousands of years old, shine on these [the dragon's] scales; and thus speaks the mightiest of all dragons: "All value of all things shines on me. All value has long been created, and I am all created value. . . ."

> . . . The creation of freedom for oneself and a
> sacred "No" even to duty—for that, my brothers,
> the lion is needed. To assume the right to new
> values—that is the most terrifying assumption for
> a reverent spirit that would bear much.[32]

According to Nietzsche, it is within the lion's power to defeat the "Thou shalt" and to create new freedom for itself. But not even the lion can create new values. The lion's power lies in resistance; it still operates according to the boundaries between self ("I will") and other ("Thou shalt"). For the creation of values a "sacred Yes" to existence is needed. This last transformation of the human spirit is symbolized by the child.

The emergence of the child in the parable of the three metamorphoses of the spirit clearly represents the self-overcoming of the dualism between good and evil. The child is innocence, the forgetting of dualism's induced guilt, a new beginning, a "sacred Yes."[33] The child's spirit symbolizes the wheel of recurrence and the dynamic continuity of life. The child has transcended the pairs of opposites that plagued the spirit of the camel and of the lion. The transcendence of dualism is made possible by the child's boundless affirmation of life.

The child of the human spirit is also a metaphor for Nietzsche's *Übermensch*. The *Übermensch*, too, symbolizes the wholeness of the spirit that is missing from alienated human life. In *Zarathustra* Nietzsche tries to show how the natural culmination of the love of knowledge and truth is for human beings to transcend dualism, to revere our origins in the earth, and to reach out to the vision of life symbolized by the *Übermensch*. Often Zarathustra addresses his speeches to the lovers of knowledge, whom he believes to be divided against themselves due to dualistic influences. Zarathustra tries to show that the fulfillment of the moral consciousness that identifies itself with the camel's bearing of what is difficult finally lies at the stage of the *Übermensch*-child. The *Übermensch*, then, does not represent the mere negation of morality but the transcendence of all dualistic categories of thought and action.

Interpretations of Nietzsche's *Übermensch* symbol have been varied. When dealing with this notion, as with the will to power, one is faced with one of Nietzsche's central metaphors. The meaning of the *Übermensch* needs to be gathered from the context in which Nietzsche uses the symbol. In *Zarathustra,* it is a symbol of wholeness, creativity, and affirmation. But it is clear that the *Übermensch* is also something that stands beyond the human condition, or at least beyond the present historical condition of human beings. Nietzsche does not simply encourage his audience to overcome their human weaknesses while at the same time retaining their strengths. His message is far more radical. He encourages human beings to *lose* their humanity in order that they might point the way to the *Übermensch.*[34] What does this mean? What is called for is the complete transformation of the divided self which claims us at present. As already explained, the dismissal of the ego-consciousness as the ruler of the organism as well as the overcoming of resentment indicates the types of radical psychological changes that need to take place before one can approach the possibility of living a fully creative life. But social and political changes also are needed. Alienated communities will be recovered and transformed into authentic communities.[35] One of the reasons that Zarathustra's disciples are asked to go into solitude is to revitalize their spirits so that one day they can be leaders of new communities. These communities will be founded upon the principle of respect for the earth. Individuals living in these communities will not be socialized according to dualistic codes of values and punitive legal systems.[36]

Nietzsche can therefore be seen to use the idea of the overcoming of morality to confront dualism and alienation in both its cultural and psychological dimensions. Nietzsche charges that the highest values ruling Western culture not only originate in decadence, nihilism, and resentment against the earth but that through their rule they pass on this system of alienation from one generation to the next. He envisions radical changes in future human beings and in institutions. The idea of the *Übermensch* is not offered as a private goal to be attained by a few individuals. It is a symbol which may be viewed collectively as unifying the "thousand and one goals" that humanity has posited so far.[37]

The critical edge of Nietzsche's idea can be seen in the fact that he claims there has never yet been an *Übermensch.* The reason for this is clear. One cannot create an *Übermensch* (even if this person is to be oneself at some future moment) in the midst of a nihilistic and dualistic culture. One cannot create an *Übermensch* as long as human beings and their culture stay alienated from the earth and as long as the revenge against time has not been healed at the psychological and cultural levels. Two principal tasks face those who wish to work toward integration: the task of healing the self and the task of healing the social environment from alienating values and institutions. For human beings, the choice of working toward the health of the self and of society is part of the process of self-overcoming which, although it may involve a significant struggle at times, still confers a creative meaning on life.

The critical nature of Nietzsche's symbol is ignored when the *Übermensch* is thought to be an attainable goal for "superior" human beings. Contrary to Nietzsche's statement that there has never been an *Übermensch,* Walter Kaufmann and Arthur Danto argue that the *Übermensch* must be an attainable ideal for contemporary human beings. Danto has the better philosophical reason for this. If it is not to be an ascetic ideal—the type of ideal Nietzsche so often criticized and in juxtaposition to which he set down his philosophy—then, argues Danto, the *Übermensch* must be an attainable human goal.[38] Danto's point is well taken, but incomplete. As already noted, the *Übermensch* is, for Nietzsche, the "child" of the human type. It is both a reminder of one's origins and a symbol of fulfillment beyond the dualism of good and evil. In *Zarathustra* the coming to be of the *Übermensch* is portrayed as the result of a gradual evolution. What is attainable for human beings now is the "working toward," not the ideal itself. For today's human beings this ideal implies the sublimation of final attainment in the same sense that parents may work to create a better society and a better environment for the future of their children without actually coming to enjoy the fruits of that environment themselves. The *Übermensch* is not an ascetic ideal because the symbol both arises from and returns to the meaning of the earth. "God is a conjecture; but I desire that your conjectures should not reach beyond your creative will. Could you *create* a god? Then do not speak to me of gods. But you could well create the overman. Perhaps not you yourselves, my brothers. But into fathers and forefathers of the overman you could re-create yourselves: and let this be your best creation."[39] Human beings are not asked to direct their energies to a lifeless beyond; they are asked to work toward the goal of making a more creative life possible for other human beings.

It is also important to note that the *Übermensch* is not to be identified with the idea of either a superior or else a free-spirited individual. There is a very strong line of demarcation in Nietzsche between the *Übermensch,* who has not yet existed, and the superior type of human being which includes literary geniuses, military heroes, great philosophers, and other exceptional persons. The *radical* transformation of the self that is implied by the symbol can in no way be reduced to the personality structure of a superior or free-spirited type. Such portraits of the *Übermensch* are given by Kaufmann and Danto, respectively. In Nietzsche's psychological sketches these human beings are called higher men and free spirits. They are not *Übermenschen.* Kaufmann and Danto both quote and dismiss as superfluous the following statement from *Zarathustra:* "Never yet has there been an overman. Naked I saw both the greatest and the smallest man: they are still all-too-similar to each other."[40] Kaufmann goes on to say that Zarathustra's statement "matters little," for Goethe was an overman.[41] The problem is that Kaufmann's interpretation is based on a misleading fusion of three Nietzschean ideas: the higher man, the *Übermensch,* and the artist–free spirit. The latter is characterized by Nietzsche as a type of higher man, but it is certainly not his sole conception of what constitutes an exceptional human being. Kaufmann's confusion is most noticeable when he states that "Caesar came closer to Nietzsche's ideal" of the overman than Goethe. Here Kaufmann mixes together three different types. Goethe is an example of a free spirit, Caesar, of a military higher man, and neither of them, of the *Übermensch.* Kaufmann concludes his brief exposition of the overman idea in the same confused manner, stating that the person who has become an overman "has overcome his animal nature, organized the chaos of his passions, sublimated his impulses, and given style to his character."[42] As an example Kaufmann refers to Nietzsche's praise of Goethe. But the quotation from Nietzsche describes Goethe as a free spirit. Kaufmann goes on to blend "free spirit" with "overman." Possibly influenced by Kaufmann's analysis of the "overman" idea, Danto concludes: "It is something of an irony that Nietzsche is least original where he has been most influential. Here is an ancient, vaguely pagan ideal, the passions disciplined but not denied. . . ."[43]

The attempt of these philosophers to bring the symbolic idea of the *Übermensch* down to the level of actual persons, present or past, is contradicted by Zarathustra's speeches. In particular, the thesis proposed by Danto and Kaufmann is denied in "Zarathustra's Prologue," as well as in "Upon the Blessed Isles" and "On Priests."[44] The *Übermensch* transcends the present possibilities of human beings. It is the child and creation of human beings. The *Übermensch* is a metaphor for what it means to transcend the dualism and alienation of the human condition. To do this one must learn about life's spontaneity from children and one must prepare the world for children whose consciousness will not have been as impaired with nihilistic values as ours has. The superior man is someone who becomes a master of dualism, whereas the *Übermensch* stands for the transcendence of dualism. There could be no more telling difference between the two types.

Sometimes it is thought that in Nietzsche's eyes the *Übermensch* is tied to the eternal recurrence, insofar as anyone who accepts the idea of the recurrence becomes an *Übermensch* or insofar as the mark of such a person is to profess the idea of the recurrence. Both of these interpretations are, strictly speaking, refuted in Nietzsche's *Zarathustra*. While Zarathustra is portrayed as one who teaches the ideas of the *Übermensch* and the recurrence, and while Zarathustra is depicted as accepting the idea of the recurrence, he is not portrayed as an *Übermensch*. Nor is it specifically suggested anywhere that the *Übermensch* must affirm the eternal recurrence of all things. It is one thing, then, to teach the overcoming of dualism and fragmentation in every aspect of human existence (the *Übermensch*) and yet another to heal the fragmentation of the self in time (the meaning of the recurrence). As long as there is dualism, there cannot be an *Übermensch*. Whether Nietzsche saw this directly or indirectly is not crucial. The important thing is that this is the way that the *Übermensch* is portrayed. The most that can be said about the attainment of *Übermenschlichkeit* by human beings is that at special moments in one's life when the power of dualism is transcended one can get a glimpse of what it would mean to be an *Übermensch*. The teaching, however, remains primarily metaphorical. As a metaphor of fulfillment in transcendence, Nietzsche's idea functions as an affirmation of the process of self-overcoming and as a criticism of all forms of human stagnation. The *Übermensch* stands against the fixation of boundaries within human life (body/soul) and between the human being and the world (subject/object). There is a connection between the ideas of the *Übermensch* and the recurrence. However, the connection is that both ideas are symbols of the integration of the human

being with life, not that *Übermenschen* must believe in the recurrence or that belief in the recurrence turns one into an
Übermensch.

THE RELATIONSHIP OF THE ÜBERMENSCH TO
THE WILL TO POWER

There seems to be an interesting connection, on the other hand,
between the teachings of the *Übermensch* and the will to power.
In keeping with the interpretation of the will to power outlined
in Chapter 4, the *Übermensch* and the will to power are best seen
as interdependent metaphors. For Zarathustra, the idea of the
Übermensch is *the* projection of the will to power, the one goal
transcending all others and manifesting the meaning of the earth.[45]
But to speak of "goal" here is somewhat misleading. The meaning
of the earth is self-transcendence and self-overcoming. It is a
process, not the attainment of a specific end unless the end be
the process itself. Therefore the *Übermensch* is not the end of a
process but rather the symbol that marks the very beginning of
the ability of human beings to be at one with the process of life
and death without building up walls and mental barriers against
it. It is a Dionysian symbol reminding one of the dynamic continuity of life. The same intent as that carried by the teaching of
the *Übermensch* is carried by Nietzsche's metaphor of the will
to power. In the will to power Nietzsche celebrates the joy of the
circle, where there is no goal unless the process itself be its own
goal. Similarly in the will to power, Nietzsche celebrates the end
of all dualism: "*This world is the will to power and nothing besides!* And you yourselves are this will to power—and nothing
besides!"[46]

Why was Nietzsche's idea of the *Übermensch* not developed
further? Given that it is such a powerful symbol of human integration, why is it that its message is not expanded upon by Nietzsche in his other late works? In part the answer to this is simply
structural. The idea belongs to a poetical text. To begin to give
a discursive interpretation of this idea or an explanation that is
completely amenable to the rules of logic is to fall below the spirit
of *Übermenschlichkeit* conveyed by the symbol itself. The *Über/
Mensch* is *above* and *beyond* the structure of divided thinking
best exemplified by the law of the excluded middle and the pairs
of opposites "either/or." When logic attempts to appropriate the

idea of the *Übermensch*, it seems to end up with the notion of a superior human being rather than with a symbol of humanity's affinity with life. To the extent that the idea is a symbol of life's creativity and self-transcendence, its meaning is best conveyed by symbols which transcend the rules of discursive thought. In this way Nietzsche's use of the *Übermensch* imagery appeals both to the unconscious powers of the mind and to the power of imagination. The idea retains philosophical importance because not all interpretations of it can be said to be adequate. For example, just as the allegory of the three metamorphoses of the spirit cannot be taken literally (just as a camel will never give birth to a lion or a lion to a child), so it makes no sense to say that human beings will give birth to a higher species of *Übermenschen*. The point of calling the healed human being an *Übermensch* is to accentuate the alienation that damages the creative development of human life. The fact that Nietzsche's teaching is metaphorical does not mean that it is irrational. In fact, it is by paying heed to its metaphorical qualities that reasonable interpretations of Nietzsche's symbol may be found.

There is yet another possible reason why the meaning of the *Übermensch* is not pursued any further beyond *Zarathustra*. Nietzsche's decision not to develop the idea further may have been caused by a shift in his use of the notion of the will to power, rather than by a flaw inherent in the idea as such. In other words, just as the will-to-power metaphor (as interpreted in Chapter 4) works to eliminate dualism, so does the *Übermensch*. However, Nietzsche explored other interpretations of the will to power which depended upon dualistic ways of thinking—most importantly, the idea of the will to power as domination. The more Nietzsche settles on interpreting the will to power in the context of a psychological theory of domination, the more does his interest in human nature move completely away from the *Übermensch* and on to the notion of the higher man or superior human being who exemplifies the will to power as domination in its extremity. Where the idea of the will to power as domination is found, Nietzsche may be seen as trapped in a dualistic universe whose main pairs of opposites are master and slave. The theme of the self-overcoming of morality then loses importance, while the theme of the overcoming of morality by the higher man takes its place. The transition between the two standponts is best exemplified by the transition from the visionary style and prophetic tone of *Thus*

Spoke Zarathustra to the psychological style and historically rooted tone of *Beyond Good and Evil.*[47]

Perhaps Nietzsche thought that the *Übermensch* was still too distant a goal and that in order to be more realistic he should address the human condition in terms of the domination model of power that presently divides human beings both spiritually and socially. In *Ecce Homo* Nietzsche praises the wisdom of Zarathustra but also adds that Zarathustra stands at such a height that his gaze is more far-sighted than even that of the Czar of Russia. Nietzsche comments that his intention in *Beyond Good and Evil* is to move closer to the here and now.[48] Certainly this distinction may explain, at least up to a point, the difference in emphasis between the *Übermensch* and the higher man. What Nietzsche left unsaid is that, corresponding to his two ideals, he also had different frameworks of interpretation for the will to power. With the *Übermensch* and with the will to power as metaphor, Nietzsche was able to transcend both morality and its opposite, immoralism. He could move beyond good and evil and suggest ideas for the healthy development of human life. On the other hand, with the higher man—a concrete historical type, unlike the *Übermensch*—the will to power is narrowed down to the exercise of domination on the part of the "strong" to suppress the "weak." Here Nietzsche cannot transcend the opposites, so he takes side with the strong against the weak. He also sides *against* morality as he defines the meaning of strength and weakness. According to Nietzsche, the criteria for strength do not rest with the moral tradition. Only those who side against Christian morality and its modern derivatives have a right to define what strength is. (This right is a consequence of their power to dominate.) The stage is now set for Nietzsche's second approach to the overcoming of morality, the overcoming of morality by the higher man.

THE END OF MORALITY AND THE WILL TO POWER

The contrast between the *Übermensch* and the higher man shows that Nietzsche foresaw two ways of going beyond morality in the project of the transvaluation of all values. One was through the self-transcendence of morality, whose integrative goal is symbolized by the *Übermensch*. The other way is through the overcoming of morality by the higher man. The *Übermensch* stands for the goal of transcending the dualism of good and evil (as well as the dualism between master and slave). Nietzsche seems to have thought that as long as social conditions remain what they are—i.e., modeled upon a structure of domination—the person who seeks to go beyond good and evil must enter the path of solitude, leaving all social relationships behind. It is possible that having shed the "Thou shalt/I will" dualism within oneself in solitude, one may wish to return to a human community to teach other human beings about the overturning of dualism. The problem, though, is that the process of overcoming dualism is an ongoing task. One cannot simply retreat, heal oneself, and come back to society (as Zarathustra attempted to do more than once) with the expectation that all will turn out well. Self-healing is relative to one's situation in the world, and one's situation is never static. A highly protective measure like complete withdrawal from the social world (Zarathustra's final answer) does not seem to be the most realistic way to find an integrated way of living. And yet, Nietzsche portrays the hermit as one who is aware of his continuity with nature, as opposed to the city-dwellers, who have forgotten what it means to be human as well as their indebtedness to the natural world.[49]

Although Nietzsche did not develop the idea of the *Übermensch* apart from the *Zarathustra* text, the idea is important in the transvaluation period because of its contrast to other goals Nietzsche derived from the basic concept of the will to power. The *Übermensch* stands for will to power as creativity. The higher man stands for will to power as power. Despite the similarity between creativity and power, Nietzsche tends to limit the higher man's use of power to activities structured by the concept of domination. It is not surprising that, given the contrast between domination and creativity, Kaufmann, Danto, and others should relate the *Übermensch* to the artist–free spirit, thereby giving Nietzsche's extramoral ideal a humanistic interpretation.

The idea of the *Übermensch* results from an aesthetic-ontological conception of the will to power. "The beauty of the overman came to me as a shadow. O my brothers, what are the gods to me now?"[50] On the other hand, the category of the "higher man" results primarily from a psychological-political interpretation of the will to power. Both types, however, have affinities toward one another. Nietzsche emphasizes the psychological superiority of the *Übermensch* with respect to human beings as well as the aesthetic superiority of the higher man with respect to the herd.

But the two types would be indistinguishable if the *Übermensch* did not represent an ontological wholeness that the higher man lacks, precisely because the latter is still a divided human type.

In this interpretation I have associated the symbolic significance of Nietzsche's idea with none but positive traits. The *Übermensch* has been portrayed as a symbol of integration, regeneration, creativity, and so on. But since the *Übermensch* stands beyond good and evil, one should note, if only briefly, that Nietzsche in principle allows the *Übermensch*-child the freedom to create as well as to destroy. Because the *Übermensch* also stands beyond alienation and resentment, it is reasonable to think that it would not be a destructive spirit—just the contrary. But Nietzsche does not qualify his statements as I have just done here. The freedom to create and destroy, however, means something very different to someone suffering from alienation, to someone who is not yet an *Übermensch*. Even the creators of value to whom Zarathustra wishes to address himself may not be completely free from resentment, and yet Zarathustra grants them complete freedom to create and destroy as they will. This is one aspect of Nietzsche's message that idealistic interpretatins of his thought fail to address. And yet it is essential not to overlook the implications of this aspect.

An important problem arises if we limit ourselves to a purely metaphorical reading of Nietzsche's symbols. It is one thing to declare loosely that all creation involves destruction; it is another to have to decide what specific values shall be created or destroyed. To be fair to Nietzsche, one must recall that traditional and Christian morality have not been exempt from practicing cruelty and domination. In the *Genealogy* Nietzsche quotes Christian theologians who celebrate the punishment of those who suffer in hell.[51] But the burning of witches and heretics in this life would be just as good an example. Still, to defend destruction as a necessary part of life (in the way Nietzsche does) is to justify violence in all of its forms. Although Nietzsche has argued that life should be a healthy and integrated activity, he has not given a method for testing what integration means. The rhetoric of integration does not necessarily represent the reality of integration. With such a vague and appealing ideal, the risk of self-deception is high. Because in Nietzsche's analysis the will to truth is the power that counteracts self-deception, it is imperative to bestow upon the will to truth a very high value as one moves beyond the restraints imposed by the rules of morality. The creation of new values and the practice of self-criticism need to go hand in hand. Moreover, if the values to be created are to affect the lives of more than one person—as most values do—and if, especially, they are to be posited as the highest values of the emerging culture, then it is imperative that they be held accountable to the criticism of all those whose lives are going to be limited or strengthened by the values selected. Granted that the practice I am recommending may be too idealistic, still it is the only way in which a truly human society can be developed.

The strength of Nietzsche's child-image is that the child represents the energy of life, the impetus of spontaneity and creativity, and the transcendence of resentment. However, the freedom from guilt needs to be balanced with a willingness to listen to the needs of others.[52] The child symbol must not be used to justify the unlimited or unconditional expression or expansion of the self. Limitations are necessary to guarantee that care be given to others. Otherwise, in the name of pursuing his or her own activity, the child grows into a tyrant who cannot endure the meaning of "No." The "sacred Yes" symbolized by the child must not be read uncritically as a mandate to create and destroy at will or as a license to exercise one's energy so intensely that one is blind to the needs of the world around one. The problem with Nietzsche's metaphors is that these other types of interpretations not necessarily contained in the text may still be suggested by the text, since there is no disclaimer against them.

In the case of the interpretation of the will-to-power metaphor, I noted that the best reading of the metaphor is one that acknowledges the metaphorical elements in the teaching while also incorporating into them a critical philosophical interpretation of what Nietzsche meant by "will," "power," "self," and so on. In the case of the *Übermensch*-child, I suggest that the metaphor needs to remain tied to a critical philosophical interpretation of the meaning of human activity. Without the critical approach, the will-to-power idea turns into a device for justifying all forms of domination, just as the *Übermensch* symbol turns into a preliminary justification for the creation of a solipsistic monster. The fact that Nietzsche does not put sufficient critical checks on these ideas shows that there is a structural deficiency in his work. If he seriously wants to argue for human integration, he needs to rule out explicitly those immediate applications of his symbols that work precisely against integration. On the other hand, if he wants to keep *all* possibilities open for the interpretation of teachings such as the *Übermensch* and the will to power, then he cannot also claim that these metaphors will take human beings beyond fragmentation. He needs to support his rhetorical statements with more specific philosophical clarifications so that his message against fragmentation (where such a message is intended) will be unequivocally understood. For example, when in *The Antichrist* Nietzsche states that what is good is whatever enhances the feeling of power in a person, he leaves the meaning of "power" too ambiguous. Therefore, it means both the flow of energy and the capacity of an individual to come out on top, to direct, to dominate.[53] A critical approach, on the contrary, would distinguish between all of these senses of power and would inquire further into the effects and implications of each. The reason that Nietzsche's symbols of integration—like the will to power and the *Übermensch*—are so easily misunderstood and misused is that not enough critical checks are placed on them to distinguish them from the dualistic, alienating structures of consciousness that Nietzsche intends to heal by means of these symbols.

At the root of the structural deficiency in Nietzsche's project of the transvaluation of all values is the nature of the task he assigns to the will to truth once morality is overcome. It is important to conclude Nietzsche's analysis of the self-overcoming of morality by giving critical attention to this problem.

The End of Morality and the Will to Truth

It will be recalled that Nietzsche's thesis of the self-overcoming of morality states that through the work of morality's offspring, the will to truth, morality now commands itself to be left behind. The will to truth recognizes that morality has been dualistic and has falsely claimed an independent or absolute foundation for its rules apart from the great totality of life. According to Nietzsche's dramatic way of depicting this, while morality in its old form perishes, the will to truth lives on and is reunited with life. But what does this reunion mean? Nietzsche offers a very vague sketch of the present and future course of the will to truth. It is clear that he did not intend to make the will to truth the sole heir to the previous authority of either God or morality. The will to truth that tells the individual to leave morality behind is already not speaking solely for itself, it is speaking for life. So it is not simply truth as such that speaks against morality, it is truth-in-alliance-with-life. The philosophical question then becomes: what criteria apply to determining the meaning of both "truth" and "life" in this fundamental Nietzschean formula?

Because Nietzsche did not philosophize by defining criteria for arguments, the exploration of this issue necessarily places the reader in a dialogue with Nietzsche. Even though all interpretations are grounded in finitude and everyone is limited from knowing the totality of life and all its possibilities, one cannot help but ask: who speaks for life? Who speaks for the truth of life? Here Nietzsche fell back on the genealogical method and sought to answer the question in part by an appeal to origins. His first claim is that what arises from overfullness speaks for life.[54] However, does not the life that is lacking something speak for life too? On another occasion he states that what arises from love of life speaks for life whereas what arises out of hatred for life is antilife, and therefore lacks truth.[55] But this, too, may be contested. Does not life include both the loving and the hating of life? Besides, who defines what "hatred of life" means—Nietzsche or, say, Wagner? Nietzsche's other recourse is to claim that what arises out of strength speaks for life. Does this mean that what arises from weakness does not? And again, who defines the meaning of "strength"? Who shall be the judge?

In *The Antichrist* Nietzsche states: "The weak and the failures shall perish: first principle of *our* love of man. And they shall be given every possible assistance."[56] If Nietzsche judged himself to be speaking here for truth and life, he was surely suffering from self-deception. It is not enough simply to consider oneself a spokesperson for "life," or to offer criteria for the meaning of "strength" that merely anticipate the value of what one is going to say after one speaks "out of strength." No matter how impressive the qualifications of any one person or perspective, the person's authority must always be *limited* and *open to challenge* both with respect to subject matter treated and with respect to the rules of the game.

The structural problem of what happens to the will to truth following the negation of traditional morality is never resolved in Nietzsche's late writings. His intention was to free individuals from an ascetic notion of truth and from the alienating distancing of truth from life. But who controls the meaning of "life" in whose service truth is to recover its essence? Perhaps it is still the ascetic consciousness in disguise. An unexpected relapse into nihilism, dualism, and resentment is quite possible. Unfortunately, many relapses are found in Nietzsche's work, especially in themes dealing with the question of authority. The failure of the will to truth to develop in a healthy way beyond traditional morality is due to Nietzsche's unwillingness to allow some of his own authoritarian positions to face criticism. Hence the principle of domination is elevated and the will to truth perverted or silenced, especially at those times when the will to truth's tendency toward criticism is needed most. In order to confirm this it is best to examine in detail one of Nietzsche's most alluring but also inherently nihilistic doctrines, the overcoming of morality by the higher man.

6

The Overcoming of Morality
by the Higher Man

Another way of looking at Nietzsche's thesis of the self-over-coming of morality is to say that the process of the will to truth turning against itself can only be realized in a few exceptional individuals. Reflecting upon the origin and nature of morality, these individuals arrive at the conclusion that morality has no absolute authority to command them or anyone else. But also believing that human beings need some sort of moral system to regulate and appraise their behavior, these exceptional human beings take it upon themselves to become, as it were, the guardians of morality. Specifically, they will work to create new values and moralities designed to enhance the will to power of the people whom they feel destined to rule.

Briefly, then, this is the origin of Nietzsche's idea of the over-coming of morality by the higher man. With this thesis Nietzsche does not advocate the dissolution of moral practice, at least for the majority. Only the limited displacement of moral authority is intended. Roughly speaking, an elite set of individuals takes over the power that once was attributed to an absolute ruler—God—or to a council of the gods. Looking back at the history of religions, Nietzsche speculates that what he advocates openly (the will to power of an elite dictating the moral standards of a society) is the natural way of things and also their rightful order. Christianity is interesting in that, following Judaism, it developed a "herd re-bellion in morals"; as a result, the will to power of the weak, by force of numbers, has gradually become the measure of morality.[1] Nietzsche also argues that instead of describing the conflict of rulers and ruled for what it is, moral authority—whether of the weak or of the strong—has always relied upon a "holy lie" to enforce its commands. The idea of the noble lie, derived from Plato's *Republic,* is applied by Nietzsche to the practice of all moral rulers who impose their ideologies upon the people over whom they exercise control.[2] Nietzsche would like to believe that the difference between his theory of the order of rank (*Rangord-*

nung) and all other theories of value consists precisely in his honesty and his lack of appeal to a holy lie to give his theory a divine or eternal sanction.[3] This Nietzschean claim is questionable since the justification he gives to his theory rests on appeals to the inevitability of destiny or of natural laws. The appeal to destiny or nature may well rest upon a mystification. Furthermore, since lying is a prerogative of the creator of values, it is acceptable in principle for Nietzsche and other creators of value to lie if the situation warrants it. However, toward the end of his career Nietzsche comes to think his position is so strong that it has no need of lies to support it.[4]

But is Nietzsche honest with himself? Is he not self-deceived about the virtually unlimited power that the few may exercise over the many? And does not this theory of a strict order of rank actually come in conflict with Zarathustra's idea that all beings seek to become something higher than themselves? In the static schema of ruler and ruled, leader and herd, there is no opportunity for individuals to grow beyond the confines of strictly limited roles: one set of ideas applies to the herd, another to the rulers. There is to be no crossing of boundaries nor a surpassing or cancellation of boundaries by either leaders or herd. "My philosophy aims at an ordering of rank: not at an individualistic morality. The ideas of the herd should rule in the herd—but not reach out beyond it: the leaders of the herd require a fundamentally different valuation for their own actions, as do the independent, or the 'beasts of prey'. . . ."[5] The limited roles given to individuals here displace the constant process of learning and transcending oneself which characterizes the teachings of Zarathustra.

Starting with the Dionysian idea of a universe of endless change (becoming) and of an innate drive on the part of all that lives toward self-transcendence, Zarathustra argues that morality is damaging to the creative drive of human beings because morality seeks to prevent diversity and change. The force of the moral tradition wants to make past values rule the future. This prevents not only an individual's spiritual development in time but the spiritual development of the species. All future values are rendered illicit or unwarranted when present or past values are believed to be absolute. This thesis is also presented in *The Gay Science* in the context of an evolutionary view of the formation of values. Nietzsche argues there that always the moral establishment is held to be "good" while any alternative system of values that begins to threaten the moral establishment is considered "evil."[6] Reversing society's expectations, Nietzsche assigns to the "new" and "evil" values a higher significance than to the old. The notion of moral rigidity is indirectly attacked. In other words, the inability to accept what is new—what creates conflict or contradictions in a moral system—signals the beginning of the end of that system. A moral system that cuts itself off from new life damages the development of the species by holding human beings back from their own future.

In *Zarathustra* a very similar type of argument is developed in the lengthy discourse "On Old and New Tablets." Nietzsche refers to the crucifixion of Christ as a paradigm of the judging of a moral thinker "evil" because of his opposition to the moral establishment of his time. It is suggested that the Pharisees hated Christ because Christ was a creator of values. The point is stressed further when Zarathustra credits Christ with the insight that "in their hearts" those who consider themselves "the good and the just" *must be Pharisees.*[7] In other words, Nietzsche charges that "the good and the just" must penalize whoever has the power to create a conception of virtue other than that of the ruling ideology.

Zarathustra goes one step further in his justification of the right of human beings to move beyond the established moral values of a society. Because "the good" who remain fixed in their ideologies are unable to accept other creators of value, they are said to block humanity's historical progress. "They sacrifice the future to *themselves*—they crucify all man's future."[8] The good cannot transcend their own values. They remain fixed in their opinions. Sometimes they believe they have a special access to goodness or truth and they think this gives them the right to be intolerant of others. What is somewhat extreme is the conclusion Zarathustra draws from all of this. Zarathustra urges his followers to crush to pieces the good and the just.[9] Because they represent decadent life they must be destroyed.

The overcoming of morality by the higher man begins with the justification of the elimination of "the good and the just" and of their tables of values. Zarathustra portrays his opponents as Pharisees. The destruction he urges for them is said to be justified because through it one is ridding the world of decadent life. "O my brothers, am I cruel? But I say: what is falling, we should still push. Everything today falls and decays: who would check it? But I—I even want to push it. . . . And he whom you cannot teach to fly, teach to fall faster."[10] From this perspective people no longer count as people but as bearers of either promising or decadent life. Those that represent decadence, it is suggested, would be fulfilled by their own extermination. Indeed, as mentioned in Chapter 3, there is some evidence to suggest that Nietzsche considered using the idea of the eternal recurrence as the kind of teaching that would induce the decadent not to wish to continue living.

The justification for destroying decadent life goes further than the suggestion that decadent persons might be fulfilled by death or suicide. The murder of the decadent is not ruled out.

> "Thou shalt not rob! Thou shalt not kill!" Such
> words were once called holy; one bent the knee
> and head and took off one's shoes before them.
> But I ask you: where have there ever been better
> robbers and killers in this world than such holy
> words?
>   Is there not in all life itself robbing and killing?
> And that such words were called holy—was not
> truth killed thereby? Or was it the preaching of
> death that was called holy, which contradicted
> and contravened all life? O my brothers, break,
> break, the old tablets!
>   . . . O my brothers, when I bade you break the
> good and the tablets of the good, only then did I
> embark man on his high sea.[11]

It is possible to interpret the "breaking" of the good and the just in less harsh ways than murder. It is also possible to interpret the identity of the good and the just as not reducible to living individuals but as referring to aspects of a person's character. In this case, Nietzsche's intent might be interpreted simply as a recommendation to individuals that they destroy or change the Pharisee within themselves. This reading would suggest a healthy moral change within individuals and would definitely exclude the justification of violence upon other people. Furthermore, the judgment of "decadence" would not be attributed to others—only to oneself. Still, while this would be the most favorable interpretation that could be given to these passages, there is substantial evidence to show that Nietzsche did not wish to rule out the more cruel interpretations. Otherwise, there would be little or no point to the thesis of the overcoming of morality by the higher man.

First, it can be shown specifically that Nietzsche reserved for himself the right to judge others as decadent and, further, to condemn these so-called decadent persons to die or to suffer exploitation for the sake of the enhancement of "life." In *Twilight of the Idols,* for example, he states:

> If [the individual] represents the ascending line [of life], then his worth is indeed extraordinary—and for the sake of life as a whole, which takes a step farther through him, the care for his preservation and for the creation of the best conditions for him may even be extreme. . . . If he represents the descending development, decay, chronic degeneration and sickness . . . , then he has small worth, and the minimum of decency requires that he take away as little as possible from those who have turned out well. He is merely their parasite.[12]

In *The Antichrist* he writes: "The weak and the failures shall perish: first principle of *our* love of man. And they shall even be given every possible assistance."[13] Zarathustra's ideas are not expressed as explicitly, nor is the structure of Zarathustra's reasoning as narrow as this. However, Nietzsche nevertheless gradually usurps the role of the hangman-judge that he had condemned in the priest and metaphysician. He chastises people not for being "evil" but for being "decadent"—that is, for not being sufficiently evil. In any case, while the charges that lead to the sentencing may be reversed, the structure of domination, cruelty, and punishment is not. There is no "transvaluation of all values" here—only an unfortunate and extreme repetition of some of the alienation and fragmentation against which Nietzsche had objected in another context.

Second, it can also be demonstrated concretely that one reason the destruction of or cruelty to individuals was not unthinkable to Nietzsche is that he bypassed the reality of the living individual in favor of the formula "ascendent life" or "descending" or "decadent life." This means that the person responsible for inflicting cruelty upon an individual thinks only in terms of types, as in the following: "I (i.e., ascending life) am inflicting cruelty upon decadent life." In this way the individuality of both exploiter and exploited is erased. The exploited is seen as a representative of something ill-formed, that is, a parasite or something that, to begin with, has no right to exist or to claim a continued right to existence. The metaphysical doctrine of the innocence of becoming is perverted under this model of domination. In Nietzsche's original model of the Dionysian, the thesis that individuality is an illusion was used to defy the notion of the *alienated* individual. In other words, it was the individual perceived as an atom or as a fully separate entity from the rest of reality that was declared to be an illusion. But under the model of domination this opposition to alienated individuality is discarded or forgotten. The domination model of individuality posits individuality as real where it finds it convenient for it to be real and declares individuality to be unreal where it is inconvenient to recognize individuals. For example, under the domination model of existence, the "few" are allowed to be individuals: "Independence is for the few; it is the privilege of the strong."[14] The rest, who are expected to be dominated by these few, are ontologically barred from the possibility of being individuals. This is why the dominating party can exploit or kill them—why, indeed, it often *must* do this as a duty to "ascending life." The complete subordination of the reality of concrete individuals to human types (to abstractions) allows Nietzsche to speak of the destruction of individuals as if he were only destroying abstractions. But "the good and the just," as pharisaical as they may be, are also concrete human beings. Before it is suggested that they ought to be crushed, at least the issue of the killing of individuals ought to be raised in a direct and explicit way.

The view of the extraordinary powers of "higher men" was not without precedents in Nietzsche's time, although Nietzsche seems to have promoted the domination view of power to its extreme conclusion. Concerning the special prerogative of some "destined" individuals to stand above the strict guidelines of morality, Hegel had already stated: "A World-historical individual is not so unwise as to indulge a variety of wishes to divide his regards. He is devoted to the One Aim, regardless of all else. It is even possible that such men may treat other great, even sacred interests, inconsiderately; conduct which is indeed obnoxious to moral reprehension. But so mighty a form must trample down many an innocent flower—crush to pieces many an object in its path."[15] Hegel qualifies the statement, noting that human beings should be the last form of life to be treated as an object. Nietzsche leaves unqualified the suggestion that the good and the just be crushed to pieces. It is up to the reader to decide where the qualification will be placed.

In the "new tablets," Zarathustra advocates the destruction of the decadent. In *Beyond Good and Evil* Nietzsche moves to a more conservative and yet more insidious position. Here he favors the subordination of the weak and the decadent to the strong. Nietzsche interprets the modus operandi of nature to be that of always subordinating whatever is weak to what is strong. This is a redundant principle of explanation but it seems to be accepted without question in a culture such as ours, where it is morally acceptable for persons and nations to thrive on the use of force. The principle of the subordination of the weak to the strong becomes Nietzsche's model of order and continuity (*Rangordnung*) under the standpoint of the will to power as domination. Unfortunately, when this model of explanation is used, nothing can be experienced that is not made to fit the dominator-dominated duality. All transactions in biology, physiology, morality, religion, epistemology, and so on are given an explanation according to the master-slave paradigm of activity and order. Every breath one takes, every metabolic function, and even the absence of apparent movement are interpreted as a struggle between "ascending" and "descending" forces in life. This is the ultimate dualism, a dualism Nietzsche could not understand fully because it is so firmly imbedded in one of Western culture's most pervasive ideologies—the glorification of the war of all against all.[16]

Nietzsche's Exploitation of Truth

How does Nietzsche, a philosopher, resolve this apparent inconsistency in his views? In *Zarathustra* he condemns moral systems for resisting change and for outlawing the creator; but in *Beyond Good and Evil* he upholds moral systems for keeping everything in place and for compelling human beings to obey moral commands no matter how absurd the content. The second view is defended in *Beyond Good and Evil* in the context of a justification of slavery.

> Slavery is, as it seems, both in the cruder and in
> the more subtle sense, the indispensable means of

spiritual discipline and cultivation, too. Consider
any morality with this in mind: what there is in it
of "nature" teaches hatred of the *laisser aller,* of
any all-too-great freedom, and implants the need
for limited horizons and the nearest of tasks—
teaching the *narrowing of our perspective,* and
thus in a certain sense stupidity, as a condition of
life and growth.

    "You shall obey—someone and for a long time:
else you will perish and lose the last respect for
yourself"—this appears to me to be the moral imperative of nature. . . .[17]

One suggestion with respect to this would be to say that when he
himself is the outlaw, Nietzsche defies the moral establishment,
whereas when he is in command he justifies the obedience and
even the enslavement of any possible opponent.[18] A more theoretical answer based on the problem of truth is also worth exploring.

Nietzsche must believe that the principle which justifies the
destruction of the moral tradition as well as the endorsement of
slavery is the synthesis between truth and life offered in his theories of the order of rank and the will to power as domination.
But Nietzsche's assumptions under the model of domination are
superficial. There are better ways of discovering the relationship
between truth, morality, and life than by appealing to a blind
principle of obedience in nature or to a natural order of superiority
based on the power of the superior type to dominate the inferior.
To posit these hypotheses as irrefutable truths appears to be a
violation of the will to truth whose guidelines one was following
when one was led to question the authority of traditional morality.

For Nietzsche, morality stands to truth as a lie or an illusion;
but lies and illusions are necessary for life. Because Nietzsche is
committed to a philosophy that will affirm life, he will not forego
the power of morality as long as it can be used to further life. In
Beyond Good and Evil the so-called "lies" Nietzsche discusses
are no ordinary indiscretions. They are all metaphysical fictions.
He refers to the belief in the subject, in causality, and in the self-
identity of objects as lies without which the human species could
not preserve itself in existence or even grow.[19] Although he does
not specifically name morality among these conventional fictions,
it is clear that moral valuations are very important to human
beings. In *Zarathustra* he had noted that "no people could live

without first esteeming'' and that ''Zarathustra found no greater power on earth than good and evil.''[20] In *Beyond Good and Evil* Nietzsche argues that the preservation of the species demands a practical belief in morality.[21] This is the same practical belief which, in a different sphere, is directed toward metaphysical fictions like the external world, causality, and freedom of the will. Morality is a regulative agent for life.

Truth, for Nietzsche, is the very power that defies such stability and regulation. Truth demands that the philosopher see that life is fundamentally a constant process of self-overcoming—the will to power. The demand of truth is constant exposure to destruction and creation; this also involves the repeated risk of self-destruction (if one has a static concept of self). Nietzsche considers courage the determining factor as to how much truth an individual can stand in order to go on living. ''We are all *afraid* of truth.''[22] The transvaluation of values, however, was an effort to reconcile truth and life. On the one hand, truth would acknowledge the value of illusion, therefore placing itself on the side of life. On the other, the value of some of these initially undesirable truths would be changed from negative to positive (e.g., ontological change would be viewed positively rather than negatively). Truth and life would be reconciled because these ''hard'' truths would become more acceptable once their value for individuals would be reversed. The ''apparent world'' would become an incitement to life (to human living) rather than an objection to life as in the greater part of the Western philosophical tradition.

In his theory of *Rangordnung* Nietzsche may have intended a reconciliation between truth and life. The concept of an order of rank promotes the idea of preservation (by keeping things in their proper place), thereby benefiting the stability of life. On the other hand, the order of rank promotes the idea of the subordination of some things to others, according to their inherent value. This subordination justifies Nietzsche's view of justice: ''To *me,* justice speaks thus: 'Men are not equal. Nor shall they become equal!' ''[23] Given Nietzsche's strong belief in social inequality, his view of the order of rank, presented as a natural given, is precisely what needs to be questioned. Even if the concept of an order of rank contains some measure of truth, could there not be other ways of valuing that are just as truthful, or even more so, than what he proposes? He cannot deny this a priori unless he wants to make of the order of rank an absolute. But his own principles of the will to power require him to do away with all absolute values. The principles of the transvaluation, moreover, require a thorough questioning on the part of human beings of their most valued assumptions.[24] Unless Nietzsche violates his own tenets, he cannot dispose of Christian morality and replace it with his cherished *Rangordnung* without subjecting the latter to as intensive a critique as he applied to the former.

I have suggested that Nietzsche only achieves a superficial reconciliation between morality (the morality of the higher man) and life. In fact, any morality whose fundamental principle is the superiority of some human beings over others has to be superficial because there is no way to confirm such a belief. At best, the view is oversimplified; at worst, it can be an inexcusable prejudice. The connection between morality and the will to truth is either suspended or eclipsed. Nietzsche's doctrine of the self-overcoming of morality posits the movement of a will to truth which eventually uncovers the fraudulent authority of an absolute morality. From this point on, however, truth points only to one source—the will to power as the nature of all that is. "Life" becomes the predominant manifestation of the will to power, and then Nietzsche ascribes to life the authoritative status that once belonged to an absolute. One need only say " 'A' is antilife, therefore 'A' must be overcome." For example, morality is antilife, therefore it must be overcome. The will to truth that once caused morality to question itself recedes into the background. The logical point is that *once the break between truth and morality has taken place, the doctrine of the self-overcoming of morality through the will to truth is no longer needed.* In other words, the theory of the self-overcoming of morality is *used* by Nietzsche as an intermediary step to arrive at the theory of the overcoming of morality by the higher man.

Of particular interest are two unpublished notes from the fall of 1884 where Nietzsche refers to his philosophy as "die neue Aufklärung," the new Enlightenment. The date of these notes places them between the composition of *Zarathustra* III and IV. In the first note, Nietzsche mentions three steps or stages of the new Enlightenment. The first stage is the discovery of fundamental errors, such as the error of free will, of causality, and of the morality of taming. (An exposition of what he means by the morality of taming is given several years later in *Twilight of the Idols.*)[25] The second stage is the discovery of the creative instinct or drive. But the third and final stage is the overcoming of human beings.[26] By this Nietzsche means the overcoming of human decadence, but decadence is interpreted in an extreme way. According to Nietzsche, the principle or activity of self-overcoming is to be a step toward the overcoming of (decadent) humanity. This shows that the idea of self-overcoming is being used by him to further other ends. The note which follows makes these other ends more explicit. The note is entitled "The Eternal Recurrence: A Prophecy."[27] Nietzsche states here that the old Enlightenment was conducted for the democratic herd whereas the new Enlightenment is intended for the rulers. The new Enlightenment will give the rulers the principle that for them *everything is allowed.* In these notes, none of the ideas of the transvaluation are related to truth or to the affirmation of life. The eternal recurrence is not taken here as an expression of the affirmation of life but as a tool (Nietzsche's favorite word for this is "Hammer"). The idea of the recurrence is depicted as an instrument of manipulation by which the most powerful human beings may mold the rest of humanity into conformity with their goals. Although this is done in the name of an "artistic" vision, Nietzsche's rhetoric is especially misleading in such cases. The intent is to provide a "moral" justification for the unlimited use of power by the higher human being.

Nietzsche's obsession with the need of the superior type to rule makes him reinterpret all of the life-affirming ideas of the transvaluation of values as tools used to justify the unchecked use of power by the dominating type of person. For the higher type, "everything is allowed." This travesty of the meaning of life, however, does not follow from the other principles of the transvaluation. It occurs through the exploitation of the will to truth. When the role of the will to truth loses significance, the doctrine of the overcoming of morality by the higher man not only gains importance but the connection between the higher man and truth is not always preserved. This distancing of the higher man from truth occurs because the original ontological meaning of the will to power is forgotten in favor of a domination view of power which is used to justify the interests of the higher man. The domination view of power aims at strength through containment. One builds power by not giving of oneself as well as by containing the power of others as much as possible. The structure of domination is actually a temporary negation of the Dionysian will to power that is characterized by self-transcendence, self-destruction, and self-overcoming. The truth of the whole process is displaced by the narrow instincts of a part of life to preserve itself, to accumulate as much power as possible for itself, and to do all in its power to resist change.

With respect to morality, a paradox develops. As soon as truth is set aside, morality quickly reappears on the scene under the patronage of the need for illusion. Morality, with its illusory and powerful "Thou shalt" (*Du sollst*) is now appreciated for what it can contribute to life—not simply stability but domination, control, discipline. Kant's concept of moral obligation (*das Sollen*)—lifeless, empty, and formal—now enters Nietzsche's philosophy as an ally of life. No longer categorical, it becomes "the moral imperative of nature."[28] It has the form of a threat—unless you obey some authority blindly for a long time, you shall not survive. And yet one knows that the standpoint of preservation and survival is precisely what Zarathustra wanted to overturn through the teaching of self-transcendence. The paradigm that Nietzsche followed in his Dionysian theory of truth is that whatever aids human survival is usually a lie or a fiction; its value lies simply in its convenience for maintaining life. Truth liberates one from such fictions and leads one to attain inner stability without belief in fictive regulators. The Nietzsche who wrote *Thus Spoke Zarathustra*, then, stands opposed in these respects to the one who wrote *Beyond Good and Evil*.

In *Ecce Homo* Nietzsche observed that *Beyond Good and Evil*, in form and theme, represented for him a "recuperation" from *Zarathustra*.

> In every respect . . . you will find [in *Beyond Good and Evil*] the same *deliberate* turning away from the instincts that had made possible a Zarathustra. . . .
> All this is a recuperation: who would guess after all *what* sort of recuperation such a squandering of good-naturedness as Zarathustra represents makes necessary?[29]

What Zarathustra stood for, however, is not good-naturedness. It is the desire to inspire others with ideas and teachings *without forcing these ideas upon people*. Even the extreme attacks against the good and the just are not presented as a moral imperative of nature. The recommendation is to overthrow the "Thou shalt." Therefore it is offered in the spirit of freedom. Although Zarathustra may be mistaken about the value of a particular course of action, his instincts are to liberate the future of life. The so-called recovery from these instincts in *Beyond Good and Evil* indicates that Nietzsche wished to counteract those fine instincts by moving on to theories that would repress life's future.

FROM CREATIVITY TO AUTHORITARIANISM

Nietzsche's defense of an authoritarian morality (after Zarathustra's critique) represents a decision on his part to repress his own Dionysian instincts. These were the instincts to transgress all boundaries, to let his passions and his spirit overflow, to allow himself continuity with the play of existence. These instincts are looked upon retrospectively as a "squandering" of the spirit. "Squandering" is an economic metaphor here; it indicates the concern for a quantified view of gain and loss. This concern already shows that the Dionysian perspective has been abandoned. Instead, one begins to view human living from the point of view of quantification. One's time and energy are meticulously measured and monitored so as to make sure none of it is wasted. It is clear from this standpoint why Nietzsche would then think that the will to power of a healthy individual must be marked by the deliberate restraint of the passions. Compared with the restraint favored by the standpoint of quantification and domination, Zarathustra's passions appear self-destructive. What is left out of the analysis is the critical consideration that Zarathustra did not want to destroy the self but only those controls within the self which blocked the dynamic continuity of life—and, in human life, the process of creativity.

It is a misrepresentation to portray the Dionysian flow of life as something chaotic. There is order and perspective within the Dionysian affirmation of all there is, only it is not the order of domination. One does not need to move outside the Dionysian perspective to consider that, without some guidance, order, or measure of restraint, the process of instinctual liberation may lead to the destruction of self or others. This is particularly true given Nietzsche's insistence that the ban on the "evil" side of human beings also be lifted. The psychological-political question one must raise, however, is not whether some measure of control is necessary but *in whose interest* the control is being exerted. This is the same question that Nietzsche directs against his opponents when he criticizes the sterile values of the good and the just. A reading of *Zarathustra* shows that Nietzsche argued in that work for instinctual liberation in the interest of creativity, since the meaning of the will to power was related both psychologically and metaphysically to a philosophy of creativity. I would argue, therefore, that as long as the goal of creativity is kept in mind, there is no special reason to think that the release of the passions should lead to any great psychological danger. On the other hand, if the goal of creativity were missing and the passions were to be released blindly, Nietzsche's very concept of a Dionysian affirmation of life would lose its meaning. Without a healthy psychological base the Dionysian perspective could not retain its stability in anyone's consciousness for very long.

Further dispelling the myth that the Dionysian perspective is psychologically dangerous—a myth which, possibly to enhance his power, Nietzsche helped to further—is the fact that Nietzsche was well aware that to enhance the possibility of a creative life for human beings, certain psychological and social conditions would first have to obtain. He argued explicitly for the view that physical and mental health are necessary conditions for the release of the creative instincts. His criticism of Christian and cultural nihilism speaks to this. In his critique of Christianity Nietzsche shows that creativity is directly roted in the natural functioning of a healthy body. His aim in *Zarathustra* is to restore to human beings the trust and pride in the body that had been called into question by Christian doctrine. With its alienating and repressive doctrines of sinfulness, guilt, punishment, and the afterlife, Christianity has shattered the possibility of a healthy relationship between the body and consciousness. In contrast to the moralists' condemnation of sinfulness and license, Nietzsche condemns the social and physiological conditions that have led to the disintegration of instinctual strength. "The church and morality say: 'A generation, a people, are destroyed by license and luxury.' My *recovered* reason says: when a people approaches destruction, when it degenerates physiologically, then license and luxury follow from this. . . ."[30] It is clear that Nietzsche thought of Christianity as the major ideological and emotional cause of the violation and repression of the instincts. In *The Antichrist* he exposed his

objections to Christian values, taking as his criterion the demor-
alizing psychological consequences of Christian belief upon the
individual. Basically, Nietzsche argued that Christianity repressed
human beings' sexual and intellectual nature (the church's distrust
of scientific progress, its insensitivity to sexual activity). "Really,
how can one put a book in the hands of children and women
which contains the vile dictum: 'to avoid fornication, let every
man have his own wife, and let every woman have her own husband. . . . It is better to marry than to burn.' "[31] In addition,
Nietzsche believed that a religion which glorified unconditional
love and suffering ("God on the cross") left human beings weak
and incapable of dealing with the necessarily aggressive aspects
of life.

In contrast to Christianity's alienating and repressive view of
the body, Zarathustra's early speeches bring into sharp focus the
psychological necessity of rooting the self in a healthy body.[32]
Nietzsche argues that the healthy (life-oriented) body is by nature
a creative body. A healthy body wants to participate in the life-
process, which means it instinctually shares in the wheel of recurrence and wants to create something beyond itself. On the
other hand, when this instinctual disposition toward creativity is
repressed, an unhealthy disbalance occurs in the organism, resulting in a resentment against the body. "That is why you have
become despisers of the body! You are no longer able to create
beyond yourselves."[33] Nietzsche analyzed the repression of creativity as codetermined with the repression of the instincts, and
both types of repression as a perversion of life. He sought above
all else to heal the fragmentation and alienation in human nature
by negating the values that had previously served as enemies of
life. As long as he does not force upon his values the structure
of domination, he is able to carry across to his readers the message
of human integration.

Aside from proposing a radical change in the meaning of personal health, Nietzsche also argued in favor of a reappraisal of
the type of social conditions needed for the advancement of creativity. This accounts for his contempt for democratic "leveling"
and his exaltation of the age of the Greeks. However, his defense
of authoritarian principles for aristocratic purposes led him to
violate his separate critique of psychological repression. Nietzsche needs to be reminded that he has sufficient order in his
philosophy of creativity to dispel the need for the so-called "moral

imperative of nature"—blind obedience to authority. This principle is introduced in *Beyond Good and Evil* not to justify morality but to lend support to Nietzsche's reactionary political views. His theory of instinctual liberation is sufficiently strong because he qualifies it with supplementary theories on a healthy body and social order. That he may have been mistaken about the specific type of social order most conducive to creativity does not detract from the formal strength of his theory, which takes into account the importance of social conditions for the development of a more balanced human life.

Nietzsche presented a goal toward which people might strive either alone or with others. He was aware that the goal did not represent an absolute and that its attainment depended upon given psychological and social conditions. This philosophical standpoint is not likely to result in nihilism or self-destruction, for to reason in terms of the material and spiritual conditions for the possibility of something is to withhold faith in the unconditional with respect to that question. And Nietzsche believed that it is precisely the faith in the unconditional that tends to trigger the nihilistic and self-destructive tendencies of human beings.

What Nietzsche was faced with as an author of both a positive and negative philosophy (criticizing the practices of his time, trying to offer an alternative vision to his readers) was the problem of persuading people to destroy certain aspects of themselves and their mores which, he believed, were holding them back from a higher type of life. Were persuasion to fail, however, Nietzsche considered outright manipulation. This manipulation will be shown to be both ideological and physiological. But if the course of manipulation is taken, the claim to a philosophy of creativity must be dropped. Nietzsche's idea that the higher men coordinate the breeding of human types reduces the dignity of the elite by transforming them into manipulators of other human beings. The same observation can be used against Nietzsche's insistence on the interdependence of master and slave moralities, which, in a different context, predicates the freedom of a select few upon the oppression of the masses. Yet as long as the master depends on the slave for his freedom, the master is not free (a point already made by Hegel in the *Phenomenology of Mind*). If the creator of values is forced to become a breeder of values or a dictator of values, the title of creator is lost and the person's work no longer commands the respect due to a creative spirit.

The idea of manipulation gives the problem of elitism a political dimension, for it involves the belief that superior individuals have both the right and the obligation not only to be leaders of society but to dominate the personal destinies of others. These others are impersonally referred to as the masses, the herd, the weak. Nietzsche's idea of domination exhibits all the weaknesses of the patriarchal model of responsibilty, use of power, and authority— the need to control the lives and values of others and the need to use force to maintain that control, if necessary. Part of Nietzsche's rationale for the domination of the many by the few lay in a feeling of protective paternalism toward the masses. One is reminded of Zarathustra's moments of compassion toward the crowds. But Nietzsche was also motivated to support a narrow elitism on account of his contempt for the values of the masses. He believed someone must defend the future of noble values against herd values. Someone must also be responsible for modifying the herdlike judgment of the masses, as well as for elevating their taste. In *Beyond Good and Evil* Nietzsche stated that the task lay in the hands of the creators of value, and its promise lay in the overcoming of morality by the higher man.

Free-Spiritedness versus Breeding

The idea of the self-overcoming of morality is not based on a psychology of power and privilege. In this respect it differs from Nietzsche's schematic contrast between master and slave moralities, which is made from the standpoint of the overcoming of morality by the higher man. The self-overcoming of morality is based on the logical consequences unfolding from the idea of a will to truth which attains self-consciousness of its own foundations (or lack of foundations). However, the self-overcoming of morality does not merely refer to the logical movement of an idea, that is, it does not refer merely to the logical implications that may be derived from the lack of an absolute truth. It is also a moral (or more precisely, a postmoral) event requiring from human beings an unusual spiritual capacity to both experience and overcome nihilism. In Nietzsche's view this "overcoming" of morality and of nihilism cannot be the achievement of the many. The subtitle of *Thus Spoke Zarathustra*, "A Book for All and None," expresses the existential openness as well as the forbidding closure of the possibility of this experience. There is always the acknowledgment that the doctrines of Zarathustra, including that of the self-overcoming of morality, can only be grasped, at least initially, by a few individuals. However, these individuals do not constitute a social or political elite as envisioned in *Beyond Good and Evil*. On the contrary, the few are the lonely ones. "Wake and listen, you that are lonely! . . . You that are lonely today, you that are withdrawing, you shall one day be the people: out of you, who have chosen yourselves, there shall grow a chosen people—and out of them, the overman. Verily, the earth shall yet become a site of recovery."[34] It is clear that the test of becoming one of the forerunners of the *Übermensch* is existential. Professional success or political achievement cannot be confused with authenticity. The creators stand apart from other people because they have a further range of vision, combined with a generosity of spirit which possibly allows them to affirm the eternal recurrence of all things without resentment.

Although the invitation to become a creator of values is open to all, Nietzsche's theory depends on the presupposition of the existence of a natural elite. Only individuals who are exceptionally gifted in a complex variety of ways are capable of overcoming nihilism, or of affirming the doctrine of the recurrence, or of heralding the birth of the *Übermensch*—given what Nietzsche states about all these theories. It would be difficult to imagine how anyone who did not have at least the opportunity of a relatively good life could have his or her character tested by Nietzsche's standards. Could the poor or the uneducated members of the population realistically join Zarathustra in the quest to become artists and creators of value? Could anyone who does not have enough to eat affirm the "dance" of existence or take joy in the innocence of becoming? Could the mother of a starving child believe that the test of her character lies in the affirmation of the eternal recurrence of all things? To free his theory from nihilism Nietzsche also needs to respect the suffering that exploitation and needless oppression inflict on human beings. He needs to argue for the reversal of conditions in society such that *everyone* in principle has the opportunity to affirm life without resentment. This cannot be the privilege of a few or an elite.

While philosophers have often been in the habit of theorizing about rationality or the good in abstraction from the material conditions without which these values could not even begin to have meaning, Nietzsche was not totally remiss about giving serious consideration to the material ground of all ideals. His attacks on the false sublimity of idealism and his emphasis on a healthy body and society speak to his concerns. The problem with Nietzsche is not that he disregarded the importance of material and social conditions but that at certain important points in his thought he considered the wrong structures to be valuable. The precise way in which he envisioned bridging the material gap in his theory between the creators of value and the rest of humanity, for example, is highly controversial although worth exploring.

At stake in the controversy is the issue of manipulation versus what I would simply refer to as spiritual leadership. There is an inconsistency between Zarathustra's vision of the creator and comments Nietzsche makes elsewhere regarding higher men as a ruling class. Zarathustra demands from his followers the toughest spiritual independence.

> Now I go alone, my disciples. You too go now, alone. Thus I want it. Verily, I counsel you: go away from me and resist Zarathustra. And even better: be ashamed of him! Perhaps he deceived you.
>
> The man of knowledge must not only love his enemies, he must also be able to hate his friends.
>
> One repays a teacher badly if one always remains nothing but a pupil. And why do you not want to pluck at my wreath? . . .
>
> Now I bid you lose me and find yourselves: and only when you have all denied me will I return to you.[35]

The idea of spiritual leadership expressed in this passage seems to be at odds with the transference of this idea to a political context where leaders are granted extensive power to manipulate the masses. The inconsistency might be resolved (or avoided) by taking into account Nietzsche's distinction between the separate and unequal values of leaders and herd. However, this separation is already a denial of Zarathustra's hopes that one day the lonely ones should become the people, which means that Nietzsche also hoped for a society made up entirely of spiritually strong, self-determined human beings. Behind Zarathustra's hopes for a healing of human beings' ontological and psychological fragmentation (again, a hope that applies to everyone) there may lie the assumption that "decadent" types who cannot overcome them-

selves will in time cease to exist. This would be based on the
hypothesis that whatever organism is in a state of decadence is
also in a state of disintegration and ultimately will be unable to
reproduce itself. "And he whom you cannot teach to fly, teach
to fall faster!"[36] On the other hand this hypothesis is too general
to be verified adequately and, wishful thinking (for Nietzsche)
aside, it is too unrealistic. As an alternative to the elimination of
decadence, Nietzsche supported a political scheme wherein the
survival of the decadent types is accepted on the condition that
the stronger type always rule.

In the passage just quoted from *Zarathustra,* there is no hint
that Nietzsche might be searching for a programmatic method of
achieving a change of values. On the contrary, Zarathustra insists
that individuals must reach self-development through their own
efforts and reflection. This passage, which concludes Part I of
Thus Spoke Zarathustra, was written in January of 1883. It is
poetic and, despite its practical wisdom, it is idealistic. It is interesting to contrast it at length with another passage written a
few months later, in the spring or summer of 1883, and contem-
poraneous with Part II of *Zarathustra.* Here, in an unpublished
note, Nietzsche offers the strange suggestion that breeding should
replace moralizing if one's aim is to achieve changes in character.
"Change the characters. Breeding instead of moralizing. Working with direct influence on the organism, instead of indirectly on
ethical discipline. Another body will *construct* itself *another* soul
and morals. Therefore, *turn round! . . .*"[37] Comparing Nietzsche's published and unpublished work from roughly the same
period one sees that the notion that "another body will create for
itself another soul and morals" is the same basic thought that
Zarathustra proposed to his followers. Here is Zarathustra's statement: "Remain faithful to the earth, my brothers, with the power
of your virtue. Let your gift-giving love and your knowledge serve
the meaning of the earth. . . . Lead back to the earth the virtue
that flew away, as I do—back to the body, back to life, that it
may give the earth a meaning, a human meaning."[38] The difference
in the two passages lies in the important fact that in Zarathustra's
case the turn to the body reflects a self-conscious commitment
on the part of those changing their values. In the second case,
the change takes place without any reflection on the part of those
involved, since it is effected through breeding.

There are other similarities between the passage concluding Part I of *Zarathustra* and the note advocating change through breeding. Again, the differential element in the note is the concept of manipulation. According to Nietzsche's theory in *Zarathustra*, the "voice of the healthy body" that arises to reshape the meaning of one's life will also lead the way to the *Übermensch*.

> Let your spirit and your virtue serve the sense of
> the earth, my brothers; and let the value of all
> things be posited newly by you. For that shall
> you be fighters! For that shall you be
> creators! . . .
> . . . out of you, who have chosen yourselves,
> there shall grow a chosen people—and out of
> them, the overman.[39]

The idea of the *Übermensch* has already been connected to Nietzsche's ontological questioning of the stabilizing function of all laws. The *Übermensch* is also associated with a new psychological tendency to trust in the instincts and a turning to the meaning of the earth, as in the passage just noted. The same analysis of law and the same turning toward the instincts appear in the passage from 1883. What is added in the latter case is an interest in breeding (*Züchtung*) as well as the idea that the healthy expression of instinct is feared by the common people. These two observations which are absent from the *Zarathustra* text are connected to the suggestion that the political manipulation of the masses is a prerogative of the higher man.

> Law: the will to conserve the existing conditions
> of power. Presupposition for that is the satisfac-
> tion with these conditions. Everything venerable
> will be used to demonstrate that this law is some-
> thing eternal.
> *Practical consequences:* Change the characters.
> Breeding instead of moralizing. . . .
> Socrates' *plebeian* distrust towards the affects
> [Affekte]: they are ugly, wild—therefore something
> to suppress—that is the distinction of *Epicurus* in
> comparison with the Stoics. These however are
> easier for the common people to understand.
> Just so the Christian saint is a plebeian ideal.[40]

In the unpublished note Nietzsche considers the idea of using physical force ("working directly on the organism") to achieve the society desired by the creators of value, whereas in *Zarathustra* the change was said to occur through the power of self-awareness and self-consciousness.

What is added in the spring-summer of 1883 reveals an alternative emphasis on Nietzsche's part when considering the means to a transvaluation of values. In the writings of Zarathustra, the call for change is always free-spirited and inspirational. The change depends upon the strength of will and character of those who initiate a change of values in society. The other method (the suggested "breeding") indicates the reverse procedure. It calls for a biological means of effecting a change in character, and thereby a change in values. In *Zarathustra,* one recovers the value of one's body by the strength of one's character. By healing oneself, one helps the earth become "a site of recovery." The other method hypothesizes an initial "if" for which there is no ethical explanation. "If" one starts out with a healthy body, that body will gradually give expression to a healthy soul and morals. Nietzsche may have been right that given a reversal of the value of the instincts (from distrust and repression of the instincts to their affirmation and expression, for example) the new "soul" and "morals" of human beings would tend toward psychological healing and the possibility of a more creative existence. What appears to be a psychological contradiction is the idea that freedom, responsibility, or creativity of the sort Nietzsche eulogized might be biologically bred into the human species.

Nietzsche apparently compares breeding ("working with direct influence on the organism") with the conditioning effect of morality and ethical education ("instead of [working] indirectly on ethical discipline"). Breeding is direct and open manipulation, whereas morality has functioned as indirect manipulation camouflaged by holy lies. This analysis blends in well with Nietzsche's claim that at least his philosophy will not depend upon such holy lies to achieve its goals. But does it not? Once one has granted to *some* men the power to breed people for the sake of a specific goal, does not all reference to the present creativity of the first group (the breeders) and the future creativity of the latter group (the bred) lose its intended meaning? Why should Zarathustra say "Become creators"? Would it not be more appropriate to say "Become breeders of selected human types"? And does Nietzsche not slip, sometimes, into teaching the crude theory "Become breeders of a stronger race," so that the *Übermensch* is reduced to a meaning which was not originally intended? The turn to open manipulation of the common people undermines Nietzsche's theory from within, destroying the professed nobility of the "higher men," who are reduced to mere instruments of implementing power. It also destroys the potential dignity of the "common" people, who are reduced to manipulable animals (the "herd" and "beast" metaphors used by Nietzsche being unfailingly appropriate here). To prevent Nietzsche's theory of values from being reducible to a crude concept of will to power one has to eliminate the rhetorical endorsement of power as manipulation and domination either of oneself or of others. This needs to be done whether Nietzsche himself chose to put this limitation on his theory or not.

To the objection that Nietzsche's comments on breeding should not be taken in such a literal sense, it serves well to point to other passages, especially from his published works, where he seems to use the term "breeding" literally enough. In *Twilight of the Idols* Nietzsche devotes one entire section, "The Improvers of Mankind," to contrasting Christian morality (which he terms a morality of "taming") with the more excellent morality of breeding.

> . . . At all times they have wanted to "improve"
> men: this above all was called morality. Under
> the same word, however, the most divergent ten-
> dencies are concealed. Both the *taming* of the
> beast, man, and the *breeding* of a particular kind
> of man have been called "improvement". . . .
>   To call the taming of an animal its "improve-
> ment" sounds almost like a joke to our ears.[41]

Nietzsche refers to the human being as an animal or beast that is enfeebled by being tamed. He also remarks that these zoological terms (die *Zähmung* der Bestie Mensch, die *Züchtung* einer Gattung Mensch) must be used to express realities which the typical moral improver, the priest, will not comprehend.

In Nietzsche's view, both the morality of taming and the morality of breeding have accomplished their aims by thoroughly immoral means.[42] Of the two, the morality of breeding is regarded as something excellent. As its finest example he cites the Indian caste system, inspired by the law of Manu. Nietzsche admires the system of breeding "no less than four races at once," although he also objects to the exclusion of a fifth category of people—the Chandalas—from the privilege of being bred.[43] From this one may reasonably conclude that Nietzsche would want to see all human beings bred for a specific function—as in the castes celebrated by him where some would be priests, some warriors, some farmers and traders, some servants. It is instructive that Nietzsche selected the law of Manu rather than Plato's *Republic* for his authority.[44] This highlights the importance that the specific notion of breeding held for Nietzsche. The emphasis on the celebration of racial privilege cannot be missed. "How wretched is the New Testament compared to Manu, how foul it smells!"[45]

In *Beyond Good and Evil* Nietzsche expressed the belief that the noble man must be convinced that for his sake the fate of others must be sacrificed.

> At the risk of displeasing innocent ears I propose:
> egoism belongs to the nature of a noble soul—I
> mean that unshakeable faith that to a being such
> as "we are" other beings must be subordinate by
> nature and have to sacrifice themselves. The no-
> ble soul accepts this fact of its egoism without
> any question mark . . . [for] "it is justice itself."[46]

The theme of sacrifice which appears in this published aphorism is the masked rhetorical counterpart of the idea of the higher man's right to destroy the unfortunate. The latter theme is made explicit in the notes from 1884.

> First principle: no consideration for numbers: the
> masses, the miserable, and the unfortunate con-
> cern me little—but the *first and most splendid*
> types [concern me], and that *out of consideration
> for the ill-bred* (i.e., the masses) they *do not
> come off badly.*
> Destruction of the ill-bred—for that purpose
> one must emancipate oneself from all traditional
> morality.[47]

In another note from the spring of 1884 Nietzsche associates the idea of "breeding" with the idea of the selective annihilation of human "failures." The elite must "gain that tremendous *energy of greatness* in order to shape the man of the future through breeding and, on the other hand, [through] the annihilation of millions of failures, and [yet] *not perish* of the suffering one *creates,* though nothing like it has ever existed.''[48] Those destined to fulfill this task of breeding, says Nietzsche in *Beyond Good and Evil,* are the philosophers. The philosopher, above all human beings, has "the conscience for the over-all development of man."[49] But the fact that the philosopher is chosen to direct this proposed enhancement of humanity in no way ennobles the task to one who is familiar with the specific details of Nietzsche's political project.

The overcoming of morality by the higher man (as opposed to the idea of the self-overcoming of morality) is a doctrine laden with despotic implications. Rather than being founded on the will to truth it is founded on prejudice. What other term could better describe Nietzsche's own statement that justice itself depends on "that unshakeable faith that to a being such as 'we are' other beings must be subordinate by nature and have to sacrifice themselves"?[50] It is ironic that in a work whose first chapter is entitled "On the Prejudices of Philosophers" and where numerous metaphysical and moral prejudices are carefully unraveled, Nietzsche did not pause to question his own "unshakeable faith" in the powers he attributed to the so-called "higher man."

Nietzsche did not give up the belief in these ideas after the publication of *Beyond Good and Evil.* In a note from 1886–87 he states:

> My ideas do not revolve around the degree of freedom that is granted to the one or to the other or to all, but around the degree of *power* that the one or the other should exercise over others or over all, and to what extent a sacrifice of freedom, even enslavement, provides the basis for the emergence of a *higher type.* Put in the crudest form: *how could one sacrifice the development of mankind* to help a higher species than man to come into existence?[51]

In the fall of 1887 Nietzsche acknowledged, at least to himself, that in the process of desiring a "superman" or a "higher man" one achieves precisely the opposite.

> Man is beast and superbeast; the higher man is inhuman and superhuman: these belong together. With every increase of greatness and height in

> man, there is also an increase in depth and terri-
> bleness: one ought not to desire the one without
> the other—or rather: the more radically one de-
> sires the one, the more radically one achieves
> precisely the other.[52]

What he *achieved* was inhuman; what he desired, as can be seen from the note preceding this one, was more than human—and also more than a master race.

> Not merely a master race whose sole task is to
> rule, but a race with its own sphere of life, with
> an excess of life, with an excess of strength for
> beauty, bravery, culture, manners to the highest
> peak of the spirit. . . .[53]

However, in the same set of notes from the autumn of 1887 Nietz-sche disassociates the highest-ranking spirits from any feeling or concern for morality.

> Preoccupation with morality places a spirit in a
> low order of rank: he lacks the instinct for privi-
> lege, the *a parte,* the feeling of freedom of crea-
> tive natures, of the "children of God" (or of the
> devil—). And it is all one whether he preaches
> current morality or uses his ideal for a critique of
> current morality: he belongs to the herd—even if
> it be as the herd's supreme requirement, its
> "shepherd."[54]

In the writings from 1888, especially *Twilight of the Idols* and *the Antichrist,* the reiteration of these themes (as has already been indicated) was continued.

The overcoming of morality by the higher man is a definitive Nietzschean doctrine, a doctrine which Nietzsche supported with-out interruption from the time of *Zarathustra* to the end of his life. I have concentrated my discussion on some of the most controversial and (morally) objectionable implications that Nietz-sche drew from this theory, primarily because it is important to show what Nietzsche meant when he called himself an immoralist. The term "immoralist" is not simply something to be ignored as mere rhetoric. Nietzsche's view of *Rangordnung* and his concept of justice ("men are not equal") were important axioms of his theory of values. They are therefore essential to an understanding of Nietzsche's theory and to the interrelationship of his psychology and politics. A more detailed explanation of Nietzsche's views on justice will be given in Chapter 7. At this point by way of summary I can only try to unify some of the themes touched upon in this discussion.

A Dionysian philosophy of the instincts, as long as it is rooted in a healthy body (as Nietzsche himself recommended), does not constitute a great *danger* to humanity (as Nietzsche professed to believe). It represents, rather, a great liberation to human beings—specifically, a liberation from the power of an alienated conscience. What Nietzsche failed to do was to retain faith in his theory of instinctual liberation. He failed to see how it could apply to the "masses," given the low esteem he held for the majority. Moreover, he did not take his own advice regarding the liberation of life from the power of a punitive ego. He failed to consider the ultimate implications of the death of the patriarchal God. Because he still believed in the great patriarchal myth of Man as creator, judge, and hangman of humanity, Nietzsche did not see that the higher man, as described by him, is a sham. The deification of the higher type, the absurd belief that the higher man's will is everyone else's command, and the extremes to which this idea is carried show that in spite of his good and often invaluable suggestions for healing the human spirit, Nietzsche did not fully heal the alienation within himself. His method for handling the conflict between strength and weakness was both oversimplified and aggressive. In spite of the fact that he advocated laughter for the liberated spirit, his doctrine of the overcoming of morality by the higher man is devoid of any good-natured word. Nietzsche's fascination with domination—itself a product of Western values—ruptured the intent of his project and brought the transvaluation of all values to a halt.

The concrete result of Nietzsche's alienation can be seen in the way he handles the relationship of the elite to the masses as well as that of men to women in his mature and late works. Some of the psychological and political aspects of this problem will be discussed in Chapter 7. It should be clear so far, however, that the psychology of domination calls for the war of all against all. Out of distrust for the people, out of distrust for women, out of distrust for one's own body, the authoritarian conscience establishes the need for obedience regardless of the absurdity of the rule. Under the psychology of domination, the contribution to personal well-being that grows out of a healthy and life-affirming morality is replaced by the commanding voice of a despot who would very much like to rule the world.

This reversion to repression undermines all the liberating aspects of Nietzsche's philosophy. The Dionysian affirmation of self-transcendence is contradicted by the implementation of rigid boundaries in human life ("leader" and "herd"). The joy and pride in one's own values ("it is . . . our work—let us be proud of it") is undermined by the defense of breeding and slavery.[55] Above all, the union of truth and life which was the aim of the Dionysian transvaluation of values is completely shattered when the doctrine of the overcoming of morality is used to sever truth from life.

7

Nietzsche's Politics

The right of the strong to dominate the weak—the essential premise of Nietzsche's view of the overcoming of morality by the
higher man—translates itself politically into a justification of highly
authoritarian systems of government. Nietzsche erroneously believed that the overcoming of nihilism required the crushing of
democracy and of all movements inspired by the French Revolution's ideals of liberty, equality, and fraternity for all. The wom-
en's movement, which was beginning to gain some impetus in
Nietzsche's time, was also condemned by him. Because Nietzsche portrayed himself as an antipolitical thinker, it is not often
thought that Nietzsche's philosophy has serious political implications or that he advanced specific political views in conjunction
with his critique of morality.[1] And yet in *Beyond Good and Evil*
he states: "I am beginning to touch on what is *serious* for me,
the 'European problem' as I understand it, the cultivation of a
new caste that will rule Europe."[2] Although it would be preferable
to disregard this aspect of Nietzsche's theory, it would be a misrepresentation of his intentions to either modify or ignore the
political goals he hoped to achieve by means of the transvaluation
of all values.

On Interpreting Nietzsche's Politics

In the *Genealogy of Morals* Nietzsche argues that all systems of
values (and therefore all interpretations of existence) are inherently political. The values that ultimately triumph in any society
do not necessarily reflect any philosophical truths but rather the
interests of those who can wield the most power.[3] This implies
that one must always keep a critical attitude toward all posited
values by raising such questions as: what are the political assumptions implicit in these values? By whose power have these
values been posited? Who is to profit from the widespread acceptance of these values? These critical questions need to be

161

raised not only against opponents but must also be directed toward oneself. In *Thus Spoke Zarathustra* and *Ecce Homo* Nietzsche ties the process of self-criticism to the ongoing process of self-overcoming that characterizes the development of all life.[4] He does not, however, always carry out the mandate of self-criticism in practice. Because this matter is left unresolved in the writings of the transvaluation period, it is important to pursue the significance of the contradictions implicit in Nietzsche's position.

The method I follow here is the demystification of Nietzsche's appeal to destiny as a justification for the force or the truth of his ideas. The appeal to destiny is too close in spirit to the Christian "God wills it" to justify the theories of a thinker who proclaimed the death of God. It is especially interesting to follow Nietzsche's rhetorical use of "destiny," especially when this rhetoric is used to justify the oppression of women or the right of philosophers to rule the world.[5] Nietzsche's suggestion in *Ecce Homo* that, as the initiator of the "great politics" (*große Politik*), he is speaking for humanity's destiny, will be rejected. On the contrary, one needs to question how his political views would affect the present and future welfare of human beings.[6]

In the past there has been a tendency on the part of scholars to avoid uncovering some of the more politically controversial aspects of Nietzsche's theory of values. This can be understood as a historical reaction against the improper use of Nietzsche's ideas by the Nazis. The tendency to protect Nietzsche's political views from public criticism, however, can also be taken too far. For example, while many texts from both his early and late writings show that Nietzsche repeatedly justified slavery and the exploitation of the disadvantaged for the sake of the development of a "higher culture," standard interpretations of Nietzsche proceed to discuss the meaning of a higher culture while bypassing the issue of slavery and exploitation. Against this approach it should be noted that Nietzsche defended the right of "superior" men to exploit the "inferior" as a necessary condition for the existence of a worthy culture. In particular, Nietzsche defended the exploitation of the masses for the advantage of the "higher" individual as well as the exploitation of so-called "feminine" values for the sake of a "masculine" cultural ideal. Both of these themes are to be understood as interdependent applications of the idea that a "strong" culture cannot exist without the exploitation of "lower" beings for the benefit of "higher" ones. In contrast to Nietzsche's direct and explicit statements on these matters, the tendency of criticism has been to de-thematize the interconnection between the defense of exploitation and the endorsement of a "strong" and "masculine" ideal for Western culture. As an illustration of how some critics have overlooked Nietzsche's defense of exploitation I shall briefly cite some representative examples from the works of Jaspers and Kaufmann.

In Jaspers's analysis of Nietzsche's politics it is openly acknowledged that Nietzsche regarded war to be as much a necessity for the state as the slave is for society. Having stated this, Jaspers proceeds to investigate the philosophical meaning of Nietzsche's remarks on war without making any critical comment on Nietzsche's endorsement of slavery.[7] Jaspers's method is to defend Nietzsche's statements in the best way he can while bypassing anything that cannot be defended. This type of analysis is highly unsatisfactory.

Kaufmann follows a similar strategy. On the issue of racial prejudice, for example, he has accomplished the difficult but legitimate task of clearing Nietzsche from charges of anti-Semitism.[8] And yet Kaufmann's analysis avoids raising the more radical question of whether Nietzsche's endorsement of the superiority of some races to others lends support to a general principle of ethnic or racial discrimination.[9] Even a casual reading of *Beyond Good and Evil* will show that Nietzsche held strong views against the English.[10] While this might be dismissed as philosophically insignificant, a careful reading of Nietzsche's unpublished notes shows that on occasion he suggested that entire races (judged decadent) ought to be exterminated and/or bred out of existence.[11] To illustrate his point Nietzsche parenthetically suggests the annihilation of the English. These statements, which appear absurd to us, may be said to be "playful" or "ironic," and, indeed, either of these conjectures may be correct. But it is also the case that Nietzsche's statements fit logically into a well-defined political ideology regarding what special groups and power structures ought to control the future of Europe. It is understandable that humanistic scholars should try to give the best possible reading of passages which carry an ambiguous meaning or which may seem to be superfluous to a philosopher's major theories on metaphysics, ethics, or epistemology. However, the critical claim I wish to maintain is that Nietzsche's defense of exploitation cannot be entirely separated from his other theories. The nature of this connection needs to be investigated further.

As for the ambiguity of some of his statements, Nietzsche himself admits in his highly antidemocratic work, *Beyond Good and Evil*, that it is not in the interests of an antiegalitarian "free spirit" (such as himself) "to betray in every particular [detail] *from what* a spirit can liberate himself and *to what* he may then be driven."[12] Still, he has said enough to convey to the reader the sense that as part of his intended transvaluation of all values he expects to see a rebirth in society's appreciation for a tyrannical type of government.

There is also a more general philosophical issue at stake here. Jaspers and Kaufmann are correct in emphasizing the idea that Nietzsche was interested in laying down the conditions that would allow a regeneration of the human spirit and the quest for human fulfillment. Much of Nietzsche's work lends support to this hypothesis. But any philosophy that stresses the radical need for regeneration must also face the concrete problem of how that regeneration is to be achieved. The fact that the rebirth of the human spirit was the fundamental goal of Nietzsche's transvaluation of all values does not necessarily mean that he was always correct in delineating how this goal would be attained. The critical reader must be able to hold Nietzsche accountable for the goals that Nietzsche himself proposed as well as to insist that departures from this goal not be met with indifference by the scholarly community. The tension between the need for human fulfillment and the obstructions of decadence and various forms of prejudice is both a theoretical and practical problem for any theory of values that places an enormous stress on bringing about the possibilities of fulfillment. By confronting honestly how Nietzsche handled this tension—which may be broadly conceived as the tension between the affirmation and negation of human life—we can gain some extremely valuable insights about the strengths and weaknesses of Nietzsche's method as well as possibly keep from repeating in our own work some of the errors to which Nietzsche may have been susceptible.

RANK, ARISTOCRACY, AND EXPLOITATION

Nietzsche had a set of political opinions which surface with almost predictable regularity in his aphoristic writings. But it is often

thought that he was not interested in either the theory or practice
of politics since he neither wrote nor intended to write a political
treatise. His political opinions appear as tangential remarks in the
context of a sociocultural critique. Although the existence of a
high culture is a very important concern for Nietzsche, this is not
to say that he was either uninterested in politics or that he considered politics unimportant. While he generally presented his
political views as functions of the thesis that decadence is the
primary characteristic of modern times, this approach is always
supplemented by the judgment that decadence ought to be eliminated and by the assertion that in his philosophy he addresses
this crucial historical task. Nietzsche's logic therefore moves from
the critique of contemporary culture to the advocacy of political
and social change. The importance of articulating Nietzsche's
political opinions is that they provide us with the most accessible
yet not always evident information about the direction of his
envisioned change. Everyone agrees that Nietzsche was a ve-
hement critic of the political establishment of his time. The question remains, for what reasons did he criticize it, and to what
ends?

The political changes envisioned by Nietzsche were intended
by him to affect the course of modern history. For a base from
which to criticize modern governmental policies and structures,
he turned to the distant past—to ancient Greece and Rome. For
the realization of his political hopes he looked to the distant future.
At the end of his career, however, he seemed to think that the
time for change was imminent: "For when truth enters into a fight
with the lies of millennia, we shall have upheavals, a convulsion
of earthquakes . . . the like of which has never been dreamed of
. . . all power structures of the old society will have exploded—
all of them based on lies. . . . It is only beginning with me that
the earth knows *great politics*."[13] In *Beyond Good and Evil* Nietzsche had expressed his hopes for the political future of Europe:

> While the democratization of Europe leads to the
> production of a type that is prepared for *slavery*
> in the subtlest sense, in single, exceptional cases
> the *strong* human being will have to turn out
> stronger and richer than perhaps ever before. . . .
> I meant to say: the democratization of Europe is
> at the same time an involuntary arrangement for
> the cultivation [Züchtung] of *tyrants*—taking that

word in every sense, including the most
spiritual.[14]

Although the tone of Nietzsche's statement is descriptive, he was
well aware that he was promoting an interpretation of history.
Ultimately it is up to us to judge whether in exchange for a system
of power structures based on "lies" (as he took the political
systems of his contemporaries to be) Nietzsche proposed anything
fundamentally different. In the case noted here, Nietzsche's myth
that the future of Europe belongs to the rule of select "tyrants"
is no less false than the power structures of the old society that
he takes to be based on lies. In spite of the overwhelming power
structures that affect the lives of modern human beings, the future
belongs to those who live in it, not necessarily to tyrants. Moreover, democratic institutions *may* cultivate in people the love of
freedom rather than turn them into either slaves or tyrants. By
making it appear that the rise to power of future tyrants is either
historically inevitable or destined, Nietzsche avoids facing a much
more important issue—how to view the human condition in a way
that either corrects or transcends the master-slave dualism. Rather
than look to history for possible alternatives to this dualism,
Nietzsche tended to use history to confirm this narrow perspective.

It is important to emphasize that Nietzsche was a strongly
antidemocratic thinker. When he turned to the past—to ancient
Greece, for example—he did so for politically reactionary reasons. In ancient Greece and Rome he sought to find an alternative
to the increasingly egalitarian trends of modern political movements. While other nineteenth-century thinkers looked to ancient
Greece in order to celebrate the origins of democracy, Nietzsche
used Greek society as a standard of excellence precisely for the
opposite reason.[15] As early as 1871–72 he praised the Greeks for
their dependence on slavery, arguing that slavery is required for
the flourishing of art and culture. "Slavery belongs to the essence
of culture," he declares in "The Greek State," an unpublished
essay written at the time of his intense association with Wagner.[16]
In this early piece Nietzsche argued in favor of increasing the
misery of "toiling men" so as to facilitate for a small number of
"olympic men" the production of the "*Kunstwelt*." He offers an
economic argument for this. The working class must be exploited
so that the surplus from their labor will buy time for artists.

> In order that there may be a . . . fruitful soil for
> the development of art, the enormous majority
> must, in the service of a minority, be slavishly
> subject to life's struggle. . . . At their cost,
> through the surplus of their labor, that privileged
> class [the minority] is to be relieved from the
> struggle for existence, in order to create and sat-
> isfy a new world of want.[17]

It might be objected that the extreme use of oppression against the majority for the sake of maintaining the well-being of an elite might violate the notion of human dignity. But Nietzsche had already argued in the same essay that human dignity is not at-tainable until one is released from the need to earn a living. His argument is interesting not because it shows the influence of a Greek model of freedom but because it admits the alienating con-ditions under which human beings must often work in order to preserve their existence. Instead of taking Marx's route and call-ing for a reappropriation of one's labor power, Nietzsche takes an elitist stand against labor as well as against the people who are "destined" to belong to the working class. The influence of Greek thought and the distinction between freedom and necessity take Nietzsche and Marx in two very different directions. For the sake of preserving the privileges of an elite, Nietzsche wants to discredit all movements which offer some ideological, legal, or moral benefit to the working class. He aggressively maintains that human beings as such have no dignity:

> Such phantoms as the dignity of man, the dignity
> of labor, are the needy products of slavedom hid-
> ing itself from itself. . . . Cursed seducers, who
> have destroyed the slave's state of innocence. . . .
> Now the slave must vainly scrape through from
> one day to another with transparent lies recogniz-
> able to everyone of deeper insight, such as the al-
> leged "equal rights for all" or the so-called
> "fundamental rights of man," of man as such, or
> the "dignity of labor." Indeed he is not to under-
> stand at what stage and at what height dignity can
> first be mentioned—namely, at the point, where
> the individual goes wholly beyond himself and no
> longer has to work and to produce in order to
> preserve his individual existence.[18]

These statements deny the meaning of human dignity by restrict-
ing its attainability to an idealized minority. Nietzsche uses these
views in support of an elitist ideology. But it must also be remembered that he opposed the system of quantifying human
work—this would include what is today referred to as "productivity." Nietzsche always thought of the quantification of value
as one of the most divisive and alienating features of Western
culture.[19] Therefore, in his alternative theory of values he struggled to transcend all conceptions of value subject to measure
through quantification. In order to achieve this, he had to disengage himself from society and from society's market ideology.
In the world of art, in the ideas of the *Übermensch,* the will to
power, and the eternal recurrence, Nietzsche found expressions
of the value of existence transcending criteria of quantification.
What he did not see was that in his model of domination and the
order of rank there remains another type of alienation, that of
human being from human being assumed in the justification of
slavery and the exploitation of the many for the sake of the "freedom" of a few. What can be the meaning of human dignity, one
should ask Nietzsche, if those who alone are thought to be worthy
of a human existence call for the exploitation and enslavement of
all other human beings?

THE "ETHICAL" JUSTIFICATION OF
NIETZSCHE'S POLITICS

Nietzsche uses the doctrine of the overcoming of traditional morality by the "higher" individual, developed at great length in
Beyond Good and Evil, to directly reinforce his political beliefs.
In fact, Nietzsche's politics and his doctrine of the overcoming
of morality by the superior person are inextricably connected with
each other in the writings of the transvaluation period. The aim
of Nietzsche's politics is to make the world correspond to an
ethical view in which the control of all values is placed in the
hands of a "superior type" of human being. But the very choice
of this hierarchy of control indicates a radically politicized view
of the universe. Nietzsche admits that the ethical theory of the
"higher" human being is a political morality. In his own words,
it is "a morality with the intention of training a ruling caste."[20]
And, as already noted, in *Beyond Good and Evil* he asserts that
he is most seriously interested in the cultivation of a new caste

that will rule Europe. The ethical theory of the higher man, then, is invoked in support of various political positions which promote the concentration of power in the hands of these superior individuals.

Nietzsche's critique of traditional morality—whether of the Christian, Kantian, or utilitarian type—rests on his disagreement with the notions of human equality and of the universality of moral maxims. Kant's categorical imperative is reduced by Nietzsche to an expression of Kant's will to power, that is, to an expression of Kant's will to universalize the peculiarities of his moral outlook as if this were a maxim mandated to all human beings.[21] If Kant is to be dismissed so quickly, then what about Nietzsche's values? "To *me* justice speaks thus: 'Men are not equal.' Nor shall they become equal!"[22] These are the words of Nietzsche's Zarathustra, whose disparagement of "herd" values also serves to discredit the utilitarian's democratically oriented moral calculus. In *Beyond Good and Evil* Nietzsche explicitly replaces Christian, Kantian, and utilitarian ethical theories with the notion of an order of rank where superior and inferior types have a separate value and function within the whole: "Every enhancement of the type 'man' has so far been the work of an aristocratic society—and it will be so again and again—a society that believes in the long ladder of an order of rank and differences in value between man and man, and that needs slavery in some sense or other."[23] In this way Nietzsche displaces the common bond that all human beings are capable of sharing as moral agents.

Once the egalitarian and universalist concerns of the Christian, Kantian, and/or utilitarian ethics are discredited, the way is clear for a justification of slavery and exploitation. The idea that there must be "distance" among *types* of human beings translates politically and economically into the justification of castes or classes. Nietzsche's doctrine of an order of rank called for an aristocratic class who would not be ashamed of demanding the reinstitution of slavery. The practical problem of maintaining slaves—whether slavery is conceived literally or just in terms of the notion of cheap, available labor—also called for the exploitation of human beings. These two marks of a "healthy" society—slavery and exploitation—are discussed by Nietzsche in the concluding chapter to *Beyond Good and Evil,* significantly entitled "What Is Noble." I shall quote from these passages at length so that the full intent of Nietzsche's arguments can be appreciated.

> The essential characteristic of a good and healthy
> aristocracy . . . is that it experiences itself *not* as
> a function (whether of the monarchy or the com-
> monwealth) but as their *meaning* and highest jus-
> tification—that it accepts with a good conscience
> the sacrifice of untold human beings who, *for its*
> *sake,* must be reduced and lowered to incomplete
> human beings, to slaves, to instruments. Their
> fundamental faith simply has to be that society
> must *not* exist for society's sake but only as the
> foundation and scaffolding on which a choice type
> of being is able to raise itself to its higher task
> and to a higher state of *being.*[24]

Here the exploitation of "untold human beings" is justified in
quasi-metaphysical terms, although the net effect of the argument
is strictly political.[25] The implications are clear. A "good" and
"healthy" aristocracy has been defined as one that can convince
itself and all human beings under its rule that the "lower" must
sacrifice itself to the "higher," while the ruling class has the power
of defining what the "higher" shall be. The "noble" consciousness, then, is one that demands the sacrifice of other human beings
and, convinced of its own elevated rhetoric, without the slightest
feeling of guilt reduces them to slaves and instruments.

   In the next section the perspective shifts from a highly rhetorical
defense of "sacrifice" and manipulation to a straightforward justification of violence and exploitation:

> Refraining mutually from injury, violence and ex-
> ploitation and placing one's will on a par with
> that of someone else—this may become, in a cer-
> tain rough sense, good manners among individuals
> if the appropriate conditions are present. . . . But
> as soon as this principle is extended, and possibly
> accepted as the fundamental principle of society,
> it immediately proves to be what it really is—a
> will to the *denial* of life, a principle of disintegra-
> tion and decay.[26]

Nietzsche was not speaking about exploitation in a figurative or
isolated sense. He makes it clear in the same section that he is
appealing to "life" to justify a methodical political and social
practice:

> everywhere people are now raving, even under
> scientific disguises, about coming conditions of
> society in which the "exploitative aspect" will be
> removed—which sounds to me as if they prom-
> ised to invent a way of life that would dispense
> with all organic functions. "Exploitation" does
> not belong to a corrupt or imperfect and primitive
> society; it belongs to the essence of what lives.[27]

Here Nietzsche uses a different tactic than moral rhetoric to defend exploitation. The tactic, which characterizes every justification that he gives for his political ideas and principles, is that of appealing both to necessity and destiny. He declares that while exploitation is necessary ("to life"), it is the aristocracy's destiny to use it against the oppressed. The two arguments are combined to yield a justification for his political vision. That is, the "necessity" of violence is used only to justify aristocratic control over the masses. It is inconceivable to Nietzsche to use it in support of populist movements of emancipation from aristocratic controls. The context in which Nietzsche's justification of exploitation and violence is given is therefore quite clear. In the previous section Nietzsche had reflected that "when, for example, an aristocracy, like that of France at the beginning of the Revolution, throws away its privileges with a sublime disgust and sacrifices itself to an extravagance of its own moral feelings, that is corruption."[28] The implication, of course, is that while the Revolution may be said to have been fighting a "corrupt" aristocracy, the aristocracy's corruption lay not in its extravagant exploitation of the people but in the fact that it did not exploit the people sufficiently. Surely, this was not Nietzsche's sole criticism of the French aristocracy and, surely, he is to some extent enjoying his own rhetoric. But the fact that he makes this kind of statement shows just how far he is willing to go to defend the rights of a privileged class to exploit the nonprivileged.

Through such a defense of exploitation Nietzsche intended to provide his new rulers of Europe with a good conscience. He wanted to make them strong, hard, unsentimental, uncorrupt—in other words, unmodern. He was afraid that the placing of one's will "on a par" with that of other human beings meant corruption. But, clearly, if anything is corrupt, it is to propose that any human being should reduce another human being to the status of a slave or instrument, no matter what elevated rhetoric is used to justify this reduction. How is Nietzsche's analysis of the meaning of corruption to be explained?

Certainly, many different and possibly even complementary interpretations of Nietzsche's position may be given. Insofar as he takes a strong critical stand against Christianity and democracy, Nietzsche's endorsement of an order of rank such as I have described may be taken as a negative consequence of his anti-Christian and antidemocratic position. In other words, one could say that since Nietzsche lacks belief in God and universal human rights, he is then "driven" to hold views on reducing some human beings to be the instrument of others. However, this explanation is not fully satisfactory. Consider the reasons that Nietzsche gave for opposing Christianity and democracy. One of the most important tenets Nietzsche rejected in Christianity was the dualism between good and evil. Moreover, his major opposition to universal human rights was the idea of reducing everyone to being the "same" as everyone else ("equal" to everyone else in a reductionist sense). And yet, Nietzsche's counterproposal of higher/lower, politically translated as the opposition between aristocrat and slave, involves a reduction of human beings to sameness of type within a dualistic structure of inequality.

Thus, in criticism of Nietzsche's politics it may be observed that the dualism of higher/lower is only a variation of the dualism between good and evil (positive and negative value). In spite of what Nietzsche says to the contrary in *Beyond Good and Evil* and the *Genealogy,* he has not yet overcome the dualism of good and evil; his analysis of decadence as an impurity that ought to be eliminated from society is much too reminiscent of the Manichean struggle between good and evil. Furthermore, his identification of Christians, democrats, socialists, feminists, and others with decadent forces is a drastic oversimplification. Nietzsche's counterproposals to democracy do not take him any farther along the road to a nonalienated, nonfragmented conception of human reality than the dualistic and reductionist structures of value that he himself opposed.

NIETZSCHE'S ANTINATIONALISM

The fact that Nietzsche's transvaluation of all values included the defense of privileges for an elite ruling class and the justification of a strongly repressive political ideology calls into question the relationship between Nietzsche's politics and his existential concerns for the development of the self's authenticity. I have tried to show so far that Nietzsche was blind to the damaging effects of certain forms of authoritarianism and that this blindness is manifested in the interpretation of the will to power as domination, in the theory of the overcoming of morality by the higher man, and finally in his politics. However, Nietzsche has at times been considered a major proponent of individualism as well as a major opponent of the nation-state. More than anything else this has kept readers from viewing him as an authoritarian political thinker. While it is true that Nietzsche rebelled against the political establishment of his time, the issue at stake is not whether he rebelled against established authority but what he sought to put in place of church and state. The context of his critique of the nation-state needs to be clarified.

Nietzsche's opposition to the state is sometimes mistaken for a sign of his concern for the rights of individuals to defend themselves against the power of the state. His most passionate critique of state power appears in Part I of *Thus Spoke Zarathustra*. Here the state is depicted as the enemy of the people and of their culture. It is an error, however, to interpret Nietzsche's views as representative of populism, anarchism, or individualism. From the beginning, Zarathustra's critique of the state establishes the point that it is in the interest of the creators of value to oppose the centralization of state power. Nietzsche openly criticizes the state as a rival to his own vision of society: "State is the name of the coldest of cold monsters. Coldly it tells lies too; and this lie crawls out of its mouth: 'I, the state, am the people.' That is a lie! It was creators who created peoples and hung a faith and a love over them: thus they served life."[29] Nietzsche's opposition to the state does not rest on the right of self-determination of the people but on the rivalry between state control over the people and the life-serving authority of the creators of value. The state is criticized for the constraints it can put on the creators of value, not necessarily on the people. This point is easily missed unless one is already familiar with Nietzsche's antiliberal opinions. The competitive rivalry for power between the creators of value and the servants of the state dominates much of Zarathustra's discourse. Nietzsche was aware that service to the state might provide a rival alternative to service to "culture" for those who do not believe in the most compelling service of all, service to God:

" 'On earth there is nothing greater than I: the ordering finger of God am I'—thus roars this monster [the state]. . . . Alas, to you too, you great souls, it whispers its dark lies. . . . Alas, it detects you too, you vanquishers of the old god."[30] Zarathustra's biting remarks about the "lie" of the state ("everything about it is false") should be read in the proper context of Nietzsche's assertion of traditional social authority rather than as statements on the self-realization of individuals. "Where there is still a people, it does not understand the state and hates it as the evil eye and the sin against customs and rights."[31] Here the emotional appeal to tradition is left vague enough that it could serve a variety of purposes, whether Nietzsche intended them or not. In Nietzsche's time, for example, the appeal to ethnic traditions could gain him the sympathy of those Germanic peoples who felt the burden of giving up their regional authority to the national power of the Prussian state ("Whatever [the state] has it has stolen").[32] But, on the other hand, the support of "traditional rights" often coincides with the support of ethnic, sexual, and class prejudices. The fact that Nietzsche elsewhere supported extreme forms of these prejudices does not lend credence to the thought that Zarathustra's rather vague statements were uttered in total political innocence.

In *Twilight of the Idols* Nietzsche condemns nationalism because a "nation" is still too small a unit of power in terms of its potential for making history. In contrast to the "smallness" of the European nations he praised the grandeur of Russia.[33] Moreover, he opposes nationalism because he associates the development of a national consciousness with the proliferation of democratic and Christian ideals—ideals which he never ceased to portray to his readers as petty and nauseous. After denying the value of all decadent individuals, Nietzsche immediately turns to an attack on Christians, socialists, and anarchists: "When the anarchist, as the mouthpiece of the declining strata of society, demands with a fine indignation what is 'right,' 'justice,' and 'equal rights,' he is merely under the pressure of his own uncultured state, which cannot comprehend the reason for his suffering—what he is poor in: life."[34] Individualism, democracy, socialism, and Christianity are all condemned as falling under the general categories of decadence and mediocrity. In other words, Nietzsche condemns both individualism and the state as two variations of the same decadent phenomenon.

Kaufmann has argued that Nietzsche opposed the state because it restricts the development of individuals.[35] He portrays Nietzsche as a champion of the right of "superior" individuals to self-realization, still using the "self" in the traditional sense. A different approach is taken by Tracy Strong, who emphasizes Nietzsche's interest in the transfiguration of the individual and ultimately of society.[36] But both Kaufmann's notion of self-realization and Strong's notion of transfiguration tend to depict Nietzsche's goals too altruistically. In his politics, Nietzsche was not as concerned with the transfiguration or self-realization of individuals as he was with the conditions whereby a special class of artist-philosophers would acquire power over society.[37] The main issue for Nietzsche remained, *Who would rule?*

The Nietzschean maxim, "Become who you are," is used by Kaufmann in support of his argument for self-realization. In *The Gay Science* Nietzsche wrote: "*What does your conscience say?* 'You shall become the person you are.' "[38] Several years later Nietzsche subtitled his autobiography, *Ecce Homo,* "How one becomes what one is." But this maxim, "Become who you are," is mistakenly interpreted if read solely as an individualistic teaching. In fact, "who one is" is a "piece of fate."[39] Therefore it is one's task to discover one's relationship to the laws of destiny operating in one's life. (The final chapter of *Ecce Homo* is significantly entitled "Why I Am a Destiny.") It may happen that an individual's task, like Nietzsche's, is to become a social rebel, a philosophical critic, indeed a transvaluator of all values. In this case the person's individuality—if it is considered "life-enhancing"—must be strengthened at the expense of the disruption of the established forms of social and political authority. But at the same time the person realizes that in strengthening one's power what matters is not the pursuit of self-realization but one's participation in a higher scheme of things.

A concise statement of how he regards individuality is given by Nietzsche in *Twilight of the Idols.* This statement applies both to the social and metaphysical meaning of the term "individual." "The single one [*der Einzelne*], the 'individual' [*das 'Individuum'*], as hitherto understood by the people and the philosophers alike, is an error after all: he is nothing by himself, no atom, no 'link in the chain,' nothing merely inherited from former times; he is the whole single line of humanity up to himself."[40] It was always Nietzsche's Dionysian position that the individual is part of the continuity of all life. What his "moral" position adds is the dualism between ascending and descending life. As pointed out in Chapter 6, if the individual is thought to belong to "ascending life," then his or her value is quite high, whereas if one belongs to "descending life," one's value is reversed.

Nietzsche's maxim, "Become who you are," is a Dionysian, not an individualist, motto. In its best expression, it can be used to promote self-awareness beyond the narrow perspective of the ego. In its worst application, it can be used to justify one's behavior—no matter how extreme—by means of an appeal to destiny. Like many other fundamental Nietzschean formulas, under the model of domination this Dionysian meaning of Nietzsche's teaching is delimited and even reversed.

THE DOMINATION OF WOMEN

Nietzsche's opposition to the political emancipation of women is consistent with his endorsement of a "strong" culture governed by the authority of the higher man. Also, nowhere is the tension between the "recurrence" and "domination" models of the will to power as explicit as in Nietzsche's conceptions of sexuality and of the relations between the sexes. The contrast between Nietzsche's metaphysical theories (based on a recurrence view of power) and his political ideology (based on a domination view of power) is worth noting.

Sexuality is an important and positive theme in Nietzsche's philosophy. It is a central theme in his psychology but also in his metaphysics, due to its important bearing on the concepts of the will to power and the Dionysian affirmation of life. Nietzsche believed that to affirm life meant to affirm sexuality, and in fact he made of the sexual process an almost mystical teaching. When Nietzsche refers to sexuality in the context of a Dionysian affirmation of life, the differences between "male" and "female" seem to disappear underneath a process of life-as-a-whole. At times sexual differentiation is forgotten, for only the general attributes of the "overfullness" and "overflowing" of life are reflected upon. Begetting and nurturing are recognized as complementary functions, neither one superior to the other, and both portraying the eternal recurrence of life. In some versions of the transvaluation of moral values, sexuality reverses places with asceticism, procreation with self-denial. Nietzsche used terms taken from sexual imagery as criteria of positive values: for example, the terms "overfull," "overflowing," "overabundant," "creative," "procreative," "pregnant," "well-formed," "begetting genius," "receptive genius." When he wanted to discredit a teaching or value-judgment, he used just the opposite set of terms to refer to it: castrating, castrated, ill-formed, antilife, lacking power, impotent, degenerate, decaying, decadent.

From the point of view of Nietzsche's philosophy of affirmation, all that is affirmed is value-free. Whatever occurs has its place in the whole, and the whole is seen as a play of forces eternally reaffirming themselves. From the point of view of Nietzsche's psychology of domination a very different perspective is introduced. This is the perspective of the part within the whole whose interest lies in the domination of what is alien to itself. In this context Nietzsche used the categories "male" and "female" as denoting centers of force eternally at war with each other. This is a nihilistic perspective although Nietzsche himself was not aware of it. The activity of begetting, which from the life-affirming metaphysical standpoint was seen as part of the general overflow of life, is now considered a function of emptiness, a function of not being whole. The emptiness of life is emphasized and domination is seen as a way of coping with emptiness—a nihilistic remedy for a nihilistic disease. Thus the sex drive is no longer interpreted as a sign of the eternal return of life but as an instinct of domination. For a man it means the drive to enhance his power by dominating a woman. For a woman it means either of two things: the drive to let herself be possessed and overpowered by a man or the drive to overpower him through pregnancy and childbirth. Nietzsche charged that women were inclined to use men sexually solely to satisfy the drive to have children. "Man is for woman a means: the end is always the child."[41] This attitude, however, may result from a resentment against a woman's capacity for childbirth. At the same time, it may stem from a type of dualism which exaggerates the importance of this natural capacity and therefore projects a deficiency upon those who lack it. And so, from the standpoint of emptiness, resentment, and dualism, there arises the psychology of the war of the sexes.

Occasionally Nietzsche spoke of love as an ideal that is yet to be attained by humanity. In his criticism of humanity's failure to live up to this ideal, he emphasizes the need for individuals to exercise reciprocal respect and compassion.[42] And yet, these are precisely the virtues which are excluded from his concept of self-actualization as domination. In his treatment of the relations between the sexes, Nietzsche generally relied on the latter standpoint. In *Zarathustra* he portrays the satisfaction of the male instinct as requiring that woman submit unconditionally to man's power. She must submit to him without understanding him, otherwise he could not preserve his power over her. Appealing to destiny here, Nietzsche claimed that woman is incapable of anything but obedience and superficiality.

> The happiness of man is: I will. The happiness of
> woman is: he wills. "Behold, just now the world
> became perfect!"—thus thinks every woman
> when she obeys out of entire love. And woman
> must obey and find a depth for her surface. . . .
> Man's disposition, however, is deep; his river
> roars in subterranean caves: woman feels his
> strength but does not comprehend it.[43]

From the alleged psychological and physiological destinies of man and woman, their economic and sociopolitical roles are deduced. In *Beyond Good and Evil* Nietzsche proceeded to the following conclusions: "A man . . . who has depth, in his spirit as well as in his desires, . . . must always think about woman as *Orientals* do: he must conceive of woman as a possession, as property that can be locked, as something predestined for service and achieving her perfection in that."[44] In other words, destiny orders that she be his slave, his possession, his property. And yet, this interpretation of destiny is not altogether unrelated to an economic and sociopolitical goal. Although the conclusion of Nietzsche's well-known aphorism is rarely quoted, it is instructive to note what he says. "As is well known, from Homer's time to the age of Pericles, as their culture *increased* along with the range of their powers, they also gradually became *more severe,* in brief, more Oriental, against women. *How* necessary, *how* logical, *how* humanely desirable even, this was—is worth pondering."[45] The institutionalization of woman's status as man's property is thus justified by Nietzsche, in the final analysis, by an appeal to the "greater good" of culture.

The logic of Nietzsche's analysis shows that, in his view, the higher man's need for a great culture has total priority over the needs of specific, particular human beings for a life of freedom and well-being within any given culture. But there is an unstated problem here because Nietzsche, as a self-conscious creator of cultural values, was well aware that a culture would lack value unless it was responsive to the needs of individuals. His solution to this apparent contradiction is to argue that a worthy culture need only be responsive to the needs of the creator of values. In this way it is easy to dismiss the needs of others. Their task is to be subservient to (not merely supportive of) the creator. Even if the creator should decide to act benevolently toward the people, he would still view them as instruments to be used in the development of the will to power.

Nietzsche's analysis of love is of psychological interest because in those exceptional cases where he speaks of it, he focuses on the experience of love as directed toward a larger-than-human context. The tendency to explain all human interaction in terms of the drive for domination leaves no room for love within the human sphere. Zarathustra admonished couples to love each other with a love mediated by a distant ideal, the love of the *Übermensch*.[46] In the absence of this exceptional type of mediation, Nietzsche reduced his psychological principles of explanation to the most basic assumption. In the case of love he determined that love is just another term (an "ingenious" term) for egoism.[47] One thirsts after new possessions and calls this "love." But what one loves is the feeling produced in oneself by the object of love— one loves the feeling, not the other person.[48] It is only in this sense that Nietzsche speaks of the harmony, rarely achieved, between the sexes. Harmony results from the fulfillment of certain expectations generated by man's and woman's so-called natural drives. "Will is the manner of men; willingness that of women."[49]

In none of the examples considered does love exist directly between the sexes or between two individuals. If there is love, what exists is the love or acceptance of one's role in the larger scheme of things. For example, the couple who love each other as precursors of the *Übermensch* qualify for this type of love. Although he does not state this explicitly, Nietzsche postulates that the only object worthy of love is something nonhuman or superhuman. In his psychological portraits he observes not only the selfishness of human love but even the unworthiness of human beings to be objects of love: "Discovering that one is loved in return really ought to disenchant the lover with the beloved. 'What? This person is modest enough to love even you? Or stupid enough?

Or—or—' "⁵⁰ What exists for Nietzsche as a reality is the love of fate, *amor fati*. He turns his love toward something impersonal, something that is worth loving because it is incapable of loving him in return.

Nietzsche's exclusion of the possibility of love between the sexes and among human beings in general has important effects upon his sociopolitical thought. The result may be seen especially in his lack of concern for human happiness, in his disregard for human rights, and in his tendency to distrust the human need for community. As he ironically states, the virtue of cleanliness demands that one refrain from human contact. Community makes human beings "common."⁵¹ The lack of trust in human contact leads Nietzsche to place a very high value on impersonal goals. The results of the psychology of domination are striking, especially when seen in light of the price Nietzsche is willing to pay for his objectives. All of his "high" goals—such as a high culture, the breeding of a higher man, and the maintenance of authoritarian social institutions—are set up at the price of methodically exploiting, enslaving, or otherwise dominating the great majority of human beings. When the desires of human beings are reduced to the drive to domination, all human association or interchange must also be reduced to the functioning of this drive. Nietzsche has argued with a good conscience for physical, emotional, economic, and political exploitation because he has been able to transfer all instincts toward harmony, love, play, and devotion from the sphere of personal relationships to highly impersonal objects: either life or destiny. Unfortunately, in such a depersonalized universe, the tendencies that remain to be discharged in human conduct are none other than the instincts of domination and aggression. This implies an eternal order of social repression from which there is no escape as long as one is involved in human affairs.

Sexism and the Order of Rank

The authoritarian ideology that Nietzsche supported in the case of aristocratic government is, not surprisingly, replicated in Nietzsche's theory of the ideal family structure as presented in *Twilight of the Idols*. In this work Nietzsche confirms and develops his earlier pronouncements in *Beyond Good and Evil* by continuing to oppose democracy, the equal rights of women, and the rights of workers to organize. Because the family functions as the smallest and yet the most important social institution affecting all aspects of daily existence, the principles of *Rangordnung* must be applied just as strictly here as in the political order at large. Again, Nietzsche used a critique of modern society from the political standpoint of the "far right" to destroy the relatively liberalizing trends in modern marriages and to introduce his own views on the principles that ought to guide the institution of marriage. As any other modern institution, marriage shares the weaknesses of the present age.

> *Critique of modernity.* Our institutions are no
> good any more; on that there is universal agree-
> ment. However, it is not their fault, but ours. . . .
> In order that there may be institutions, there must
> exist the kind of will, instinct, or imperative,
> which is anti-liberal to the point of malice: the
> will to tradition, to authority, to responsibility for
> centuries to come, to the solidarity of chains of
> generations, forward and backward *ad infinitum.*
> When this will is present, something like the *im-
> perium Romanum* is founded; or like Russia . . .
> the concept that suggests the opposite of the
> wretched European nervousness and system of
> small states. . . .[52]

Any departure from an authoritarian view of order is held to be a sign of decadence.

Nietzsche claims that modern marriage has lost its meaning because it has lost its rationality. But in the same section he notes that the rationality (*Vernunft*) of an institution lies in its structure of domination.

> The rationality of marriage—that lay in the hus-
> band's sole juridical responsibility, which gave
> marriage a center of gravity, while today it limps
> on both legs. The rationality of marriage—that lay
> in its indissolubility in principle, which lent it an
> accent that could be heard above the accident of
> feeling, passion, and what is merely momentary.
> It also lay in the family's responsiblity for the
> choice of a spouse. With the growing indulgence
> of love matches, the very foundation of marriage

has been eliminated, that which alone makes an institution of it.[53]

Nietzsche goes on to say that love is an idiosyncracy upon which no institution can be founded. Marriage must be founded not on a "feeling" but on an instinct, "on the sex drive, on the property drive (wife and child as property), on the drive to dominate, which continually organizes for itself the smallest structure of domination, the family."[54] While this may be an accurate description of some essential features of the patriarchal family structure, the claim does not follow that only where this structure obtains can there be a marital relationship between men and women. By reducing the nature of love to a mere accident or feeling Nietzsche is able to argue that some of the most personal of human relationships (relationships between the sexes and between parents and children) should be founded on such impersonal (instinctual) characteristics as the sex or property drive.

Two main motifs of repression may be abstracted from Nietzsche's conception of a "rational" or uncorrupt marriage. These are the repression of love and the domination of women and children. These themes, of course, are closely interconnected. The outcome of Nietzsche's conception of marriage is the repression of individual feeling, especially the feeling of love between the spouses. He states that marriage "ought" to be indissoluble, and further that the choice of a spouse ought to be dictated by the familial authority structure. His idea of a nondecadent marriage requires, along with the repression of feeling, the domination of the wife and children by the husband-father figure. Both types of repression are interconnected in that the subordinate role assigned to women and children in marriage is analogous to the role assigned to emotion and love. Since in this context the "male" instincts stand for rationality and duty (moral self-righteousness) while the "female" instincts stand for emotion and play, Nietzsche's preferences are quite clear when he states that the husband must be the center of power in the marriage, that the marriage is decadent if it "limps on both legs." Here Nietzsche has defended a master-slave hierarchy as essential to the family as well as to society at large. The family, as the smallest but most important social structure, consists of a master-slave structure in which duty suppresses emotion, man suppresses woman, and parents suppress the children (even after they grow up). The latter relationship—parents versus children—provides the form through which the structure of domination is passed from one generation to the next.

Given the extreme authoritarian statements Nietzsche makes about the family (nothing less than *total* domination of the feelings of the spouses is demanded), and also given Nietzsche's intelligence, his critical nature, and his acknowledged unhappiness with the authoritarian structure of his own limited family life, one may question whether he really held these opinions about the institution of marriage seriously. Could he have voiced these opinions without caring much about them, simply to provoke thinking and discussion on these issues? Or could this be one of several opinions he might have held? It must be admitted that in so unsystematic a writer as Nietzsche one cannot expect a single view on any topic, including marriage. However, one may note a logical pattern to his views, even when noticing several variations in his statements. For example, in an unpublished note from the same period as *Twilight of the Idols* Nietzsche cites the possibility of short-term marriages ("for years, for months, for days"), but these were envisioned primarily as an alternative to prostitution and as a way of allowing the birth of more children in the society.[55] In these arrangements sex is also unrelated to love and women are explicitly regarded as means to satisfy men's short-term sexual needs and society's need for children. Although Nietzsche's statements on the repression of feeling seem to be psychologically inconsistent with the unhappiness of his own limited family experience and although they are somewhat out of line with his defense of spontaneity and the affirmation of life, they are not inconsistent with his views on modernism, decadence, the order of rank, the "war" of the sexes, the psychology of domination—in short, with all of the fundamental themes of the narrow psychology of the will to power. He himself states that the dissatisfaction that is felt with modern marriage should constitute "no objection to marriage but to modernity." Nietzsche's counterproposal to "modern ideas" is to reintroduce an extreme form of authoritarianism into the power structure of all social and economic institutions. Authoritarianism becomes the alternative to the "decadence" of modern life, while its censorship agent, intolerance, becomes the weapon of "justice" against the threat of criticism and (progressive) change.

The link between intolerance and justice had been made by Nietzsche in *Beyond Good and Evil*. In this work he praises the aristocracy for its intolerance "in the education of youth, in their arrangements for women, in their marriage customs, in the relations of old and young" and he adds, "they consider intolerance itself a virtue, calling it 'justice.'"[56] Here we are not simply confronting the antiegalitarian view of justice professed by Zarathustra that "men are not equal—nor shall they become equal." What is clear from this passage is that there appears to be a logical connection between Nietzsche's defense of intolerance, his defense of aristocratic privilege, and his defense of a sexist and authoritarian social and family structure. The master-slave dualism which Nietzsche proposed for society at large also operates *within* the ruling class in the form of a rigid structure of subordination in which the established men of the upper class control the younger men of that class and where women and children can be legitimately viewed as man's property. The "intolerance" which Nietzsche commends is aimed at the preservation of this tradition. Thus intolerance must call itself justice—otherwise in the name of justice one would question the validity of the tradition.

Nietzsche's authoritarian interpretation of an order of rank is an artificial and intellectually unacceptable doctrine based on a rigorously oversimplified view of reality. This rigid adherence to fixed categories is a special example of self-deception in a thinker whose primary metaphysical project was to show that all being is in flux, that there is no being, only becoming. It represents an attempt to generate in society at large an ethical and political structure which would simply duplicate the distorted experiences of a highly isolated and socially alienated individual. Rather than being the incarnation of natural justice, Nietzsche's order of rank is the attempted institutionalization and objectification of a highly distanced and alienated view of human relations. A compulsive distance among individuals (even among those of the highest rank) is required. Even friends must obey the rules of distance dictated by the order of rank. Nietzsche's Zarathustra teaches that the friend must always be regarded as standing at a height. He counsels that one must never reveal one's true nature to one's friend. The point of the disguise is to cover up all of the weaknesses that make one human, as well as to exclude the possibility of love and compassion from the friendship. Men who do not live up to Zarathustra's model of friendship are devalued to the status of women and animals.[57] Moreover, Nietzsche's overall position is dualistic. The "higher" human being must draw the meaning of his existence from the distance he perceives between himself and those others whom he calls the herd, the slave, the wife, the effeminate. The distance insulates the "higher" person from the impurities of the "lower" and helps to maintain the myth that the distant person is superhuman. Thus the dualism between good and evil appears to plague Nietzsche's theory of values from beginning to end—both in the doctrines that he undertook to fight and in some of the principal alternatives that he set up in their place.

NIETZSCHE'S POLITICS REVERSED

Having said this much, however, I want to consider, finally, whether Nietzsche's political ideas have anything positive to contribute to the future justice and well-being of human life. One of the more interesting political questions that can be directed at Nietzsche's politics is one he suggested himself when the object of his attack was the democrat or the Christian. When applied to Nietzsche, the question is: who is to profit from Nietzsche's proposed system of values? Who is to profit from the exploitation of the many by the few, of the "lower" by the "higher"? At once it is evident that it would be the "few," although not the "higher." Anyone whose "higher" qualities demanded the conscious exploitation and/or enslavement of others would be neither "high" nor "deep," as Nietzsche recurringly claimed. But that is another matter.

While Nietzsche's ideas are targeted against socialism and egalitarianism, I believe that it is a mistake to draw the inference from this alone that he must be taken as a spokesman for capitalist and imperialist ideologies. His ideology was necessarily elitist, but he did not perceive the elite as those who have the most money or wield the most military power. The "imperialism" advocated by Nietzsche is of a much more subtle nature. It is an imperialism of "rank," of "moral authority," of "philosophic vision." Its elevated rhetoric and tone, however, do not match the blind and mediocre suggestions with which these phrases are associated as a matter of practical application. Nietzsche's rhetoric of rank is therefore highly misleading. Who would not want to see Europe led by men and women of the highest philosophical vision? But already we find in *Beyond Good and Evil* a major obstacle to the practical application of this ideal when we are told that the role of women is to be silent in politics and furthermore that women are incapable of speaking truthfully.[58] Even so, some would say, who would not want to see Europe led by *men* of the highest philosophical vision, these "philosophers of the future" to whom Nietzsche dedicates his thoughts in *Beyond Good and Evil?* But when we inquire what these thoughts are in practical terms, we see the elevated rhetoric as an empty effort to make a political and ethical myth out of a few banal and destructive attitudes, such as considering oneself a member of a highly select group or devaluing others so that, by contrast, one appears to be heroic.

Here I would call attention to the distinction between Nietzsche's "philosophical" and nonphilosophical thoughts which, given the nature of his aphoristic writings, has often been used to separate the essential from the nonessential elements in his writings. For example, Kaufmann has claimed that Nietzsche's views on women are inessential to his theory of values.[59] Danto has claimed that Nietzsche's defense of slavery is a thoughtless error.[60] The distinction between what is essential to Nietzsche "as philosopher" and what is not has been used to either disclaim or deemphasize the connection between Nietzsche's high-sounding rhetoric ("order of rank," "higher man," "philosophers of the future") and the idiosyncratic opinions Nietzsche associated with these words (tyranny "in every sense," slavery in every sense, breeding in every sense).[61] I suggest, as a counterthesis, that the weeding out of the least attractive elements in Nietzsche's work amounts to either self-deceit or censorship, and that, in any case, this practice keeps us from understanding the whole of Nietzsche's vision. I have stressed that both the elevated rhetoric and the banal application of such terms as the "order of rank" and the "higher man" belong to Nietzsche's legacy. His work needs to be understood both where it is critical and where it is anticritical. The issue raised here is that there is a highly anticritical streak in Nietzsche's *entire* theory of the "order of rank" and the practical applications derived from it. By his own admission, the morality of *Rangordnung* upon which his political vision and his vision of "destiny" rest is highly uncritical. Here one encounters Nietzsche as Anticritic. In advocating the theory and practice of *Rangordnung,* Nietzsche becomes the Anticritic par excellence.

As long as one gives philosophical credibility to the rhetoric of the "superior type" or "higher" person and sets aside the political and practical implications of how this rhetoric is instantiated, both by Nietzsche and by the historical patriarchal tradition in which we still live, we are defending what I shall call "the politics of unspecified prejudice." While the logic of unspecified prejudice calls for the higher/lower distinction without committing itself to any particulars to fill those categories, Nietzsche has made it quite clear what groups by "nature" or "destiny" are higher and what lower. Here are two statements regarding women and workers, two groups Nietzsche has condemned to the "low." Reversing Goethe's statement that "the eternal feminine draws us higher," the author of *Beyond Good and Evil* wrote: "I do not doubt that every nobler woman will resist this faith, for she believes the same about the Eternal-Masculine."[62] The criterion of a woman's "nobility," then, is her "faith" that the male, as male, is more noble than herself. This insidious rhetoric is also applied to the slave, who is urged to believe that his exploitation is justified because the master/aristocrat is more noble than he. When one unmasks the realities of this rhetoric, one sees that the practical advantages do not go to "superior" persons—even assuming there were so pure a type—but simply to the privileged classes of the established society. Nietzsche himself points this out in *Twilight of the Idols:*

> *The labor question.* The stupidity—at bottom, the degeneration of instinct, which is today the cause of *all* stupidities—is that there is a labor question at all. Certain things one does not question: that is the first imperative of instinct. . . . But what was done? . . . The instincts by virtue of which the worker becomes possible as a class, possible in his own eyes, have been destroyed through and through with the most irresponsible thoughtlessness. The worker was qualified for military service, granted the right to organize and to vote: is it any wonder that the worker today experiences his own existence as distressing—morally speaking, as an injustice? But what is *wanted?* . . . If one wants an end, one must also want the means: if one wants slaves, one is a fool if one educates them to be masters.[63]

The theme of the "strength" of *not questioning* the structure of power that serves the interests of a privileged class is not simply antiliberal to the point of malice (as Nietzsche suggests in the aphorism that precedes this one). It is anticritical to the point of malice. These statements on women, the working class, and the need of the privileged class for thoughtless and obedient "slaves" are not simply isolated opinions on Nietzsche's part, as sometimes they tend to be read. They are logically tied to other notions that Nietzsche is commended for holding—such as the distinction between the "superior" person and the "herd," the belief in a "strong" culture, and even the love of one's fate. The fact that we ignore the concrete side of the issue while holding on to the more abstract side shows that in this case we are much less logical than Nietzsche, for we are the ones caught in a logical dilemma, while Nietzsche is not. Nietzsche, however, is caught in a much larger type of contradiction even though his logic is tight with respect to the connection between elitism and oppression. This is the contradiction between his intended affirmation of life and his reactionary and nihilistic politics.

Still, the political implications of Nietzsche's thought can be turned around to some extent if we ask: was not Nietzsche correct in insisting upon a logical connection between a "strong" masculine ideal, a "strong" culture, and a blind system of political exploitation and psychological repression? Is it not true that if the goal of one's values is to implement a "strong" patriarchal system where a few will command and the rest will obey, it is then foolish to allow moral codes which favor the notions of the universal brotherhood and sisterhood of human beings? Does not the morality of universal human dignity entail in theory, if not also in practice, the elimination of all forms of elitism, domination, and oppression? In Nietzsche's idea of "greatness" one finds the logic of the extreme—of this he was well aware. But thanks to his uninhibited articulation of the extreme he has exposed the logic of patriarchal domination in its essence. While Nietzsche has outlined various incentives for overturning the democratic influences of modern times and for instituting a "purer" system of patriarchal domination under the banner of overcoming the "evils" of "effeminacy" and "decadence," it is up to us, not him, to make the choice as to what we want our political future and our moral values to be. His appeals to destiny, intolerance, and the suspension of critical questioning of authoritarian political institutions are not convincing.

Conclusion

The main problem that appears to delimit Nietzsche's philosophical affirmation of life is his failure to value human life as much as life in its totality. His advances over nihilism are rooted in the notion that there is no need to invent a more perfect form of life (as in the notion of an afterlife) since life already has sufficient meaning and value. The Dionysian struggle against the Socratic approach to existence is based on the view that reason has exceeded its role when it purports to define the meaning of life in terms of reason itself. And yet, the same opportunity that Nietzsche would like to see given to life is denied to human life. There is an irresistible tendency on Nietzsche's part to deny the value of human life as such and to accept it as valuable only if it is perfect, noble, or strong. The dualism between good and evil is maintained as a measure of human worth. The fact that the dualism remains, however, means that the broader project of the affirmation of life in its totality is blocked.

Zarathustra's position serves as an illustration of this dilemma. His love of life is stifled by the torture he experiences at the thought that "small" human beings will recur eternally. Human weakness and failure elicit in Zarathustra a sense of nausea for the whole of existence. His perception and appraisal of reality appear to be out of balance. Even though Zarathustra finally accepts the idea of the recurrence, he makes his choice at the cost of his separation from humanity. He drops all human contact and stays in the mountains, desiring intercourse with eternity alone. There is an important split between his desire to affirm life and his inability to affirm human life. Human life still appears to be too small, too insignificant and wretched to Nietzsche. Thus he constantly seeks grandeur.

Nietzsche noted that human life has dwindled because human beings lack opportunities for integrated and creative activities. It is a mistake, however, to link creativity and integration with the quality of greatness. The demand for greatness involves a value-judgment against anything that is not exceptionally powerful or distinguished. This involves a devaluation of the ordinary aspects of human life. If these aspects do not count toward making human life meaningful, however, then one is still exhibiting a nihilistic attitude toward human existence. Nietzsche is right in claiming that nihilism must be overcome in order for human beings to lead creative and resourceful lives. On the other hand, when he associates the latter values with the creation of a strong and majestic culture, he delimits the meaning of creativity. The expectations he places upon it are nihilistic as long as creativity is made to fit under a paradigm of domination.

Traditionally, the answer to the split between Nietzsche's critique of human life and his affirmation of life has been to explain his reaction against human weakness as a reaction against nihilism. His position might be justified this way if one viewed the rejection of human nature not as a devaluation of human nature as such but as a rejection of the nihilism that has "overtaken" humanity. Certainly, Nietzsche's work—at least significant portions of it—lends support to this hypothesis. Nevertheless, his analysis of nihilism is insufficiently radical. It does not point to the dualism inherent in the notions of strong versus weak, of master versus slave. In order to overcome nihilism, one must transcend *all* forms of dualism, not merely some of them. The use of the notion of nihilism as one of two poles of an opposition between "right" and "wrong" must also be avoided. If "nihilistic" human life stands to "life-affirming" human life as evil to the good, and if, furthermore, one considers the "prolife" forces as being commanded by "destiny" to chastise the "evil" forces, then one falls back precisely upon the problem of self-division that plagues the nihilistic consciousness. The question that emerges out of this is whether it is indeed possible for human beings to transcend dualism.

I believe it is possible to transcend the metaphysical and moral types of dualism that Nietzsche attacked in the Western tradition as well as the remnants of that dualism still appearing in Nietzsche's work. Nietzsche made an excellent start in the direction of overcoming dualism when he called attention to its origins in the psychological desire to divide reality into good and evil and then to punish one side of reality at the expense of the other. The origin of dualism, then, is in the need for self-punishment. But whether this is a natural need is highly questionable. Rather than view the need for self-punishment as a natural need, it is reasonable to view it as a culturally induced habit based on reverence for a patriarchal model of authoritarianism. Nietzsche contributed significantly to the investigation of this problem by tracing the need to punish oneself or others to a resentment against time, the body, and the earth. Still, the temptation remains to reverse the dualism and bestow on time, the body, and the earth the authoritative voice that once belonged to their opposites. The quest for integration must be taken beyond this stage. One must question whether the meaning of authority remains the same and whether the need to appeal to authority is even applicable once the understanding of value has shifted to a life-affirming foundation. Unless this is done, the "healer" of past resentment may view himself or herself as a new "authority" in morals and proceed to behave dualistically against antagonists in the same way his or her predecessors had.

Despite Nietzsche's contribution to the problem of resentment, he cannot see through completely to its solution because he fails to reconsider the meaning of authority under a "transvaluated" perspective on values. The answer he sought at this level—the idea of will to power as domination—is in no way a radical answer to what authority would mean under a new system of values. It simply reconfirms the traditional meaning of authority—namely, the power of command and the enforcement of rules—although, instead of grounding the power of command upon a "sublime" or a "moral" basis, Nietzsche gives it an extramoral foundation. In doing this he is not carrying Western culture to a new ground of values. He is simply taking away some of the more hypocritical trimmings from the attitude toward power that has generally prevailed in the culture.

A reconsideration of the meaning of authority would question the need for appealing to authority under a life-affirming conception of values. If the aim of overcoming nihilism is the healing of human beings from fragmentation and alienation, and if it is the philosopher's task to achieve this aim, should the philosopher invent various appeals to the authority of reason or life to make his or her contributions to human understanding more acceptable or enticing? Must the approach to the investigation of a vital issue be mystified in this manner? Obedience to authority binds the self. To end an argument by stating "Thus life wills it" does not lend any additional support to the argument. Moreover, it would seem that dependence upon authority is the mark of a restless consciousness, of a consciousness that cannot provide its own foundations for values. Such a consciousness seeks to lose itself in an authoritarian formula or, if it is somewhat bolder, it will seek compliance with its values by others as a way of reassuring itself that its values have a foundation.

The ideology of superior/inferior reinforces the dependence of individuals upon authoritative systems of value. Because one can always be judged inferior to something superior to oneself, one is always subject to the power of that which is deemed superior to one's performance and values. This creates in some the desire to conform to external standards of conduct so as to prove one's value. However, the result of this type of alienation is the mentality of the "herd" criticized by Nietzsche. On the other hand, in others the ideology of superior/inferior may create a need to compete and either rival or overcome the previous authorities. And yet there seems to be only one permissible way of being successful in this respect, and that is to become a "new" authority. The circle of alienation, however, is not broken by the latter procedure. The person who attains the more valuable or "superior" status simply moves to a different position in the circle of nihilism.

Moreover, because one cannot be "superior" in every respect, the organism remains fragmented and alienated. Standards of values outside its own needs are held up as measures of its value in every conceivable area of the individual's appearance and performance. Indeed, this panorama of existence yields the scene laid out by Nietzsche where modern human beings are depicted as either completely manipulated by standards of value external to themselves or else, in rebellion against this, rising as dictators over the masses. In a society or culture where everyone has to account for one's value to a "higher" authority, the possibility of emptiness and fragmentation will always stay with human beings. The need to prove one's value to a higher authority may keep one from developing those talents and virtues that would be most meaningful to oneself. The origin of the depreciation of human life, then, is in the need to make human life fit the expectations of a "superior" authority.

The divided consciousness resulting from this cannot transcend nihilism until and unless it can transcend the dependence on authoritarianism. The nihilistic mind wants to control reality; it does not want reality simply to be. Where it can no longer control, it only knows how to suspend its desire to grasp by submitting to a higher force. This reinforces its sense of helplessness and its inordinate need always to keep in control of things. Like "superior" and "inferior," the opposites "good" and "evil" serve to reinforce the authoritarian mentality. It is not so much the opposition of terms as the authoritative confinement into which the self is trapped when these terms are employed that reveals their nihilistic nature. One must remember that Zarathustra, the superior teacher, is just as confined to his mountain top—despite the appearance of freedom—as the "inferior" people living in the valley. Once the ideology of superior/inferior and good/evil sets in, one is confined, restricted, and immobilized in the quest for personal integration and a healthy sense of values. One escapes individuality by placing one's identity within the boundaries of one or both of these categories (superior/inferior, good/evil). Escaping individuality, one never succeeds in learning what it means to be a healthy individual.

Nietzsche was correct in suspecting that one simply cannot value human behavior in the same way as one values phenomena like trees or flowers. And yet, the answer to the problem of human value—or the affirmation of human life—cannot be given through the duality of strength versus weakness. Nietzsche also knew that the key to understanding the value of human life lies in the liberation of the self from a nihilistic understanding of itself. Breaking through the chains of command through which human experience is generally understood, dissected, and evaluated is the most liberating act and yet the most threatening act against the values presently controlling the self-understanding of human beings. Despite the setbacks affecting Nietzsche's theory of values, such a future is nevertheless promised in Nietzsche's image of the child's "sacred Yes" to life and in the symbol of the *Übermensch*.

Chronology of
Nietzsche's Major Works

1872   *Die Geburt der Tragödie* (*The Birth of Tragedy*)

1873–76 *Unzeitgemaße Betrachtungen* (*Untimely Meditations*)

1873   I. *David Strauss, der Bekenner und Schriftsteller* (David Strauss, the Confessor and Writer)

1874   II. *Vom Nutzen und Nachteil der Historie für das Leben* (*On the Use and Disadvantage of History* [*for Life*])

1874   III. *Schopenhauer als Erzieher* (*Schopenhauer as Educator*)

1876   IV. *Richard Wagner in Bayreuth*

1878   *Menschliches, Allzumenschliches* (*Human, All-Too-Human*)

1879   First sequel: *Vermischte Meinungen und Sprüche* (*Mixed Opinions and Maxims*)

1880   Second sequel: *Der Wanderer und sein Schatten* (*The Wanderer and His Shadow*)

1881   *Morgenröte* (*The Dawn* [*of Day*])

1882   *Die fröhliche Wissenschaft* (*The Gay Science* [*The Joyful Wisdom*])
         Book V published in 1887.

1883–85 *Also sprach Zarathustra* (*Thus Spoke Zarathustra*)
         First public edition of Book IV in 1892.

1886   *Jenseits von Gut und Böse* (*Beyond Good and Evil*)

1887   *Zur Genealogie der Moral* (*On the Genealogy of Morals*)

1888   *Der Fall Wagner* (*The Case of Wagner*)

1889   *Die Götzen-Dämmerung* (*Twilight of the Idols*)

1895   *Der Antichrist* (*The Antichrist*)

1908   *Ecce Homo*

1895   *Nietzsche contra Wagner*

Abbreviations

A	*Der Antichrist* (*The Antichrist*)
EH	*Ecce Homo*
FW	*Die fröhliche Wissenschaft* (*The Gay Science*)
G	*Die Götzen-Dämmerung* (*Twilight of the Idols*)
GM	*Zur Genealogie der Moral* (*On the Genealogy of Morals*)
GT	*Die Geburt der Tragödie* (*The Birth of Tragedy*)
J	*Jenseits von Gut und Böse* (*Beyond Good and Evil*)
M	*Morgenröte* (*The Dawn*)
NCW	*Nietzsche contra Wagner*
Z	*Also sprach Zarathustra* (*Thus Spoke Zarathustra*)
WM	*Der Wille zur Macht* (*The Will to Power*)
KGW	*Nietzsche Werke. Kritische Gesamtausgabe.* (Berlin, 1967–82)
KGB	*Nietzsche Briefwechsel. Kritische Gesamtausgabe.* (Berlin, 1975–)
CWFN	*The Complete Works of Friedrich Nietzsche.* (New York, 1909–11, 1964)
PN	*The Portable Nietzsche* (New York, 1954, 1968)
K	Kaufmann translations of *The Birth of Tragedy, The Gay Science, Beyond Good and Evil, On the Genealogy of Morals,* and *Ecce Homo* as cited in the Bibliography.

Notes

Since this is primarily a study of Nietzsche's mid-to-late works and these have already been translated and published by Walter Kaufmann, I have used the available Kaufmann translations in my notes unless otherwise specified. In the case of notes not previously published or not previously translated into English I have provided my own translations. These are based on the recently compiled critical edition of Nietzsche's works (KGW) by Giorgio Colli and Mazzino Montinari. Because the KGW supersedes all other previous editions of Nietzsche's works, I have relied on it for bibliographical purposes, although I have also benefited from access to the Kröner and Schlechta editions of Nietzsche's works. The collection known as *Der Wille zur Macht* (*The Will to Power*) is superseded both in format and in content by the KGW edition of Nietzsche's un-published notes. Yet at the present time the one-volume edition of *The Will to Power* (English translation by Kaufmann and Hollingdale) is much more accessible to readers than the many volumes of notes collected in the KGW edition. For the reader's benefit all notes I have used from the KGW edition which have appeared in *The Will to Power* have been cross-referenced and dated according to the findings by Colli and Montinari. Moreover, textual departures from the KGW, whether in the form of word omissions or textual tampering, have been recorded in my notes. The dates given always refer to the KGW information (not all dates in the WM collection are reliable). This system of cross-reference should save the reader much time should she or he wish to consult the notes under consideration.

The format for my notes is as follows. If the citation is to individual works by Nietzsche, there will generally be the abbreviated title of the work, followed by the title or section number in which the passage appears. This enables readers who are using editions of Nietzsche's works other than the ones I have cited to locate the passage speedily for their own reference. If a passage is quoted, the page numbers refer to the source used. Generally, for the translations, that source is Kaufmann, while for the untranslated or previously unedited material, the source is the KGW. See the Bibliography, under "Selected Works by Nietzsche," for the specific bibliographical data on the sources used.

INTRODUCTION

1. G, "The Problem of Socrates," § 1; PN, p. 473.

2. Z, II, "The Soothsayer" and "On Redemption."

3. The problem of the resentment and revenge against time will be discussed in Chapter 2.

4. The incompatibility of endorsing the value of domination within a life-affirming theory of values is one of the main themes of this study. Specific critiques of Nietzsche's use of the theme of domination will be found in Chapters 3, 6, and 7 as well as elsewhere.

5. FW, §§ 1, 125, and 342; Z, IV.

6. See especially Chapters 6 and 7.

7. GM, III, §§ 1 and 28.

8. Z, I, "On the Thousand and One Goals."

9. EH, "Thus Spoke Zarathustra," § 1.

10. WM, § 1059, p. 545; KGW, VII$_2$, 223 (1884).

11. GT, §§ 5 and 24. For the relevance of *The Birth of Tragedy* to Nietzsche's fundamental ideas on the Dionysian affirmation of life, see Chapter 1.

12. The text of *The Will to Power,* as presently available, is no indication of the work that Nietzsche contemplated under that title. In the early 1900s, after Nietzsche's death, two editions of *Der Wille zur Macht* were published under the direction of Nietzsche's sister, Elizabeth Förster-Nietzsche. The first edition, published in 1901, contained approximately four hundred notes. The second edition—the version with which we are familiar today—was first published in German in 1906 and contains one thousand and sixty-seven notes. This edition of *The Will to Power* should be compared with the arrangement of Nietzsche's unpublished notes and fragments compiled by Giorgio Colli and Mazzino Montinari in *Nietzsche Werke. Kritische Gesamtausgabe* [KGW], 20 vols. (Berlin: Walter de Gruyter, 1967–82). The work of Colli and Montinari shows that the collection of notes known as *The Will to Power* contains many errors, omissions, and distortions of Nietzsche's unpublished notes. The *Will to Power* collection is relatively useful, however, insofar as it provides a certain thematic continuity for some of Nietzsche's notes from 1883 to 1888.

Nietzsche provisionally outlined a set of notes to be included in a collection to be entitled *The Will to Power* (see KGW, VIII$_2$). However, Nietzsche's correspondence from February 1888 shows that he was completely dissatisfied with his efforts. In the fall of 1888 the project of "The Will to Power: Attempt at a Transvaluation of All Values" was changed to a four-part series under the general title of "The Transvaluation of All Values" (*Umwertung aller Werte*). Only the first part—*The Anti-*

christ—was completed by Nietzsche. For Nietzsche's outlines from the fall of 1888, see KGW, VIII₃, 347, 397, 402, and 423.

13. G, "Maxims and Arrows," § 26; PN, p. 470.

14. Nietzsche's theories are usually interpreted from a non-Dionysian stand. When his concept of art is referred to, very often what is taken to be artistic is only seen from an Apollonian perspective. Among the Apollonian categories influencing the reading of Nietzsche we find the notion of the perfect individual, morality as self-perfection, and knowledge as an artistic (shaping) process. These are genuine Apollonian categories in Nietzsche, but they need to be supplemented by their Dionysian counterparts. Dionysian categories corresponding to these are the union between the individual and the totality, morality as self-overcoming, knowledge as self-transcendence. In order to be consistent in the use of a Dionysian category one needs to read all of its elements in a Dionysian context. For example, for a consistent interpretation of the Dionysian notion of self-transcendence one also needs a Dionysian reading of Nietzsche's notion of the self and of transcendence. This point is often missed by readers who are unfamiliar with Nietzsche's Dionysian teachings. Specific arguments relating to these points will be offered as we proceed with our investigation.

15. GT, § 10.

16. The term "progressive" is being used here in the sense of "directed forward" rather than "oriented toward progress." "Regressive-progressive" is roughly equivalent to "backward-forward." Nietzsche's method of reasoning should not be confused with Sartre's progressive-regressive method (*Search for a Method,* 1963). Sartre follows a dialectical logic; Nietzsche's logic is oriented toward cycles. The term "progressive" has a Marxist connotation in Sartre. This would, of course, not apply to Nietzsche. Sartre's analysis focuses on social and economic as well as psychoanalytical issues. Nietzsche uses the regressive-progressive method through the mediation of ontological and symbolic categories, e.g., past/future and origin/rebirth. On the metaphysical issue of whether there is infinite time Nietzsche endorses the notion of a *regressus in infinitum.* On the issue of social progress, he denounces the concept of historical progress. Cf. WM, § 1066 (KGW, VIII₃, 166–68).

17. This discussion does not touch on Nietzsche's theory of the eternal recurrence. Yet a similar conception of backward-forward movement and/or awareness results from the thought of the eternal recurrence of all things. Every moment in time may be seen as potentially having a past precedent (in a previously recurring cycle) and a future issue (in a cycle not yet actualized). Cf. Z, III, "On the Vision and the Riddle."

18. See especially Gilles Deleuze, *Nietzsche et la philosophie* (Paris: Presses Universitaires de France, 1962), pp. 1–3ff.

19. According to Kaufmann, Nietzsche should have ended his book at the end of section 15, thus dropping all references to Wagner. Kaufmann's judgment resembles that of Nietzsche's contemporaries. His academic peers did not view favorably the inclusion of statements on Wagner in Nietzsche's study of Greek tragedy. These critics give no importance whatsoever to the main Dionysian thesis of Nietzsche's work— the origin, death, and rebirth of tragedy. Without the section on Wagner (or the rebirth of tragedy) Socrates would come out as the conqueror of Dionysus. See Walter Kaufmann, *The Birth of Tragedy,* Translator's Introduction §§ 2–3 and n.11, pp. 98–99.

20. GT, § 10; K, p. 73.

CHAPTER ONE

1. Human beings are finite beings rooted in the earth. There is no absolute knowledge, only a manifold of perspectives. See also "Perspective and Politics," below, and n.33.

2. Søren Kierkegaard, *Concluding Unscientific Postscript,* trans. David F. Swenson and Walter Lowrie (Princeton: Princeton University Press, 1941), pp. 99–113.

3. GT, Preface, § 2.

4. Ibid., § 10.

5. Ibid., § 8; K, p. 65.

6. Ibid., § 1; K, p. 37.

7. Ibid. § 20; K, p. 123.

8. Ibid.

9. Ibid.; K, p. 124.

10. Ibid., § 2.

11. Ibid.

12. Ibid., § 21; K, p. 128.

13. Ibid., § 12; K, p. 81.

14. Ibid., § 1.

15. Ibid., § 12; K, pp. 83–84.

16. Ibid.; K, p. 85.

17. Ibid., § 15; see also Z, II, "On the Famous Wise Men."

18. G, "The Problem of Socrates," §§ 9–10.

19. GT, § 15.

20. Ibid., § 12; K, p. 85.

21. Ibid., p. 83.

22. Ibid., § 13; K, p. 87. Cf. § 15; K, p. 95.

23. G, "The Problem of Socrates," § 9.

24. GT, § 13.

25. Ibid., § 14; K, p. 92.

26. Ibid.; K, p. 93.

27. Z, II, "On Redemption."

28. GT, §§ 16 and 24.

29. EH, "Thus Spoke Zarathustra," § 1.

30. Z, I, "On Reading and Writing."

31. "Among School Children," *The Collected Poems of W. B. Yeats,* 2d ed. (New York: Macmillan, 1950), p. 242.

32. It is interesting to note in this respect that even though the German language is able to combine several nouns (or verbs) together, it also demands separate words for subject, verb, and object. Nietzsche's observations on the reification of the subject and the failure of grammar to show a sense of unity or process in the subject-verb-object structure are more applicable to some languages than others. For example, in Spanish it is possible to combine subject/verb and verb/object constructions such as "Take-this-with-you" or "Bring-it-to-me" by merging verbs and pronouns into a single word. The use of the personal pronoun as grammatical subject is also optional; one need only state the verb to make such statements as "I think" or "Have they arrived?" In these cases the subject is part of the verb, as it were. The Nietzschean point might be to conclude that the Spanish language is not as metaphysically deceptive as the German language.

33. G, " 'Reason' in Philosophy," § 5.

34. More precisely, Nietzsche states in one of his notes that "what can be thought of must certainly be a fiction" (WM, § 539; KGW, VIII₃, 124). Nietzsche is saying here that conceptual frameworks are contrived instruments for perceiving a reality that is always in flux.

35. WM, § 481, p. 267; KGW, VIII₁, 323 (1886–87).

36. WM, § 1067; KGW, VII₃, 339 (1885).

37. See, for example, J, §§ 18–19 and 203.

38. GM, III, § 27; Z, II, "On Self-Overcoming."

39. Z, II, "On Self-Overcoming," p. 115.

40. G, "Maxims and Arrows," § 8; PN, p. 467.

41. Z, I, "Zarathustra's Prologue," § 3.

42. Ibid., "On the Despisers of the Body."

43. Ibid., "Zarathustra's Prologue," § 3.

44. "Ueber Wahrheit und Lüge im aussermoralischen Sinne" (1873), KGW, III₂, 375; "On Truth and Falsity in Their Ultramoral Sense," CWFN, II, 180.

CHAPTER TWO

1. The Idealist tradition dominated Nietzsche's attention. He was most influenced by the work of Plato, Schopenhauer and some of the pre-Socratics. The Christian view of sin, guilt, and redemption also exerted a significant influence upon him. Nietzsche was generally critical of Kant and Hegel, while he spoke favorably of Spinoza and Heraclitus. Nietzsche's style was to speak on metaphysical issues without developing

a systematic critique of metaphysics. For information on his metaphysical views we must rely primarily on his discussions of specific issues such as the nature of becoming or the metaphysics of guilt and punishment.

2. *Philosophy in the Tragic Age of the Greeks,* trans. Marianne Cowan (Chicago: Henry Regnery, 1962), § 5, pp. 50–52. The original draft, "Die Philosophie im tragischen Zeitalter der Griechen" (in KGW, III₂, 293–366), was written in 1873 and revised in 1876 but never published by Nietzsche.

3. Ibid.

4. G, "The Problem of Socrates," § 1; PN, p. 473.

5. Z, II, "Upon the Blessed Isles."

6. Ibid., "On Redemption," pp. 138–41.

7. G, "The Four Great Errors," §§ 7–8; PN, pp. 500–501.

8. Z, II, "On Redemption," pp. 139–40.

9. Ibid., p. 140.

10. Ibid., "The Soothsayer," p. 133.

11. WM, § 521; KGW, VIII₂, 81–82 (1887). See also WM, § 568; KGW, VIII₃, 63 (1888).

12. This theme is tied to Nietzsche's view of the Dionysian, as expressed in 1888. The Dionysian takes one across the abyss of forgetfulness (*Vergessen*), that is, beyond what one normally considers to be one's real self. The memory that keeps this "self" together is actually the forgetting of one's unity with life. See KGW, VIII₃, 16–17, for a corrected version of WM, § 1050.

13. Z, I, "On the Despisers of the Body," pp. 34–35.

14. Ibid., p. 34.

15. Ibid., III, "The Convalescent," § 2, p. 217.

16. WM, § 1067; KGW, VII₃, 338–39 (1885).

17. One of the more significant passages is GM, I, § 13. Nietzsche accepts the idea of force as a category of explanation but states at the same time that we are deceived by the metaphysics of language when we say "force causes" or "force moves." This, he argues, is to make force responsible for something. His denial of causality is therefore an aspect of his conception of the innocence of becoming. This important section in the *Genealogy* contradicts Nietzsche's hypothetical argument in section 36 of *Beyond Good and Evil.* There Nietzsche attempts to reduce the meaning of all efficient force to will force, particularly will-to-power force. Several premises in his argument advocate positions that he does not hold, e.g., the notion that every change is caused by a will. (Nietzsche's standard position on this issue is that the will does not cause anything because it does not exist.) In any case, if every change were the result of an act of will, this would also go against his arguments on the innocence of becoming. I therefore regard section 36 of *Beyond Good and Evil* as a very unreliable source of Nietzsche's views on causality.

This section should be read in the context of statements Nietzsche makes elsewhere on the same subject.

18. J, § 21. The alternative Nietzsche proposed was merely a different *sense* of force—force not paired into relationships of cause and effect but viewed as the dispelling of energy.

19. KGW, VII₃, 386 (1885).

20. See especially *The World as Will and Representation*, trans. E. F. J. Payne (New York: Dover Publications, 1969), I, 18–22.

21. Translated from KGW, VII₃, 386.

22. WM, § 551, p. 295; KGW, VIII₃, 66–67 (1888).

23. G, "The Four Great Errors," § 3; PN, p. 495.

24. Ibid.

25. WM, § 551, p. 296; KGW, VIII₃, 66–67 (1888).

26. WM, § 552, p. 297; KGW, VII₂, 47 (1887).

27. G, "The Four Great Errors," § 5; PN, p. 497.

28. PN, pp. 497–98.

29. G, "The Four Great Errors," § 7; PN, p. 500.

30. PN, p. 499.

31. J, § 21; K, p. 29.

32. See G, "The Four Great Errors," §§ 3, 6, and 7.

CHAPTER THREE

1. KGW, VII₃, 386.

2. WM, § 1067, p. 550; KGW, VII₃, 338–39 (1885).

3. See Chapters 6 and 7.

4. WM, § 1067; KGW, VII₃, 338–39 (1885).

5. This may be clarified through an analogy with literary interpretation. If someone has a special gift for writing poetry (but not prose), the person should not be expected to forsake poetry for prose on the grounds that the later might be more readable. Some authors are better poets than writers of prose. In the philosophical tradition, some authors may have more to contribute to knowledge by presenting their thoughts systematically, others by opposing or questioning systems. In my judgment Nietzsche belongs with the latter.

6. The main sources for Nietzsche's exposition of the idea of the eternal recurrence are the following: FW, IV, § 341; Z, III, "On the Vision and the Riddle," "The Convalescent," "The Other Dancing Song," and "The Seven Seals"; EH, "Thus Spoke Zarathustra"; WM, §§ 1053–67. For works interpreting Nietzsche's teaching, see Karl Löwith, *Nietzsches Philosophie der ewigen Wiederkehr des Gleichen*, 3d ed. (Hamburg: Felix Meiner, 1978); Bernd Magnus, *Nietzsche's Existential Imperative* (Bloomington: Indiana University Press, 1978); Joan Stambaugh, *Nietzsche's Thought of Eternal Return* (Baltimore: Johns Hopkins Press, 1978). See also Arthur Danto, *Nietzsche as Philosopher* (New York: Macmillan,

1965); Gilles Deleuze, *Nietzsche et la philosophie* (Paris: Presses Universitaires de France, 1962); Martin Heidegger, *Nietzsche,* 2 vols. (Pfullingen: Günther Neske, 1961).

7. Z, III, "The Convalescent," § 2, p. 221.

8. Ibid.; K, p. 220.

9. FW, IV, § 341; K, pp. 273–74.

10. This theme is best pursued by reading some of the more specialized literature on the subject. Magnus and Danto are especially helpful, while Deleuze offers some interesting thoughts on the matter. The *Will to Power* collection (§§ 1053–67) contains some of Nietzsche's unpublished notes on the recurrence. Some of these give sketches of logical arguments for the eternal recurrence, including an appeal to the principle of the conservation of energy.

11. See Chapter 5.

12. Nietzsche praises Zarathustra as having a driving need for seeing far into the distance (as opposed to focusing on what lay nearest to him, his own age). See EH, "Beyond Good and Evil," § 2.

13. Nietzsche seems to have been familiar with the work of two leading researchers on the principle of the conservation of energy, Friedrich Mohr and J. Robert Mayer. According to Karl Schlechta's *Nietzsche Chronik* (Munich: Carl Hanser, 1975), one of the books taken out of the Basel library by Nietzsche in 1873 was Mohr's *Allgemeine Theorie der Bewegung und Kraft als Grundlage der Physik und Chemie* (Braunschweig, 1869). Several years later (and approximately four months before Nietzsche's acclaimed vision of the eternal recurrence by Silvaplana Lake) Nietzsche read the work of another proponent of the conservation of energy, Julius Robert von Mayer. The new critical edition of Nietzsche's letters compiled by G. Colli and M. Montinari shows that Peter Gast (Heinrich Köselitz) thought highly of Mayer and sent Nietzsche a copy of Mayer's book in April 1881 (*Nietzsche Briefwechsel. Kritische Gesamtausgabe* [KGB], III,$_2$, 148 and 158). The essay celebrated by Gast, "Dynamik des Himmels," is one of several contained in Mayer's *Die Mechanik der Wärme in gesammelten Schriften* (Stuttgart: J. G. Cotta, 1867). In this work Mayer argues for the principle of energy conservation and the convertibility of heat and light into energy. Mayer also links his scientific views to a vision of metaphysical and cosmic harmony. Nietzsche's initial response to Mayer's work was enthusiastic on the basis of Mayer's vision of the totality of life and energy as a great cosmic harmony (KGB, III,$_1$, 84). A year later, however, in another letter to Gast from March, 1882, Nietzsche openly criticized some of the theses advocated by Mayer (KGB, III,$_1$, 183–84). I will return to Nietzsche's disagreements with Mayer shortly.

We do not know to what extent, if any, Nietzsche was influenced by Mohr, whose work came to his attention in 1873. But Nietzsche's thoughts bear some affinities to those of a collaborator of Mohr's, Ludwig Büchner. Büchner, an advocate of scientific meterialism, was known, among other things, for popularizing Mohr's research on the conservation of energy in an 1857 piece entitled "Die Unsterblichkeit der Kraft" (see Frederick Gregory, *Scientific Materialism in Nineteenth Century Germany* [Dordrecht: D. Reidel, 1977]). Although there is to my knowledge no record of Nietzsche having read Büchner, I think it is revealing to cite Gregory's account of Büchner's 1857 paper to indicate the similarities between Büchner's popularization of the law of the conservation of energy and Nietzsche's ideas on the will to power and the eternal recurrence.

> [According to Büchner] nature did not know a standstill. . . . it was rather a never-ending cycle of motion that corresponded to diverse kinds of force. These forces were not able to be created or destroyed, but they were interconvertible into one another in such a way that their sum was a constant, and force itself was immortal. . . . A force could be transformed into another form, but the total amount of force in the world remained equal in amount. (Gregory, p. 160)

Readers familiar with Nietzsche's Dionysian vision of the will to power will remember his words: "This world: a monster of energy, without beginning, without end; a firm, iron magnitude of force that does not grow bigger or smaller, that does not expend itself but only transforms itself. . . ." (WM, § 1067, p. 550 [1885]).

Büchner offered an explanation of the second law of thermodynamics in a manner which also shows similarities with Nietzsche's idea of the eternal recurrence. In *Licht und Leben* (Leipzig, 1882) Büchner addressed the law of increasing entropy by saying that only parts of the universe would die but that other parts would go on living. After reviewing several cosmological hypotheses about the death and rebirth of the solar system, Büchner concluded that our world " 'must and will . . . celebrate its resurrection some day' " (Gregory, p. 163). Büchner's popularization of the first and second law of thermodynamics fits in with Nietzsche's sketchy explanation of what the eternal recurrence would mean from a logical standpoint. The ideas on the conservation of energy and the death and rebirth of the universe were very much in the air in Nietzsche's time. The element Nietzsche added was the thought that all possible configurations of energy states which were once actualized would reproduce themselves eternally. The ethical component of the idea (the total affirmation of life in spite of all suffering) also had precedents in the nineteenth century. Schopenhauer came close to articulating Zarathustra's most profound thought in *Welt als Wille und vorstellung* (§ 54). This work was discovered and enthusiastically read by Nietzsche in 1865.

Having noted similarities between some of the scientific analyses of energy conservation and Nietzsche's theory of the recurrence, I should also point out some differences. Although Nietzsche accepted the concept of energy, he did not accept the concept of matter. In March 1882, Nietzsche wrote to Peter Gast saying that Mayer (*Mechanik der Wärme*) did not realize that matter (*Stoffe*) is one great prejudice (KGB, III₁, pp. 183–84). These scientists may have had interesting data but, according to Nietzsche, they were still metaphysically confused. It appears that Nietzsche accepted the idea of the conservation of energy but did not identify energy metaphysically with either matter or spirit. He probably assumed that, whichever of the two categories he chose, he would be caught in some latent if not explicit form of dualism.

14. FW, IV, § 341; EH, "Thus Spoke Zarathustra," § 1.

15. WM, § 617; KGW, VIII₁, 320 (1886–87).

16. WM, § 1056; KGW, VII₂, 69 (1884). See also WM, § 1053 [KGW, VII₂, 248 (1884)] and WM, § 1054 [KGW, VIII₁, 130 (1885–86)]. The Colli-Montinari edition shows no specific reference to the idea of the recurrence in the note equivalent to WM, § 1053. It shows several textual changes (additions and deletions of material) in the notes corresponding to WM, §§ 1056 and 1054. However, in all textual versions it is clear that Nietzsche views the idea of the recurrence as a kind of weapon through which the decadent will be destroyed, and that he is not merely referring to an individual's overcoming of his or her own potential or actual decadence.

17. On Nietzsche's arguments regarding the destruction of weakness and/or the weak, see Chapters 5–7.

18. Kierkegaard, *Concluding Unscientific Postscript,* pp. 178–82.

19. Z, III, "The Convalescent," § 2, pp. 219–21.

20. See the passages referred to in n.16 above.

21. Z, II, "On Redemption," pp. 139–41.

22. Ibid., pp. 141–42.

23. Ibid., III, "The Convalescent," § 2, p. 221.

24. Nietzsche claims, it seems, that there is no such thing as "same" with respect to any object or individual. Everything is always in flux. However, the "great year" of becoming that brings us back to life brings us back to the same life. In other words, the pattern of the great cycle is the same but within the cycle everything is in flux.

CHAPTER FOUR

1. WM, § 1067, p. 550; KGW, VII₃, 338–39 (1885).

2. Z, II, "On Self-Overcoming"; J, §§ 13 and 36.

3. See above, pp. 5–7.

4. Stern, *A Study of Nietzsche* (Cambridge: Cambridge University Press, 1979), pp. 94–96.

5. Walter Kaufmann, *Nietzsche: Philosopher, Psychologist, Antichrist,* 4th ed. (Princeton: Princeton University Press, 1974).

6. Selections from several French studies on Nietzsche, including the work of Deleuze, have appeared in English translation in *The New Nietzsche: Contemporary Styles of Interpretation,* ed. David Allison (New York: Delta Books, 1977). For recent Spanish criticism, see Fernando Savater, *Conocer Nietzsche y su obra* (Barcelona: Dopesa, 1977) and Eugenio Trias et al., *En favor de Nietzsche* (Madrid: Taurus, 1972). Among recent French critics, Nietzsche's use of metaphors has gained some attention and prominence. The reader may find the work of Eric Blondel and Sarah Kofman of interest. Still, Blondel offers primarily a Freudian reading of Nietzsche, equating metaphor with transference, while Kofman centers her valuable insights on metaphor primarily on Nietzsche's early works (where the notion of the will to power is not yet stated). See David Allison, ed., *The New Nietzsche,* pp. 150–78 and 201–14.

7. For example, Kaufmann rejects a "metaphysical" interpretation of the will to power and instead proposes a "psychological" interpretation of Nietzsche's theory (*Nietzsche,* p. 204).

8. A psychological interpretation of the will to power would need to address Nietzsche's conception of human nature in light of his critique of the self and traditional morality. Insofar as Kaufmann discusses Nietzsche's psychology his aim is to show how Nietzsche's ideas fit a conservative model of morality.

9. See Z, II, "On Self-Overcoming," pp. 113–16.

10. Kaufmann, *Nietzsche,* pp. 213–216.

11. See Chapters 6 and 7.

12. Kaufmann claims that Nietzsche's theory of sublimation antedates Freud's (*Nietzsche,* pp. 218–19). However, there is only a superficial similarity between Nietzsche's and Freud's notion of sublimation. Freud saw sublimation as the final process of a psychological mechanism originating primarily in the castration complex and Oedipus complex of (male) children. For Nietzsche, on the other hand, the sublimation of sexual energy is simply one of many manifestations of the creative process of *Selbstüberwindung* underlying all forms of life.

13. " 'I' [Ich], you say, and are proud of that word. But greater is that in which you do not wish to have faith—your body and its great reason: that does not say 'I,' but does 'I' " (Z, I, "On the Despisers of the Body," p. 34).

14. See J, §§ 16–17 and G, "The Four Great Errors," §§ 3, 7 and 8. See also WM, §§ 480–92 and passim.

15. Stern, *A Study of Nietzsche,* p. 114. For Stern's discussion of the will to power, see pp. 114–25.

16. Ibid., pp. 93–96 and passim.

17. Ibid., p. 123.

18. See especially J, § 259 and GM, I and II.

19. For Nietzsche's critique of morality as domination, see primarily Part I of *Thus Spoke Zarathustra*. See also G, "The Four Great Errors," §§ 7–8. On other occasions Nietzsche exposed morality as domination but praised the value of domination in morality (e.g., J, § 188, and G, "The Improvers of Mankind"). Nietzsche's uncritical acceptance of aristocratic domination is responsible for his endorsement of domination whenever he takes the latter standpoint.

20. Cf. WM, §§ 481 and 482.

21. As noted in Chapter 3, Nietzsche tends to alternate between a recurrence-oriented and a domination-oriented model of explanation. See also Chapters 5–7.

22. Heidegger, *Nietzsche*, I, 517–27, 590–602, 613–16.

23. Ibid., p. 628.

24. Ibid., pp. 657–58; cf. p. 495.

25. For Heidegger's theory see *Nietzsche*, I, 551–77, 632–34.

26. WM, § 551; KGW, VIII₃, 66–67 (1888).

27. Translated from KGW, VII₃, 386.

28. Z, II, "On Self-Overcoming."

29. Heidegger, *Nietzsche*, I, 488–91.

30. Stern, *A Study of Nietzsche*, pp. 95–96.

31. For the relationship between asceticism, nihilism, and silence, see Z, III, "The Convalescent," and Nietzsche's critique of the soothsayer in Z, II and IV.

32. Deleuze, *Nietzsche et la philosophie*, pp. 50–53.

33. See especially Chapter 2, "Actif et réactif," pp. 44–82.

34. Nietzsche takes the individual (understood as separate from the rest of reality) as a fiction (G, "Skirmishes of an Untimely Man," § 33). This point is often bypassed in interpretations of Nietzsche.

35. See Deleuze, *Nietzsche et la philosophie*, pp. 61–62. Nietzsche's thesis on the contrary is that (1) all meaning is perspectival and (2) all perspectives are value-laden.

36. GM, III, §§ 1 and 28.

37. Deleuze, *Nietzsche et la philosophie*, pp. 63–65, 74–77, and passim.

38. Ibid., pp. 44–48.

39. Ibid., p. 77.

40. See, e.g., J, § 16–17, and G, " 'Reason' in Philosophy," §§ 2, 5 and 6.

41. These themes constitute Nietzsche's conception of healthy creativity and intellectual honesty during his "Zarathustra" and "will to power" periods.

42. In most of his mature works Nietzsche argues that the belief in the existence of the will is a metaphysical error, but, depending on the context of the discussion, this argument is unevenly applied to other, more specific problems. See, e.g., FW, § 127; J, § 19; WM, §§ 664–66, 670–72, and 692; G, "The Four Great Errors," §§ 3, 7 and 8.

43. This is the intent of J, § 36, where Nietzsche relies upon more than one premise he regarded as false in order to reach this conclusion.

44. In contrast to Kaufmann, Danto finds it very important to question what Nietzsche meant by the will to power if the term is used in the same sense to refer to both human and nonhuman reality. See Arthur Danto, *Nietzsche as Philosopher*, pp. 214–28. Kaufmann prefers to keep these two categories separate. Although Kaufmann does not omit a discussion of the metaphysics of the will to power, he begins and ends with the human factor. Kaufmann commits himself only to accepting a psychological interpretation of the will to power. He regards Nietzsche's position that all life is the will to power as an unconvincing generalization. Even as he quotes the poetical verses where Nietzsche's statement appears in *Thus Spoke Zarathustra*, Kaufmann omits viewing Nietzsche's statement as a metaphor. See Kaufmann, *Nietzsche*, pp. 204, 206–7, 235–43, and 261–69.

45. GM, I, § 13. In section 11, Nietzsche praises "the innocent conscience of the beast of prey" which allows human beings to murder, rape, and torture "as if it were no more than a students' prank" (K, p. 40).

46. This view is argued most eloquently by Tracy Strong in *Friedrich Nietzsche and the Politics of Transfiguration* (Berkeley: University of California Press, 1975).

47. I am not arguing here that Nietzsche had a theory which he forgot or which he set up and then let relapse. The order of my discussion is not chronological, although I take it that the order in which Nietzsche wrote his work shows the development as well as the changes in his point of view. The logic I am tracing in Nietzsche (and the context in which his development is being judged in this study) is simply the logic of the transvaluation of all values. This project shows Nietzsche's attempt to take philosophy from nihilism to the joyful affirmation of life. If successful and true to its intent, the logic I am tracing in Nietzsche does its job as long as it operates in a nonnihilistic manner and does not justify nihilistic ends. It suffers a relapse when it does the latter, as when it is used to ennoble or justify cruelty in the name of affirming life. Regardless of whether living entails cruelty or not, or the degree to which it may entail cruelty, it does not follow (except to the sadistic or masochistic mind) that the joyful affirmation of life requires the affirmation of cruelty. Therefore I show here and as the study progresses that it is inconsistent for Nietzsche to claim to present a viewpoint which tran-

scends nihilism and, at one and the same time, to endorse the notion of power as domination and cruelty.

48. J, §§ 259 and 265; GM, I, § 16, and II, § 3. Cf. WM, § 1027 [KGW, VIII₂, 90 (1887)].

49. See Chapter 2.

50. WM, § 1067, p. 550; KGW, VII₃, 339 (1885).

51. See "On Truth and Falsity in Their Ultramoral Sense" (1873), CWFN, II, 171–92.

52. This theme is developed in *The Gay Science,* with its combination of poetry and aphorisms, its critique of realism, its mood of exaltation, and the emphasis on the creative life as "the great health." It is also implicit in *Thus Spoke Zarathustra.*

53. Translated from KGW, VII₃, 385 (1885).

54. WM, § 1067, p. 550; KGW, VII₃, 339 (1885).

CHAPTER FIVE

1. Cf. FW, III, § 270. Nietzsche later subtitled his autobiography, *Ecce Homo,* "How One Becomes What One Is." None of this makes Nietzsche a believer in individualism. See Chapter 7, pp. 175–76.

2. Nietzsche's critique of traditional morality is developed at length in *Thus Spoke Zarathustra, Beyond Good and Evil, On the Genealogy of Morals, Twilight of the Idols,* and *The Antichrist.* For interpretations emphasizing some of the "immoralist" aspects of Nietzsche's teachings, see Arthur Danto, *Nietzsche as Philosopher,* pp. 130–61, and J. P. Stern, *A Study of Nietzsche,* pp. 93–170. See also Philippa Foot, "Nietzsche: The Revaluation of Values," in *Nietzsche: A Collection of Critical Essays,* ed. Robert C. Solomon (New York: Anchor Books, 1973), pp. 156–68.

3. For Nietzsche's references to himself as an immoralist, see especially J, § 32; G, "Morality as Anti-Nature," § 6; EH, "Why I Am a Destiny," §§ 2–6.

4. Kaufmann, *Nietzsche,* pp. 374–75.

5. The details of Nietzsche's views will be discussed in Chapters 6 and 7.

6. Danto, *Nietzsche as Philosopher,* p. 160.

7. Ibid., p. 161.

8. "Jenseits von Gut und Böse / Versuch einer Überwindung der Moral. / Von Friedrich Nietzsche" (KGW, VIII₁, 27 [1885–86]). According to Colli and Montinari, this note has only been published previously by Erich F. Podach in *Ein Blick in Notizbücher Nietzsches* (Heidelberg, 1963). The note has been left out of all previous editions of Nietzsche's works.

9. EH, "Beyond Good and Evil," § 2.

10. GT, "Attempt at a Self-Criticism" § 5; K, p. 24.

11. Translated from KGW, VIII₁, 121–22 (1885–86).

12. Z, I, "On the Adder's Bite," p. 68.

13. EH, "Why I Write Such Good Books," § 1; K, p. 261.

14. J, § 32; K, pp. 44–45. See also GM, III, § 27.

15. Z, I, "Zarathustra's Prologue," § 5, p. 17.

16. WM, § 404, p. 219; KGW, VIII₁, 210 (1886–87).

17. M, Preface, § 4.

18. J, § 32; K, p. 44.

19. GM, III, § 27.

20. "Selbstüberwindung" is used in J, § 32, GM, III, § 27, and EH, "Why I Am a Destiny," § 3. "Selbstaufhebung" appears in M, Preface, § 4 and GM, III, § 27. "Selbstvernichtung" (as in KGW, VIII₁, 28 [1885–86] or WM, § 405) is used more rarely. But Nietzsche uses the term "Vernichtung" when referring to the destruction of morality by the higher man (e.g., KGW, VII₁, 262 and VII₂, 241).

21. The latter point is best developed in Part I of *On the Genealogy of Morals*.

22. J, § 23; K, p. 32.

23. Ibid., § 201; GM, I, § 2.

24. KGW, VII₂, 31–33 (1884).

25. GM, III, § 27; K, p. 161.

26. J, § 230; K, pp. 161–62.

27. FW, IV, § 342.

28. See FW, V, § 343.

29. Z, I, "Zarathustra's Prologue," § 3, p. 12.

30. Ibid., pp. 12–13. See also "On the Afterworldly," pp. 30–33.

31. Ibid., "On the Three Metamorphoses," p. 26.

32. Ibid., pp. 26–27.

33. Ibid., p. 27.

34. Ibid., "Zarathustra's Prologue," §§ 3–4, pp. 12–16.

35. Ibid., "On the Gift-Giving Virtue," § 2, p. 77.

36. Cf. GM, II, § 10.

37. Z, I, "On the Thousand and One Goals," p. 60.

38. Danto, *Nietzsche as Philosopher,* p. 199.

39. Z, II, "Upon the Blessed Isles," pp. 85–86.

40. Ibid., "On Priests," p. 93.

41. Kaufmann, *Nietzsche,* p. 316.

42. Ibid. One cannot help but notice the alienation from nature and the body implicit in Kaufmann's portrait of the "overman."

43. Danto, *Nietzsche as Philosopher,* p. 199.

44. Z, pp. 14–16, 85–88, and 93.

45. This is implied in Zarathustra's discourse "On the Thousand and One Goals." See also "Zarathustra's Prologue," § 3, p. 13.

46. WM, § 1067, p. 550; KGW, VII₃, 339 (1885).

47. This is not to say that in *Zarathustra* Nietzsche does not pursue the theme of domination but that he is not limited to this perspective and in fact often transcends it.

48. EH, "Beyond Good and Evil," § 2; K, p. 311.

49. Z, I, "Zarathustra's Prologue," §§ 2–5, pp. 10–19.

50. Ibid., II, "Upon the Blessed Isles," p. 88.

51. GM, I, § 15.

52. Zarathustra's inability to receive love is lamented by him in "The Night Song."

53. A, § 2.

54. FW, V, § 370.

55. NCW, "We Antipodes"; PN, p. 671.

56. A, § 2; PN, p. 570.

CHAPTER SIX

1. GM, I, §§ 7, 10, 13, and passim.

2. See *Republic,* III, 414ff., and G, "The 'Improvers' of Mankind," § 5.

3. Cf. J, § 257.

4. EH, "Why I Am a Destiny," § 1.

5. WM, § 287, p. 162; KGW, VIII₁, 288 (1886–87). This note was originally part of a long fragment entitled "Die Guten und die Verbesserer" intended for one of Nietzsche's drafts of *The Will to Power.* Nietzsche's editors later divided the fragment into sixteen different sections which appear scattered throughout the second edition of *The Will to Power.*

6. FW, I, § 4.

7. Z, III, "On Old and New Tablets," § 26, p. 212.

8. Ibid., p. 213.

9. Ibid., § 27, p. 213.

10. Ibid., § 20, p. 209.

11. Ibid., §§ 10 and 28, pp. 202 and 213.

12. G, "Skirmishes of an Untimely Man," § 33; PN, p. 534.

13. A, § 2; PN, p. 570.

14. J, § 29; K, p. 41.

15. G. F. W. Hegel, *The Philosophy of History,* trans. J. Sibree (New York: Dover Publications, 1956), p. 32.

16. The existence of conflict (both at the individual and social level) cannot be denied. But the glorification of conflict which has come down to us by myth, poetry, and other records of history goes well beyond the observation that conflict exists. Greek myth exalts conflict at every level of interpersonal or social interaction. For example, one of its many legends tells of Zeus's father, Cronos, who swallowed alive his five oldest children because it had been prophesied that one of his children would

deprive him of his power. Christian myth, too, exalts conflict and war as much as it does peace and quietude. For instance, even when condemning Lucifer, it glorifies his power, which is sometimes believed to be almost complete over the world. In poetry, positive representations of the war hero are found systematically in three of the most important genres—tragedy, the epic, and the romance. By the time we get to the nineteenth century, we find the ideology of struggle and war even in science and philosophy. Evolutionary theory referred to the struggle of every living organism for survival. Hegelian idealism ennobled struggle as the dialectical movement of the Idea in history. In more recent times, militant socialism has also ennobled the idea of struggle and armed conflict by employing the notion of class struggle to justify the revolutionary rights of the working class. Struggle is a given in human experience, and sometimes it may be morally justified. But is it something that should be idealized? I am not trying to excuse Nietzsche's idealization of conflict. On the other hand, I am calling attention to the pervasiveness in our culture of the assumptions he takes for granted.

17. J, § 188; K, p. 102.

18. Another possibility is to say that Nietzsche projects upon nature (or natural law) the authoritarian structures which he saw operating in his social environment (e.g., "Obey superiors"). The rebel could follow this logic quite strictly ("I am superior to others, therefore they should obey me"). Yet this explanation does not cover the case of the creator of values who lives and acts beyond the polarity of superior/inferior. Such a possibility is at least envisioned in parts of *Thus Spoke Zarathustra*.

19. J, §§ 4 and 21.

20. Z, I, "On the Thousand and One Goals," p. 58.

21. J, § 188.

22. EH, "Why I Am So Clever," § 4; K, p. 246.

23. Z, II, "On the Tarantulas," p. 101.

24. EH, "Why I Am a Destiny," § 1; K, p. 326.

25. G, "The 'Improvers' of Mankind," §§ 2–5.

26. KGW, VII₂, 294–95 (1884).

27. Ibid., p. 295.

28. J, § 188; K, p. 102.

29. EH, "Beyond Good and Evil," § 2; K, p. 311.

30. G, "The Four Great Errors," § 2; PN, p. 493.

31. A, § 56; PN, pp. 642–43. The reference is to 1 Cor. 7:2, 9.

32. Z, I, "On the Despisers of the Body," pp. 34–35.

33. Ibid., p. 35.

34. Ibid., "On the Gift-Giving Virtue," § 2, p. 77.

35. Ibid., p. 78.

36. Ibid., III, "On Old and New Tablets," § 20, p. 209.

37. Translated from KGW, VII₁, 283.

38. Z, I, "On the Gift-Giving Virtue," § 2, p. 76.

39. Ibid., p. 77.

40. Translated from KGW, VII₁, 283 (nn.7 [96] and 7 [97]).

41. G, "The 'Improvers' of Mankind," § 2; PN, p. 502.

42. Ibid., § 5; PN, p. 505.

43. Ibid., §§ 3–4; PN, pp. 503–505. Walter Kaufmann, commenting on this passage, observes that Nietzsche objects to the caste system as a whole due to his alleged sympathy for the oppression of the Chandalas (*Nietzsche*, p. 297). Actually Nietzsche has no objection to the caste system, only the the exclusion of a part of society (the Chandalas) from participation in a specific caste status.

44. Cf. WM, § 142; KGW, VIII₃, 233–34 (1888).

45. G, "The 'Improvers' of Mankind," § 3; PN, p. 503.

46. J, § 265; K, p. 215.

47. Translated from KGW, VII₂, 71 (1884).

48. WM, § 964, p. 506. Some sections of this note not published previously will be found in KGW, VII₂, 94–95 (1884). All previous editions fail to print the sentence that follows in the text: "Conviction of the ill-bred, that they must sacrifice themselves: this is the meaning of the religious orders that take a vow of chastity."

49. J, § 61; K, p. 72.

50. Ibid., § 265; K, p. 215.

51. WM, § 859, p. 458; KGW, VIII₁, 288–89 (1886–87). The original note is part of a fragment called "Die Guten und die Verbesserer." See n.5 above.

52. WM, § 1027, p. 531; KGW, VIII₂, 90 (1887).

53. WM, § 898, p. 478; KGW, VIII₂, 88–90 (1887).

54. WM, § 879, p. 470; KGW, VIII₂, 88 (1887).

55. WM, § 1059, p. 545; KGW, VII₂, 223 (1884).

CHAPTER SEVEN

1. EH, "Why I Am So Wise," § 3. Cf. G, "What the Germans Lack," § 4.

2. J, § 251; K, p. 189.

3. Nietzsche's critique of how Christianity acquired political power may be seen as an elaboration of this thesis. See GM, I, § 6, and passim.

4. Z, I, "Zarathustra's Prologue," § 4, pp. 14–16; II, "On the Famous Wise Men," pp. 103–5, and "On Self-Overcoming," p. 166. See also EH, "Why I Am a Destiny," § 1.

5. Both positions are argued in *Beyond Good and Evil*. Nietzsche's arguments will be discussed in this chapter.

6. In one unpublished note Nietzsche argues for "The annihilation of *suffrage universel*. . . . The annihilation of mediocrity and its

acceptance. (The onesided, individuals-peoples for example Englishmen. Dühring. To strive for fullness of nature through the pairing of opposites: race mixture to this end.)'' The words ''for example Englishmen'' and ''Dühring'' were left out of WM, § 862. KGW, VII₂, 65, 25 [211] (1884).

7. Karl Jaspers, *Nietzsche,* trans. C. R. Wallraff and R. J. Schmitz (Chicago: Henry Regnery, 1965), p. 256ff.

8. Kaufmann, *Nietzsche,* pp. 287–306.

9. In *Twilight of the Idols* Nietzsche shows admiration for the breeding of four separate races as stipulated in the law of Manu. See ''The 'Improvers' of Mankind,'' §§ 3 and 4.

10. J, §§ 252 and 253.

11. KGW, VII₂, 65 (1884). The particular reference to the English was omitted from WM, § 862. See n.6.

12. In this section Nietzsche criticizes democratic free spirits who believe in the equality of rights and the alleviation of human suffering. He argues that ''everything evil, terrible, tyrannical in man'' should be seen as serving the enhancement of the human species. At the same time, he maintains that it is not his role to be more explicit about his position, linking his guarded attitude to his solitary nature. The appeal to solitude here is used ambiguously. There is the sense of keeping separate from the crowd but also of hiding something from it. This type of rhetorical ambiguity, inserted at just the right place in an argument, serves the function of exempting and protecting Nietzsche's statements from legitimate criticism. See J, § 44; K, pp. 54–56.

13. EH, ''Why I Am a Destiny,'' § 1; K, p. 327.

14. J, § 242; K, p. 177.

15. See Georg Lukács' discussion of Nietzsche's philosophy in *Die Zerstörung der Vernunft* (Neuwied am Rhein: Hermann Luchterhand, 1962), pp. 270–350.

16. ''Der griechische Staat'' (1871), KGW, III₂, 258–71. All references hereafter are to ''The Greek State,'' trans. Maximilian Muegge, CWFN, II, 3–18.

17. ''The Greek State,'' CWFN, II, 6–7.

18. Ibid., pp. 4–5.

19. See the discussion of the eternal recurrence in Chapter 3.

20. WM, § 957, p. 502; KGW, VII₃, 308 (1885).

21. J, § 187. Here Nietzsche comes close to using the notion of the will to power in the literal sense.

22. Z, II, ''On the Tarantulas,'' p. 101.

23. J, § 257; K, p. 201.

24. Ibid., § 258; K, p. 202.

25. Nietzsche then proceeds to a biological justification of aristocratic rights. He compares the splendor of the aristocratic spirit, attained at the expense of enslaving other human beings, with the biological

fulfillment of a clinging vine in Java whose happiness is attained by overtaking an oak tree and using it as its support. The attribution of happiness to a plant is typical of Nietzsche's personification of nature, while the combination of appeals to biology and destiny in support of aristocratic privilege exemplifies his approach to defending exploitation in *Beyond Good and Evil*.

26. Ibid., § 259; K, p. 203.

27. Ibid.

28. Ibid., § 258; K, p. 202.

29. Z, I, "On the New Idol," p. 48.

30. Ibid., p. 49.

31. Ibid.

32. Ibid.

33. G, "Skirmishes of an Untimely Man," § 39.

34. Ibid., § 34; PN, p. 534.

35. See Kaufmann, *Nietzsche,* pp. 157-77.

36. Strong, *Friedrich Nietzsche and the Politics of Transfiguration,* p. 210ff. Strong argues specifically against viewing as an oppressor the dominant individual created by Nietzsche. "The activity of Nietzsche's masters is *not just the converse of that of slaves* (oppressing rather than oppressed), but it is in fact a *different* form of activity" (p. 253). Here Nietzsche's defense of the right of the superior type to exploit the inferior is ignored, as in other politically liberal interpretations of Nietzsche's theory of values.

37. J, § 36.

38. FW, III, § 270; K, p. 219.

39. G, "Morality as Anti-Nature," § 6; PN, p. 491.

40. Ibid., "Skirmishes of an Untimely Man," § 33; PN, p. 534.

41. Z, I, "On Old and Young Women," p. 66.

42. "Reverence for each other . . . is what I call marriage" (Z, I, "On Child and Marriage," p. 70).

43. Ibid., p. 67.

44. J, § 238; K, p. 167.

45. Ibid.

46. Z, I, "On Child and Marriage," p. 71.

47. FW, I, § 14; K, pp. 88-89.

48. J, § 175.

49. FW, I, § 68; K, p. 126.

50. J, § 102; K, p. 84.

51. Ibid., § 284; K, p. 226. If solitude is a virtue, it need not entail the condemnation of community that one finds here.

52. G, "Skirmishes of an Untimely Man," § 39; PN, p. 543.

53. Ibid., p. 544.

54. Ibid. For the idea of woman as property, see also J, § 238.

55. KGW, VIII₃, 291 (1888). The statement also appears in WM, § 733, where the words "for days" are left out.

56. J, § 262; K, p. 210.

57. "Woman is not yet capable of friendship: women are still cats and birds. Or at best, cows. Woman is not yet capable of friendship. But tell me, you men, who among you is capable of friendship?" (Z, I, "On the Friend," pp. 55–58).

58. J, § 232.

59. Kaufmann, *Nietzsche,* p. 84.

60. Danto, *Nietzsche as Philosopher,* p. 161.

61. Throughout most of *Beyond Good and Evil* Kaufmann translates "Zucht" and "Züchtung" as "cultivation." In his study of Nietzsche, however, Kaufmann admits that Nietzsche's use of these terms comes closer to "breeding" than to "cultivation." Still, he disclaims that Nietzsche meant "breeding" in the literal sense. See Kaufmann, *Nietzsche,* pp. 304–6.

62. J, § 236; K, p. 165.

63. G, "Skirmishes of an Untimely Man," § 40; PN, p. 545.

Bibliography

SELECTED WORKS BY NIETZSCHE

Collected Works

Nietzsche Werke. Kritische Gesamtausgabe. Ed. Giorgio Colli
and Mazzino Montinari. 20 vols. to date. Berlin: Walter de
Gruyter, 1967–82. Divisions are marked by Roman numerals.
Divisions are subdivided into separate volumes by Arabic nu-
meral subscripts.

Nietzsche Briefwechsel. Kritische Gesamtausgabe. Ed. Giorgio
Colli and Mazzino Montinari. Berlin: Walter de Gruyter, 1975–.
Approximately nineteen volumes of Nietzsche's correspon-
dence have been published so far.

The Complete Works of Friedrich Nietzsche. Ed. Oscar Levy. 18
vols. 1909–11; reissued New York: Russell and Russell, 1964.

Translations by Walter Kaufmann

The Birth of Tragedy and *The Case of Wagner.* New York: Vintage
Books, 1967.

Beyond Good and Evil. New York: Vintage Books, 1966.

The Gay Science. New York: Vintage Books, 1974.

On the Genealogy of Morals (in collaboration with R. J. Hollingdale) and *Ecce Homo.* New York: Vintage Books, 1967.

Thus Spoke Zarathustra. New York: The Viking Press, 1954,
1966. All citations to *Zarathustra* will be to the 1966 Viking
Compass edition.

Twilight of the Idols, The Antichrist, and *Nietzsche contra Wagner* (in addition to *Thus Spoke Zarathustra* and other brief
selections) are contained in *The Portable Nietzsche.* New York:
The Viking Press, 1954, 1968.

The Will to Power (in collaboration with R. J. Hollingdale). New
York: Vintage Books, 1967.

Other Editions of Interest

Nietzsches Werke. Grossoktavausgabe. 2d ed. 19 vols. Leipzig:
Kröner, 1901–13. Vol. 20, an index by Richard Oehler, was
added in 1926.

219

Philosophy in the Tragic Age of the Greeks. Trans. Marianne Cowan. Chicago: Henry Regnery, 1962. Nietzsche's unpublished 1876 essay.

Selected Letters of Friedrich Nietzsche. Ed. and trans. Christopher Middleton. Chicago: The University of Chicago Press, 1969. Includes an interesting collection of letters from the period of the transvaluation of all values.

Werke in drei Bänden. Ed. Karl Schlechta. Munich: Carl Hanser, 1966. Contains Nietzsche's major works, many of his unpublished writings, and selected letters; also includes a fourth volume with a limited but helpful Nietzsche-Index.

SELECTED CRITICAL, INTERPRETATIVE, AND BIOGRAPHICAL WORKS

Alderman, Harold. *Nietzsche's Gift.* Athens: Ohio University Press, 1977.

Allison, David, ed. *The New Nietzsche: Contemporary Styles of Interpretation.* New York: Delta Books, 1977.

Brandes, Georg. *Friedrich Nietzsche.* London: William Heinemann, 1914.

Camus, Albert. "Nietzsche and Nihilism." In *The Rebel,* trans. A. Bower. New York: Vintage Books, 1956.

Copleston, Frederick. *Friedrich Nietzsche: Philosopher of Culture.* 2d ed. New York: Barnes and Noble, 1975.

Danto, Arthur. *Nietzsche as Philosopher.* New York: Macmillan, 1965.

Deleuze, Gilles. *Nietzsche et la philosophie.* Paris: Presses Universitaires de France, 1962. Trans. by Hugh Tomlinson as *Nietzsche and Philosophy.* New York: Columbia University Press, 1983.

De Man, Paul. *Allegories of Reading: Figural Language in Rousseau, Nietzsche, Rilke, and Proust.* New Haven: Yale University Press, 1979.

Derrida, Jacques. *Spurs: Nietzsche's Styles.* Trans. Barbara Harlow. Chicago: The University of Chicago Press, 1979.

Fink, Eugen. *Nietzsches Philosophie.* Stuttgart: Kohlhammer, 1960.

Granier, Jean. *Le problème de la Vérité dans la philosophie de Nietzsche.* Paris: Editions du Seuil, 1966.

Grimm, Ruediger H. *Nietzsche's Theory of Knowledge.* Berlin and New York: Walter de Gruyter, 1977.

Habermas, Jürgen. *Knowledge and Human Interests.* Trans. J. J. Shapiro. Boston: Beacon Pres, 1971.

Hayman, Ronald. *Nietzsche: A Critical Life.* New York: Oxford University Press, 1980.

Heidegger, Martin. *Nietzsche*. 2 vols. Pfullingen: Günther Neske, 1961.

———. *Nietzsche*. Vol. 1, *The Will to Power as Art*. Trans. David F. Krell. San Francisco: Harper and Row, Publishers, 1979.

———. *Nietzsche*. Vol. 4, *Nihilism*. Trans. Frank Capuzzi. San Francisco: Harper and Row, 1982.

Heller, Erich. *The Artist's Journey into the Interior and Other Essays*. New York: Random House, 1959.

———. *The Disinherited Mind*. Philadelphia: Dufour and Saifer, 1952.

———. *The Poet's Self and the Poem*. London: Athlone Press, 1976.

Heller, Peter. *Dialectics and Nihilism: Essays on Lessing, Nietzsche, Mann, and Kafka*. Amherst: University of Massachusetts Press, 1966.

Hollingdale, R. J. *Nietzsche: The Man and His Philosophy*. London: Routledge and Kegan Paul, 1973.

Jaspers, Karl. *Nietzsche: An Introduction to the Understanding of His Philosophical Activity*. Trans. Charles F. Wallraff and Frederick J. Schmitz. Chicago: Henry Regnery, 1965.

Kaufmann, Walter. *Nietzsche: Philosopher, Psychologist, Antichrist*. 4th ed. Princeton: Princeton University Press, 1974.

Klossowski, Pierre. *Nietzsche et le cercle vicieux*. Paris: Mercure de France, 1969.

Kofman, Sarah. *Nietzsche et la métaphore*. Paris: Editions Payot, 1972.

———. *Nietzsche et la scène philosophique*. Paris: Union Générale d'Editions, 1980.

Löwith, Karl. *From Hegel to Nietzsche*. Trans. David E. Green. Garden City, N.Y.: Holt, Rinehart and Winston, 1964.

———. *Nietzsches Philosophie der ewigen Wiederkehr des Gleichen*. 3rd ed. Hamburg: Felix Meiner, 1978.

Lukács, Georg. *Die Zerstörung der Vernunft*. Neuwied am Rhein: Herman Luchterhand, 1962.

Magnus, Bernd. *Nietzsche's Existential Imperative*. Bloomington: Indiana University Press, 1978.

Mann, Thomas. *Nietzsches Philosophie im Licht unserer Erfahrung*. Berlin: Suhrkamp, 1948.

Morgan, George. *What Nietzsche Means*. Cambridge, Mass.: Harvard University Press, 1941.

Müller-Lauter, Wolfgang. *Nietzsche. Seine Philosophie der Gegensätze und die Gegensätze seiner Philosophie*. Berlin and New York: Walter de Gruyter, 1971.

Nietzsche aujourd'hui? 2 vols. Paris: Union Général d'Editions, 1973.

Pasley, Malcolm, ed. *Nietzsche: Imagery and Thought.* London: Methuen, 1978.

Salaquarda, Jörg, ed. *Nietzsche.* Darmstadt: Wissenschaftliche Buchgesellschaft, 1980.

Savater, Fernando. *Conocer Nietzsche y su obra.* Barcelona: Dopesa, 1977.

Schacht, Richard. *Nietzsche.* Boston: Routledge and Kegan Paul, 1983.

Schlechta, Karl. *Der fall Nietzsche.* Munich: Carl Hanser, 1958.

———. *Nietzsche Chronik: Daten zu Leben und Werk.* Munich: Carl Hanser, 1975.

Silk, M. S., and Stern, J. P. *Nietzsche on Tragedy.* London: Cambridge University Press, 1981.

Solomon, Robert C., ed. *Nietzsche: A Collection of Critical Essays.* Garden City, N.Y.: Anchor Books, 1973.

Stambaugh, Joan. *Nietzsche's Thought of Eternal Return.* Baltimore: The Johns Hopkins University Press, 1972.

Stern, J. P. *A Study of Nietzsche.* Cambridge: Cambridge University Press, 1979.

Strong, Tracy B. *Friedrich Nietzsche and the Politics of Transfiguration.* Berkeley: University of California Press, 1975.

Trias, Eugenio, et al. *En favor de Nietzsche.* Madrid: Taurus, 1972.

Vaihinger, Hans. *The Philosophy of As If.* 2d ed. Trans. C. K. Ogden. London: Routledge and Kegan Paul, 1935.

Wilcox, John. *Truth and Value in Nietzsche.* Ann Arbor: University of Michigan Press, 1974.

Index